The

PROFESSIONAL

DEVELOPMENT

SCHOOLS

HANDBOOK

To my parents, Bea and Norman Teitel, former New York City
public school teachers: You brought me up to believe that the best and
most important thing in the world I could do was be a teacher.
Thank you. This book is for you.

The

PROFESSIONAL
DEVELOPMENT
SCHOOLS
HANDBOOK

Starting, Sustaining,
and Assessing Partnerships
That Improve Student Learning

Lee Teitel
Foreword by Marsha Levine

CORWIN PRESS, INC.
A Sage Publications Company
Thousand Oaks, California

For information:

Corwin Press, Inc.
A Sage Publications Company
2455 Teller Road
Thousand Oaks, California 91320
www.corwinpress.com

Sage Publications Ltd.
6 Bonhill Street
London EC2A 4PU
United Kingdom

Sage Publications India Pvt. Ltd.
B-42 Panchsheel Enclave
New Delhi 110 017 India

Printed in the United States of America

Library of Congress Cataloging-in-Publication Data

Teitel, Lee.
The professional development schools handbook: Starting, sustaining, and assessing partnerships that improve student learning / Lee Teitel.
    p. cm.
Includes bibliographical references and index.
ISBN 0-7619-3834-6 (Cloth) — ISBN 0-7619-3835-4 (Paper)
   1. Laboratory schools—United States—Handbooks, manuals, etc.
2. College-school cooperation—United States—Handbooks, manuals, etc.
3. Teachers—Training of—United States—Handbooks, manuals, etc.
I. Title.
LB2154.A3 T46 2003
370'.71'1—dc21

                 2002153280

This book is printed on acid-free paper.

03   04   05   06   07   7   6   5   4   3   2

Acquisitions Editor:	Rachel Livsey
Editorial Assistant:	Phyllis Cappello
Production Editor:	Diane S. Foster
Copy Editor:	Toni Williams
Typesetter	C&M Digitals (P) Ltd.
Proofer:	Olivia Weber
Indexer:	Teri Greenberg
Cover Designer:	Michael Dubowe
Production Artist:	Janet Foulger

Contents

List of Toolkit Entries

Most of the chapters in this handbook include follow-up suggestions, called Toolkit Entries, which offer worksheets, inventories, reflective writing prompts, summaries of relevant theories, and planning guides that can be used as practical next steps for partnerships.

Chapter 4. Learning Community: Improving Approaches to Teaching, Learning, and Leadership

Chapter 5. Diversity and Equity: Preparing a Diverse Group of Educators to Teach All Students

Foreword

Professional development schools (PDSs) are innovative institutions formed through partnerships between professional education programs and PreK–12 schools. They have a fourfold mission: the preparation of new teachers, faculty development, inquiry directed at the improvement of practice, and enhanced student achievement. PDS partners come together to share responsibility for all parts of their mission. Some believe that PDSs are potentially the most powerful innovation in teacher education. As hybrid institutions formed by university and school partners, they can bridge the gap between the sectors, and between theory and practice. They can facilitate renewal in both school and university as a result of knowledge shared in the partnership. Most important, they can enhance both teacher and student learning.

PDSs are often compared to teaching hospitals. Teaching hospitals are also hybrid institutions created in the early 20th century. As practicing professions, both teaching and medicine require a sound academic program and intense clinical preparation. The teaching hospital was designed to provide such clinical preparation for medical students and interns; PDSs serve the same functions for teacher candidates and inservice faculty. The basic precept in both settings is professional education through inquiry and a focus on client (student or patient) needs. The teaching hospital was a major instrument in the professionalization of medicine. PDSs can be an equally important vehicle for teacher professionalism.

In order to support this fledgling innovation, between 1995 and 2001, the National Council for Accreditation of Teacher Education (NCATE) worked with hundreds of practitioners and teacher educators to design and field-test standards for professional development schools. Draft standards were developed based on extensive input from experts in the field.

The draft standards were then piloted for three years by 16 diverse and representative PDS partnerships. The goal was to create standards that would strengthen and support PDSs, as well as be used to assess their progress.

There were several important outcomes of the NCATE work. First, a consensus emerged among educators about the definition and mission of a professional development school. Second, we refined and revised our knowledge of how professional development school partnerships function to achieve their mission. The field test helped us understand how PDS work blends the skills and knowledge of all partners and simultaneously supports professional and student learning. Through the self-studies and visiting team assessments we uncovered the central role of student achievement in the professional development school and we documented the important role of inquiry in PDS work. Field-test participants helped us to understand how inquiry, often the most overlooked part of the PDS mission, can be the vehicle for both professional development and new teacher learning. We observed how PDS partners use inquiry to determine students' needs, which in turn define curriculum for intern teachers and determine the professional development agenda for all faculty.

The PDS Standards have been broadly accepted in the community. They were endorsed by NCATE, and they are being used by both institutions and states to shape and assess their PDS partnership initiatives. The PDS Standards are also being used in research focused on measuring PDS outcomes for all learners. They provide a necessary framework for defining context or inputs in studies that seek to determine effects of PDSs on teacher quality and student learning.

This book represents another way in which the PDS Standards can be used to help partnerships move forward. We know that schools and universities coming to this work often need guidance as they form their partnerships. They need to know how to engage each other in building strong relationships and in learning how to share responsibilities that traditionally have not been shared. PDSs require the commitment of resources, and partners need to learn how to think differently about time, space, and expertise, as well as how to think collaboratively about financial support. PDS partners have to create new roles and structures to support their unique kind of work. At the same time, however, they must address the strains and stresses that they will naturally encounter as they work with new partners and maintain their traditional memberships and roles in their home institutions. This book is designed to provide much needed support to PDS partners as they encounter these and other challenges.

Dr. Teitel is well prepared to offer this assistance. He has a wealth of experience in working with PDS partnerships on just these kinds of needs.

As a principal contributor to the PDS Standards Field Test Project, he also knows the PDS Standards well. In this book he has brought his experience and the Standards together. He uses the PDS Standards to frame approaches to PDS support and implementation—ensuring that partnerships will be guided by what is most important in a PDS in its earliest stages and throughout its development. Most important, this book will help PDS partners keep their focus on students' needs—the core of PDS work—as they take this journey together.

This book is important. The PDS Standards were designed to do the hard work of both supporting PDS development and assessing PDS quality. This book makes a significant contribution to that goal. It provides concrete suggestions for what PDS partners can do in developing, implementing, and assessing their partnerships, which are framed by the Standards and grounded in their core concepts. This kind of support can help PDS partnerships fulfill their enormous potential for revolutionizing teaching and the education of teachers, and supporting the achievement of all children in our schools.

—Marsha Levine
Senior Consultant for
Professional Development Schools
National Council for
Accreditation of Teacher Education
Washington, DC

Preface

The purpose of professional development schools is to promote student learning. PDSs do that by improving schools, preparing new teachers in better ways, supporting the growth and development of all educators, and using inquiry and research to see what is working well and what is not. Given the wide gap in achievement among students of differing racial, ethnic, and economic backgrounds in this country, PDSs have a special interest in promoting the learning of all students and reducing the achievement gap.

PDSs sometimes lose sight of their focus on improving student learning and get caught up in the complicated structural and organizational changes needed to make a PDS work. This handbook is organized and written to keep the focus on student learning, even as the handbook walks partnerships through the many structural, organizational, and instructional stages that must take place. This book is aligned closely with the *Standards for Professional Development Schools*, released in 2001 by the National Council for the Accreditation of Teacher Education. The Standards represent the clearest and most comprehensive summary of what it means to be a PDS, developed through a national research project and field-tested in 16 very different sites. The Standards are developmental and acknowledge the different stages that PDS partnerships go through. With some minor modifications (see Figure A.1), the Standards can be used to illustrate the building blocks of how PDSs can improve student learning.

FOCUSING THE STANDARDS ON STUDENT LEARNING

The PDS Standards are:

I. *Learning Community.* At the heart of the PDS, this Standard represents the teaching and learning activities, philosophies, and environments created in these partnerships.

II. *Accountability and Quality Assurance.* This Standard is the assessment of the partnership and its outcomes in ways that address the PDS's accountability to its various stakeholders.

III. *Collaboration.* This Standard addresses the partnership's formation and its development of an increasingly interdependent, committed relationship.

IV. *Diversity and Equity.* This Standard focuses attention on how the PDS prepares a diverse group of educators to provide opportunities to learn for all students.

V. *Structures, Resources, and Roles.* This Standard addresses how the PDS organizes itself to support and do its work.

Figure A.1 shows these Standards aligned, with a focus on student learning outcomes.

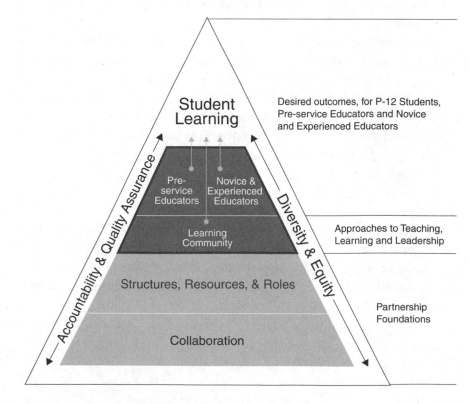

Figure A.1   PDS Standards Student Learning Pyramid

Figure A.1, the PDS Standards Student Learning Pyramid, places these Standards in relationship to one another. Standard III, Collaboration, and Standard V, Structures, Resources, and Roles, are foundational. They are necessary to build a PDS, but not sufficient. They represent the building blocks on which the all-important Learning Community (Standard I) rests. The changes brought about in the teaching, learning, and leadership environment of the learning community—the experiences of students and adults focusing together on improving student and adult learning—are what make the difference in PDSs. Student learning is enhanced in at least three ways in a PDS partnership:

- Through better preparation of interns and their enhanced roles inside and outside the classroom with PreK–12 students
- Through professional development and other experiences that the faculty, staff, and administrators at the school, university, and other partners have, engaging and focusing them on student learning
- Through the direct engagement of the PreK–12 students in an improved learning environment—improvements in curriculum and instruction as well as enhanced relationships inside and outside of class with interns, teachers, and other adults

The Pyramid places the remaining Standards, II and IV, running diagonally up the sides because attention to diversity and equity issues, and the use of accountability and quality assurance measures to assess the processes and products of the PDS, permeate all aspects of the partnerships and help maintain a focus on improved achievement for all students. The intersections this positioning creates between Standards help focus the PDS on what matters. For example, the intersection of Diversity and Equity with Collaboration focuses on how diverse the partners are and whether the PDS includes a range of partners concerned with equitable outcomes for children—parents and community agencies, for example. When this Standard intersects Learning Community, it raises the question of how issues of diversity and equity drive the content and process of the curriculum and instruction for PreK–12 students, interns, faculty, staff, and administrators at participating institutions.

Similarly, the Accountability and Quality Assurance Standard cuts through all the others, whether at the Collaboration level, ensuring accountability to the partnership's various stakeholders, including the accreditation of the participating institutions, or at the Structures, Resources, and Roles level, having the partnership use assessment to reflect on and improve its own processes.

At the apex of the Pyramid, impacts on students become paramount. The intersection of Diversity and Equity with the Assessment Standard (angling up from the other side) suggests the critical focus of PDSs on reduction of the achievement gap and evaluation of policies and practices to support equitable opportunities to learn for all students.

The use of the PDS Standards Student Learning Pyramid to organize this book does not suggest that the process of starting, sustaining, and assessing PDSs is a linear, one-way process. Some PDSs actually start with very little underlying structure or formal partnership agreements. They leap into learning community activities and only later go back to build the foundations needed for sustaining the work. However, the Pyramid does suggest that PDSs must address each of the aspects of partnership development expressed in the Standards and that each should be seen in relationship to one another and to its impacts on student learning. In this way, the Pyramid and the Standards become useful organizing tools for starting, sustaining, and assessing PDS partnerships.

WHY I WROTE THIS BOOK

For more than a decade, I have been involved in and committed to making the concept and promise of professional development schools a reality. As a researcher, I have documented the start-up and development of dozens of PDS partnerships; as a scholar, I have read and reviewed the literature on hundreds more. As a practitioner, I have been involved in starting and sustaining several partnerships between my own university and schools in Boston. As a consultant and speaker, I have talked with hundreds of people around the country and listened to their stories, challenges, and successes. I've seen and talked and read about PDS partnerships confronting all manner of tough issues. I have seen many succeed and begin to reap benefits for the students and adults in their partnerships. I have seen some founder, with relationships that limp along going nowhere or that end in the sadness and recriminations of an unpleasant "divorce." I have seen "paper PDSs" spring up overnight—places that look like traditional practice but call themselves PDSs—and I have worked closely with the PDS Standards Project to help establish some well-regarded standards for what it means to be a PDS.

Throughout this work I have developed the highest regard and respect for the thousands of parents, teachers, administrators, community members, and students who are making the PDSs across this country work. I am pleased to count many of them among my colleagues and friends and I dedicate this book to them and thank them for all they have helped me learn.

As a documentor, a consultant, and a speaker, I continue to learn a great deal from the PDSs I visit. I sometimes think of myself as a bumble-bee, traveling to different flowers, cross-pollinating ideas. What follows in this book are my gleanings. They are undoubtedly incomplete, and I invite feedback and comments from readers.

Over the past decade, I have developed a strong set of beliefs about what is important in PDS partnerships. These beliefs—some might call them biases—shape this book in many subtle and not so subtle ways, so let me try to express them.

• *PDS partnerships can and should be transformative.* John Goodlad (1988) talks about the "simultaneous renewal" of schools and teacher educational institutions through PDSs, and I am a believer. If partnerships settle with minor adjustments and don't get to improve the core missions of teaching and learning for all students, I don't think PDSs are worth the trouble.

• *Equity matters.* The Holmes Group, whose reports in the late 1980s and early 1990s provided important intellectual input into the PDS movement, made clear that PDSs need to play a critical role in addressing the inequities of our society and charged PDSs to not back away from or avoid their responsibilities due to the magnitude of the task. I think many PDSs have failed to engage that equity agenda, and much of the focus of my PDS work addresses the challenges and opportunities in high-poverty urban and rural settings.

• *PDSs should be beneficial for all partners.* I don't think you can sustain the kind of long-term partnerships that PDSs need to be unless they are benefiting all partners. I sometimes use the analogy to marriage in my thinking about PDSs, and having one partner set out to "fix" the other does not seem to me to be the recipe for long-term success and happiness with an individual or with organizations. Reciprocity and mutuality are essential.

• *Relationships are key, but systems and structures need to change for lasting impacts.* PDS partnerships work because of the strong interpersonal relationships that develop in them. These organic connections between and among people are necessary, but unless more formal organizational ties are made, partnerships will be unstable and susceptible to turnover.

• *Data and high-quality information are critical at all levels in PDS partnerships.* A range of data sources (including but not limited to test scores) is needed for the quality assurance required by external PDS stakeholders, as well as to shape the ongoing, internal decisions PDSs make when they test out new organizational and instructional approaches.

- *Leadership matters.* I define leadership broadly—it does not simply reside in the deans, superintendents, and principals with positional power, but also shows up at all levels of the partnering organizations. I think about (and invite readers of this book to think about) how the leadership tasks called for in this book get accomplished by a range of people in the partnering organizations and how spreading out the leadership tasks changes the ownership and improves the dynamics of organizational renewal.

- *Even though every context is different, the majority of the tasks and challenges facing PDSs are similar.* Most of my personal experience in PDSs has been in urban contexts, but speaking and consulting have brought me into contact with suburban and rural settings as well. I have come to learn that the equity challenges that drive my passion about PDSs not only take place in urban schools, but also exist in different ways in rural PDSs and even to some extent in suburban settings. And while I appreciate the different challenges faced in various geographic and cultural settings, I am convinced that much of the organizational work, the focus on student learning, the need to assess and use your assessments to shape what you do—much of what makes a PDS work in any context—is essentially similar and, I hope, is outlined for you in this book.

HOW THIS BOOK IS ORGANIZED

Chapter 1 is a short history of the PDS movement and an introduction to the Standards and to the convergence of what are now commonly accepted as the definitions and goals of professional development schools.

Chapters 2–6 use the ideas embedded in the five PDS Standards to organize the content of the book. Beginning with one of the foundational Standards, Collaboration, these chapters go on to address Structures, Resources, and Roles; Learning Community; Diversity and Equity; and Assessment, Accountability, and Quality Assurance. The format for each chapter organized around the Standards is as follows:

- *Overview and history:* This section describes and illustrates what the Standard looks like and how it might be met, drawing on the language of the PDS Standards and short illustrative examples. The overview includes some of the history and issues pertaining to the Standard.

- *Start-up tasks and challenges:* This section provides concrete examples of the challenges faced with this Standard in the early stages of partnership development.

- *Issues and challenges in sustainability:* This section picks up where the last stopped, moving into challenges faced in implementation and institutionalization.

- *Assessment:* This section has three parts. The first is a Quick-Check self-assessment framework—a series of questions that readers can use to quickly identify where their partnership is located developmentally for the issues discussed in the Standard. Next is an assessment template—guidelines I use with partnerships that are collecting and analyzing data on each Standard to report to internal and external stakeholders. Finally, I include excerpts from a detailed assessment framework developed for a multisite PDS partnership in the Boston area. This work-in-progress is being generously shared by this partnership as an illustration of what a detailed "real" assessment on this Standard would look like.

- *Toolkit:* This section includes specific examples and suggestions for helping readers get where they want to go with the Standard, including worksheets, ideas, and planning sheets that can be used for focusing discussions in partnership steering committee meetings.

- *Chapter resources:* This section offers a brief annotated bibliography of text and Web resources. In addition, it will refer you to http://pds. edreform.net, the PDS Development Portal developed by the National Institute for Community Innovations and edited by Douglas Fleming and myself. The portal provides updated text and Web resources as well as links to service providers that can assist you in planning for and implementing PDS development strategies.

This book concludes with Chapter 7, Next Steps for Strengthening Your PDS. This is an integration and planning document with suggestions on how to do the following:

- Use Quick-Checks to know where you are and where you want to go
- Use case studies to foster communication
- Conduct an informal self-assessment
- Conduct a formal self-study, using the NCATE PDS Standards
- Carry out self-study follow-up plans
- Work with the ideas of this book as part of a network

This book has two appendixes. The first addresses some of the special circumstances involved in applying the ideas in this book to multischool PDS partnerships. The second includes short case studies as triggers for improving communication in PDSs.

HOW TO USE THIS BOOK

- *This book can be read from the beginning in the order it is written.* This is recommended for beginning PDSs, which should find help in each chapter's background and start-up sections along with the related tools and resources. Novice partnerships may also benefit from looking ahead to where they hope to go, because this can shape and ease their transitions and next steps.

- *This book can be read as a reference manual.* Partnerships with questions about whether they are structured in the best way or are using their resources to maximum effect may turn right to the chapter on structures, roles, and resources. The Quick-Check and text sections should lead them to the tools and resources they need.

- *This book can be used as an assessment manual.* Embedded in each chapter are specific ideas for collecting and analyzing data on the Standard addressed, as well as the Quick-Check self-assessment that partnerships can use to locate themselves. A fuller discussion about assessment, types of measurement, and meeting the needs of various stakeholder audiences is included in Chapter 6.

A NOTE ON LEADERSHIP AND READERSHIP

Each chapter begins with the tasks and challenges associated with the topic (for example, start-up issues in partnership formation in the Collaboration chapter or sustaining challenges in addressing achievement gap issues in the Diversity and Equity chapter). For each task and challenge identified, I offer some suggestions for resources or ideas that might help address it. Short suggestions are presented in their entirety, in the Toolkit section of each chapter. Longer recommendations are referred to in the Chapter Resources section. I address my suggestions and recommendations to you as the reader, knowing full well that the readers of this book may vary widely in their positions or formal or informal leadership roles within their organizations. Some will be from schools and others from universities. Some will be parents or community members, or from other potential partnering organizations. The tasks and challenges identified in this book are faced by the organizations trying to partner to make PDSs work. To address them properly demands leadership from a variety of people. Some challenges can best be addressed by those in more formal authority, others by those with less authority who are closer to the partnership action. As my belief statements above indicate, I generally see a blend of top-down and bottom-up effort as working best; where I call for a decision to do something, I generally think development of a consensus on that decision will be the best approach.

WHY IS THERE SO MUCH ABOUT ASSESSMENT IN THIS BOOK?

One of my deep beliefs about PDSs is the importance of having good, high-quality data and information-shaping decisions about PDS development, teaching, and learning. Accordingly, you will find detailed assessment suggestions throughout the book, not just in Chapter 6, which focuses on the Assessment and the Accountability and Quality Assurance Standard. In Chapter 2, you will be introduced to the Urban Teacher Training Collaborative (UTTC), a PDS partnership of Tufts University and three Boston Public Schools, Fenway High School, Boston Arts Academy, and Mission Hill School. To provide some real-world grounding, in each of the chapters based on the Standards, I include excerpts from an assessment framework I designed collaboratively with the UTTC.

The strong focus on assessment in the book comes with a word of caution, however. It is probably not feasible to take every assessment suggestion in this book and apply it to your PDS—certainly not all at once. If you tried to do it all, say in a year, you would probably be so overwhelmed with data collection, analysis, and application that there would be little time for anything else. So pick and choose among the assessment choices in the book. Figure out what makes the most sense for your partnership to pursue—what information should be gathered to answer some important questions about your PDS. Think about the long-term picture of where your PDS wants to go, and what it needs to know to get there, and think in the short term about what assessments you can conduct and use now, this year. I think assessments need to be *used*—thought about, discussed, used for decision making, and shared with various audiences—or they are not worth conducting. As you develop your plans for what assessments would be powerful at your site, you will find some practical suggestions on organizing and managing long- and short-term assessments in Chapter 6. I hope they help you sort through this, so assessment really helps improve and sustain your PDS.

FINAL ORGANIZATIONAL NOTE

Dean Corrigan of the Holmes Group once described PDSs like a fishnet— when you pull on one part by making a change, it inevitably tugs on other sections. I found this to be true in organizing and categorizing this book. Many things are linked and I had to make choices about where, for instance, approaches to developing governance structures for partnerships should be. Is it part of the Collaboration chapter, or the first section of the Structures, Resources, and Roles chapter? It belongs in both, but I have tried to avoid redundancy and, where possible, have cross-referenced material.

I hope you find the book helpful and I welcome feedback and any suggestions.

ACKNOWLEDGMENTS

My deepest thanks go to the thousands of parents, teachers, students, teacher educators, and other faculty and administrators who make professional development schools have a positive impact on the lives of students. What I know about PDSs I have learned from hundreds of you—those I have worked with in PDS networks, interviewed, or met at conferences or site visits, or whose publications and reports I have read. To respect your confidentiality, I have not named you or your partnership in the text. However, I hope that you see yourselves in this book—hear your stories, see reflections of your concerns, suggestions, and ideas—and that the book inspires and helps you to continue your work in much the same way you helped and inspired me to write it.

Particular thanks go

. . . to my friends and colleagues in the Massachusetts PDS Network, where we all learned together over the last decade what PDSs are and how to make them happen—Tom Del Prete, Bob Malloy, Kathy Gagne, Marcia Bromfield, Gerry Pine, Harriet Deane, Judy Finkel, Liz Gold, Vivian Troen, Kitty Boles, Carol Pelletier, Najwa Abdul-Tawwab, and especially my co-facilitator of that network, Karen O'Connor.

. . . to Marsha Levine, Roberta Trachtman, and, in fond memory, Ellie Churins, and all the others involved in the PDS Standards Project of the National Council for the Accreditation of Teacher Education, who showed me that standards matter and can be arrived at in a careful process of consensus building.

. . . to Van Dempsey and the Benedum Collaborative, who taught me so many things about organizing and structuring a large-scale PDS partnership, and who, after several years of trying, managed to make me realize that the equity challenges of rural schools are as great as those of urban schools.

. . . to the PDS working group at the National Center for Restructuring Education, Schools, and Teaching, which more than a decade ago welcomed me into a professional community and grounded me in what matters most about PDSs—Betty Lou Whitford, Lynne Miller, Barnett Berry, Mario Borunda, Jon Snyder, Nona Lyons, Joyce Putnam, Joyce Grant, Peter Wilson, Dick Clark, Charlotte Reed, Bob Williams, and Donna Wiseman. Special thanks to Linda Darling-Hammond and Ann Lieberman, who led us all so collaboratively and purposefully, and to Velma Cobb, for helping me join that wonderful group.

. . . to Ismat Abdal-Haqq, Nancy Lauter, and the dozens of other PDS advocates across the country who worked with us each year to put together a PDS preconference at the Annual Meeting of the American Association of Colleges for Teacher Education.

. . . to Jennie Pilato, Michelle Dunkle, Kim Fleming, Maggie Madden, and Cheri Whitman of the Maryland State Department of Education, who, along with dozens of other fine Maryland educators (including Jason Karolkowski), show that a state can set the lofty goal of having every teacher prepared in a PDS and then move thoughtfully and collaboratively to make it a reality.

. . . to Linda Beardsley, Eileen Shakespear, Rosemary Sedgwick, and the faculty and staff of the Urban Teacher Training Collaborative for taking seriously the challenges of assessing their work and then being willing to share what they have done with the readers of this book.

. . . to Rachel Curtis, Mieko Kamii, Marcie Osinski, Lisa Gonsalves, Tim Knowles, and the rest of those involved in the Boston Public Schools' PDS initiative, for showing how PDS efforts can be focused on equity issues.

. . . to Bobby Belle, Jack Leonard, Charlie Desmond, June Kuzmeskus, Karen Cowan, Sandy Simpson, Chris Baumgarten, Edner Cayemite, Paul Casilli, Ed Noonan, and all the teachers and administrators involved in the Dorchester High School Partnership along with Ann Garafalo, Mary Laurenson, Sharon Norman, Jeanne Wilson, and the staff of the Condon School—for teaching me about the real work of making partnerships happen.

. . . to Peter Murrell, Rebecca Corwin, Dennis Shirley, Bailey Jackson, Nancy Roberts, Lenore Carlisle, Pam Herrup, Darlene Martin, Mari Koerner, and the rest of the Massachusetts Title II coalition, working together, learning from each other, as we try to have an impact statewide on teacher quality.

. . . to Rachel Livsey, the editor at Corwin Press who asked me to write this and guided me through the process, and to the following reviewers, whose helpful suggestions on the first draft are gratefully acknowledged.

D. John McIntyre
Associate Dean for Teacher Education and School Partnerships

College of Education and Human Services
Southern Illinois University at Carbondale
Carbondale, IL

Ismat Abdal-Haqq
Editor, Technology Leadership News
Manager, Education Technology Publications
Education Technology Programs
National School Boards Association
Alexandria, VA

Virginia H. Pilato
Director of Teacher Quality
Maryland State Department of Education
Baltimore, MD

Belinda Gimbert
Assistant Professor of Education
Pennsylvania State University
University Park, PA

Marsha Levine
Senior Consultant, Professional Development Schools
National Council for Accreditation of Teacher Education
Washington, DC

Thanks to Karlyn Morissette and the President and Fellows of Harvard College for the use of the photograph accompanying my biography.

. . . and finally, to my family—the people who give meaning to the part of my life that is not focused on professional development schools—to Laura, my lifelong partner, and to our three daughters, Joanna, Becky, and Emma, who, as they grow from girls to women, continue giving me big lessons on the meaning of life and love.

About the Author

**Lee Teitel** has been a researcher, writer, consultant, speaker, and professional development school advocate since 1989. His work focuses on PDS start-up, institutionalization, and impact issues; new leadership roles in PDSs for teachers and principals; and the development and implementation of national standards for PDSs. He has led workshops and presentations at AACTE and AERA and written numerous articles and monographs on these topics, including two PDS literature reviews, a handbook for the NCATE PDS Standards Project, and booklets on governance and documenting PDS impacts for AACTE. As a consultant, he has worked with individual PDS partnerships, as well as large and small PDS networks. He currently is working with a statewide initiative to make a PDS experience a required part of teacher preparation and with an urban district documenting the impacts their PDSs are having on student learning and teacher development. Lee is active in promoting professional development school partnerships at the University of Massachusetts at Boston, where he is Associate Professor and former Associate Dean for Community, University, and School Partnerships. He worked half-time for two years in a beginning PDS at Dorchester High School in Boston and for more than a decade has co-facilitated the Massachusetts PDS Steering Committee. He is currently one of the codirectors of the Massachusetts Coalition for Teacher Quality and Student Achievement, a statewide, federally funded, multisite school–university partnership initiative. He has developed and taught a course in "Leading Successful School/University Partnerships" at the Harvard Graduate School of Education. He welcomes suggestions, comments, and feedback at Lee.Teitel@umb.edu.

1

Introduction

*History and
Foundations of Professional
Development Schools*

Picture the following scenarios:

- A student teacher, fresh from the local university, comes into a school where she faces a whole chorus of experienced teachers who say, "You can forget everything you learned at the university. This is the real world; we'll show you how to teach."

- A university faculty member, faced with studies that show that most of the approaches he encourages his education students to use "wash off" during student teaching, complains about the schools and their readiness to support their graduates, sometimes calling them "hostile environments" and talking about how to "inoculate" his students against "bad practice."

- A superintendent invests heavily in professional development in her school district, working hard to get the experienced teachers up and running on a new approach such as standards-based education, and then complains when she notices that new teachers coming out of neighboring colleges and universities don't even know what standards-based education is.

- A university professor who is deeply committed to a particular pedagogical approach such as constructivism bemoans the back-to-basics movements and resurgence of direct instruction in her neighboring school district; committed to authentic assessment, she is horrified by the increased use of standardized tests in the district.

- A deputy superintendent for curriculum and instruction in a major urban area wonders why, with more than a dozen universities within five miles of his office, he feels like he gets no help from higher education in addressing any of what he sees as his district's research needs.

The history of the cycles of improvement of teacher education and of schooling show, at best, a lack of coordination and often a complete disconnection, along with associated finger-pointing and blaming. At a basic level, colleges and universities produce teachers for schools; PreK–12 schools prepare students for college. Despite this critical interdependence (and ignoring for a moment the other possible symbiotic connections) between teacher preparation and schools, they have often been out of sync and at odds.

Professional development schools (PDSs) are innovative types of school–college partnerships designed to address this disconnection and finger-pointing and bring about the simultaneous renewal of schools and teacher education programs—restructuring schools for improved student learning and revitalizing the preparation and professional development of experienced educators at the same time. This chapter identifies the history and roots of the PDS movement and outlines the consensus that has evolved about what it means to be a PDS. If PDSs are tools—mechanisms to improve schools and universities—it helps to understand their history and the problems they are attempting to solve. Understanding PDS roots helps us look at the present and better plan for the future.

THE ROOTS AND CONTEXTS FOR PROFESSIONAL DEVELOPMENT SCHOOLS

The PDS movement can be seen as growing out of several other strands of collaboration, reform, and renewal. Although some overlap, a few key areas (adapted from Teitel, 1998b) are outlined below:

School–University Collaboration. Professional development schools are special cases of school–university collaboration in which the experience in partnership formation provides a rich background for the efforts to "grow" PDSs. PDSs can be seen as places in which to resolve the tensions historically existing between schools and universities. For example, new approaches to teaching that develop from research conducted by universities (such as the constructivist learning mentioned above) often have had little impact on classrooms, especially when presented to classroom teachers in non-constructivist ways. PDSs can be creative ways to bridge the gap and avoid the theory–practice dichotomy (Stoddard, 1993).

School Reform. The work of John Dewey and the progressive movement shaped Abraham Flexner's advocacy of the teaching hospital in the reform of medical education; this has come full circle with the use of the teaching hospital as a model for designing professional development schools (Levine, 1992). A look at the historical roots of school reform in the past four decades identifies PDSs as evolutionary responses to reform reports such as *A Nation at Risk* of the early 1980s (Klaumeier, 1990). Sewall, Shapiro, Ducett, and Sanford (1995) describe the PDS approach as logical coalition-building between schools and universities—in part as a defensive reaction to the perception of low public esteem experienced by schools and teacher preparation institutions. Others see an eroding public support for university budgets contributing to their willingness to link themselves to school reform issues that taxpayers care about more (Frazier, 1994).

Foundation Support for School Reform. Many professional development schools got their start through the support of corporations such as Exxon and Ford, so in a sense the PDS movement can be seen as rooted in this subarea of school reform. PDSs have made sense to funders because they bring multiple players to the table at the same time and provide a structure and a mechanism for bringing about change in both sets of institutions.

Teacher Education. For teacher education, PDSs provide an opportunity to create a venue for literal praxis, the development of teaching skill and practice in context. PDSs provide an opportunity to bridge the gap between the abstract and the authentic in the preparation and development of teachers and other educators. Professional development schools can also be seen as growing out of, or in response to, the alternative certification movement (Dixon & Ishler, 1992a). They represent a response that involves universities but also tries to put some credibility back into teacher preparation in the face of the public lack of confidence that has led almost every state to provide some kind of alternative certification route (Frazier, 1994). PDSs represent a proactive response that teacher preparation programs can take to avoid a reactive response to increased regulation from legislatures (Williams, 1993). Finally, PDSs can be seen as the successors to a variety of previous forms of collaboration such as the teacher centers of the 1970s.

Evolution of the Field Experience and Its Supervision. PDS formation can be stimulated by dissatisfaction with the loose connection between the university and what is generally seen as the most important part of the teacher education experience—student teaching. The history of the distrustful, often adversarial relationship between supervisors and classroom teachers serves as an important backdrop to the role changes and reconfigurations of PDSs (Ellsworth & Albers, 1995). Evidence that the student-teaching experience has a more powerful effect than university coursework on prospective teachers makes this even more important to university educators.

Inquiry. Central to the notion of the PDS is the concept of inquiry as part of professional development and as part of the definition of teaching. Schaefer's (1967) notion of the school as a center of inquiry articulates the expectation that teachers should conduct inquiry routinely as a mechanism to understand and assess the teaching–learning process. More recent notions of action research applied to school settings are ways of improving schools and supporting the growth and development of educators.

Professionalization of Teaching. PDSs are important in the development of a knowledge base for teachers (Pugach, 1991), for thinking about the roles of teacher leaders (Collinson, 1994), for thinking about the continued professional development of experienced educators, and for developing new notions of professional accountability. In addition, PDSs can play a critical socializing role if they become the gateway by which all new professionals enter education (Darling-Hammond, 1994).

Teacher Leadership. Although in past school–university collaborations and reform efforts, teachers' roles were to "silently and blithely . . . carry out programs developed by the educational elite" (Navarro, 1992, p. 1), PDSs ask classroom teachers to take on significant new leadership roles (Little & McLaughlin, 1993). These roles are rooted in—and a departure from—earlier models in which teacher leadership was an add-on position involving a handful of individuals who were "appointed" and "anointed" (Smylie & Denny, 1990).

Standards Movement. The simultaneous renewal approach of the PDS makes it compatible with the standards and assessment approach advocated by the National Council for the Accreditation of Teacher Education (NCATE), the National Board for Professional Teaching Standards, and others, providing a framework for the concurrent development and refinement of assessment and standards. PDSs are suited to serve as sites for standards-based education, for the integration of the various standards being produced by groups such as the National Board, and for content area standards such as those of the National Council of Teachers of Mathematics (Sykes, 1997).

Teacher Quality. The report of the National Commission on Teaching and America's Future (1996) made a compelling case that good teaching matters and is the essential key to improved student learning. One of the commission's major recommendations calls for reinventing teacher preparation and professional development, with a central element being the recommendation for yearlong internships in PDSs.

Two more recent trends have given a boost to PDS and also provided some redirection.

Teacher Content Knowledge. The push in the late 1990s for enhanced teacher content knowledge has helped propel PDSs, and at the same time it has nudged them to include arts and science faculty from the university. The Federal Title II legislation for Teacher Quality Enhancement required arts and science faculty involvement in teacher education, even as it called for stronger collaborative relationships with schools—relationships like those of professional development schools.

Equity. The increase in interest in the achievement gap that shows up in schools between students of different race and class backgrounds has given a boost to PDSs as a vehicle to improve equitable outcomes in student learning. For example, the Boston public school system has provided over a quarter of a million dollars annually to fund PDS intern stipends, and has pressed for evidence that the PDS preparation will make the interns more effective in reducing the achievement gap among Boston students. The current high interest in equity has also has led to significant criticisms of PDSs for not living up to their potential. Although many PDS planning documents such as the Holmes Group's *Tomorrow's Schools* (1990) and the *PDS Vision Statement of the National Center for Restructuring Education, Schools, and Teaching* (NCREST, 1993) call for an unflagging commitment to use PDSs to increase equity in U.S. society, observers and critics have noted that much of this has not been realized (Valli, Cooper, & Frankes, 1997). Others have taken the argument further and suggested that without involvement of parents and community members, the PDS model could actually make things worse by strengthening the connection between school and university partners to the exclusion of others (Murrell, 1998).

PRINCIPLES, BELIEFS, AND GOALS:
THE COALESCENCE OF A MOVEMENT

The PDS movement has been promoted by a range of organizations: the Holmes Group, the Carnegie Forum on Education and the Economy, the National Network for Education Renewal, the American Federation of Teachers, the National Educational Association, and initiatives sponsored by Ford and other foundations. The American Association of Colleges for Teacher Education and the National Council for Accreditation of Teacher Education have supported the concept, with NCATE sponsoring the PDS Standards Project. For more than a decade, the National Center for Restructuring Education, Schools, and Teaching as well as a variety of statewide groups such as the Massachusetts PDS Network have funded research, offered conferences, and tried to shape policy in support of PDSs. The National Commission on Teaching and America's Future and its partner states have advocated for PDSs, and some of the partner states, such as Maryland, have woven requirements for PDS into regulation. Federal grants such as Eisenhower, GOALS 2000, and Title II have been used by states and grant recipients to support the work of the PDS collaborations.

Although the wording differs and there are differences in emphasis and focus among different PDS advocates, a strong convergence around the following four goals has emerged over the past 15 years:

- Improvement of student learning
- Preparation of educators
- Professional development of educators
- Research and inquiry into improving practice

This consensus was examined, field-tested, and codified by the PDS Standards Project of the National Council for Accreditation of Teacher Education. Through a careful nomination process, staff of the project identified 28 highly developed PDS sites which participated in a survey describing their practices, goals, organizational structures, funding sources, and so forth. These data were combined with other attempts to assess the state of thinking about PDSs (a literature review and other commissioned papers are published in Levine, 1998). They were used to develop a set of draft standards for PDSs, widely circulated in the late 1990s and field-tested in 16 partnership sites, and released in final form in September 2001.

While not everyone in the PDS community embraces the Standards with the same enthusiasm, they are widely seen as the best representation of the consensus of what it means to be a PDS. Even those who are critical of various segments of the Standards will likely see value in the thorough job the Standards Project did in researching, applying, and codifying. And I hope that even critics will recognize the potential of using them as they are used in this book—to establish a foundation, provide a framework, and help us maintain a focus on student learning.

CHAPTER RESOURCES

This section provides brief annotated references for further reading and Web site locations. Full text citations can be found in the reference section at the end of the book.

For a fuller history of the roots of PDSs, see Teitel (1998b, 1999); for more on general school–university collaboration, see Clark (1988, 1999) and Mitchell and Torres (1998).

For an excellent, balanced article on the notion of PDS Standards, see Sykes (1997).

Look at the Standards themselves (NCATE, 2001b; or go to http://ncate.org/newsbrfs/pds_f01.htm)

For a thoughtful review of "The Nature of Professionalism in the Context of School Reform," see Dempsey (1997).

You may also be interested in the Maryland PDS Standards and a description of the history and evolution of that statewide PDS initiative. See Maryland State Department of Education (2001) or http://cte.jhu.edu/pds/about.cfm. The online "Implementation Manual" is an excellent resource, with a helpful glossary of PDS-related terms.

2

Collaboration

*Developing Joint Ownership
of Student Learning*

At the most basic level, professional development schools are about partnership formation. PDSs start with the premise that the additional time and effort to try to work across two or more organizations is worthwhile compared with trying to achieve the same goals internally.

Partnerships might start for a variety of reasons:

- *Perception of mutual interdependence*: "We are in this together." Schools and universities (and sometimes community or other partners) can only be effective if we work more closely together.
- *Internal cost-benefit analysis*: "We can benefit from this in some way to meet our own organization's needs." Our partner(s) brings something to us that makes it worth the trouble.
- *External perception cost-benefit analysis*: "Collaboration makes us look good." This is worth doing because of how we are perceived.
- *Incentive in the environment*: "If we apply together, we can get this grant." An opportunity exists in the larger environment that makes it worth the trouble to collaborate.
- *Personal connections*: "I have an idea that might help both of our organizations." Opportunities develop out of formal or informal preexisting relationships.

I have seen partnerships get started in a variety of ways, usually in some combination of the above. Grants often serve as the trigger, since many of them call for collaborative approaches, but the underlying interest and willingness must be there. Personal connections have helped many PDSs get started—a middle school principal and a teacher education professor are neighbors, or friends. Their conversations about the issues and challenges they face at work lead to the seed of an idea. For that to ultimately blossom and go to scale, there usually needs to be interest higher up in their organizations. Perhaps the university has a public relations image problem because it is building more dorms or taking real estate off of the local tax rolls and it sees a partnership with schools as a way to give back. A school might need to get more adults into its classrooms to help more of its students pass the state standardized tests. An event may trigger collaboration—like the closing of a lab school and the need for finding good student teacher placements, along with some resources redirected from the lab school. Sometimes personal contact between a university president and a district superintendent gets things started and they then tell their staffs to form partnerships. Here again, for there to be long-term depth and success, there have to be other interests and needs met at the level of the university and school faculty and administrators who will be doing the work.

Collaborations are complex interpersonal and interorganizational undertakings. The PDS Standard calls for "PDS partners [to] systematically move from independent to interdependent practice by committing themselves and making a commitment to each other to engage in joint work focused on implementing the PDS mission" (NCATE, 2001b, p. 15).

This chapter focuses on this critical aspect of the PDS. Placed deliberately at the base of the PDS Standards Student Learning Pyramid, Collaboration quite literally forms the foundation for any and all other aspects of the partnership.

OVERVIEW AND HISTORY

As you read this, you may be in one of a variety of situations in relationship to a PDS partnership. You might be just starting out, wondering with whom to partner. You may be in a wonderful, committed relationship wondering if there could be more, or wanting to reflect on and learn from your successes. You may be in a recent or a long-term relationship that is not meeting all your expectations. You may be in several of these situations at once, perhaps expanding in a growing network of PDSs. Regardless of where you find yourself, consider the following five broad questions as ways to think and reflect about your partnership in the big picture.

- History: Are past relationships assets or obstacles to overcome?
- Change agenda: Is your partnership about minor coordination or transformative change?
- Reciprocity and power: Who is in charge and who is "fixing" whom?
- Commitment: Who is committed to what and for how long?
- Inclusiveness: Who is at the table and who is not?

History: Are Past Relationships Assets or Obstacles to Overcome?

"It was all about the fact that the principal had not been able to use the university's gym when he was a kid," the education chair of a major urban university said to me, to explain the apparent breakdown of one of their PDS partnerships. It was an initiative started by the president and the district superintendent as a way to have the university "give back" to a community where there had been tense "town–gown" relationships, but it was foundering at the building level. "Nothing I could say or do," the education chair went on, "could change or undo that baggage."

Whether the baggage is personal, as in this example from my consulting practice, or organizational, the pain and anger of past hurts and disappointments are real and often deeply felt. The history of collaborations between schools and universities is filled with unmet promises, differing expectations, and misunderstandings. These can leave scars which, if left unaddressed, will affect future partnerships. Because of their differing goals, organizational structures, work tempos, and communication patterns, it is not uncommon for there to be baggage that, unless it is addressed, can get in the way of building new relationships.

Positive past experiences provide a basis and a springboard for deeper experiences such as the formation of a PDS. Collaboration on a similar project, participation on a task force, or joining a P–16 council all contribute to trust, personal connection, and a track record—important assets for partnership development. Knowledge about potential partners and what they might bring to a partnership is helpful.

Developing trust in your potential partner is the first ingredient in partnership formation. To follow up with this, see *Ferguson's Five Steps to Partnership Formation* at the end of the chapter in the Toolkit section on p. 42.

Throughout the process is the underlying question of how much and what kinds of interdependence exist between partners. See *Who Is Depending on Whom? Joint Work Inventory* on p. 41. To look at the history with your partner, see *Unpacking the Baggage Audit* on p. 45 and *What Do We Bring to the Mix?* on p. 46.

Change Agenda: Is Your Partnership About Minor Coordination or Transformative Change?

The words "partnership" and "collaboration" are some of the most overused and misused words of the late 20th and early 21st centuries. I have seen places that called themselves partnerships because they made minor adjustments at the edges, such as having the university offer a graduate class at a later time during the day, so that it could better meet the needs of the teachers at the school. I have seen schools call themselves PDSs because the university had clustered their student teachers in one building, but no other changes were made. At the other extreme, I have seen teacher education programs totally revamped and reorganized around the partnership concept, with substantial field experiences and engagement of school-based faculty and administrators driving the redesign. I have seen schools whose relationship with their university partners was so deep and fundamental to their operation, assessment, and school planning that the principal said, "I couldn't imagine running this school without our partners." The most crucial part of your change agenda is its purpose. As you think about the continuum for change, how much focus is there on the kinds of changes that will improve student learning?

Sorting through the change dimension is challenging because it cannot be planned in a linear way, but rather evolves as a relationship does. In much the same way as the play "I Love You. You're Perfect. Now Change" captures the dimensions of this tension in personal relationships, partnerships will often not be clear about who is changing or what is on the agenda for change until they are into a committed relationship and know more about each other and have higher levels of trust. Like in a marriage or any close and long-term relationship, sorting through requires caring, compassion, honesty, and good communication. And, also as in any relationship, failure to do so will have consequences.

To look at issues of change at your own institution, see *Concerns-Based Adoption Model* on p. 36 and *ACE Depth Versus Pervasiveness Grid* on p. 37. To look at issues of change across institutions, see *How Muscular Is Your Partnership?* on p. 46.

Reciprocity and Power: Who Is in Charge and Who Is Fixing Whom?

In a phrase that draws on both of the preceding questions, Jon Snyder characterizes many historical school–university partnerships as SIPs, short for school improvement programs. Inherent in them (sometimes stated, sometimes not) is that the university will enter the partnership and, using its knowledge, expertise, and resources, try to "fix" the school. That historical pattern is complemented (less frequently) by its opposite—what he calls "flip-SIP." These are partnerships where teachers and other school-based personnel see university programs as out of touch with the needs of schools (and sometimes taught by faculty who haven't been in a classroom in decades) and see their partnership as a chance to "fix" the university (Snyder, 1994).

Embedded in these tensions are key issues of power, knowledge, and authority, as well as struggles for the direction and control of the partnership. What are the sources of power and knowledge in your partnership? If there are organizational or programmatic changes involved, is it one-way or mutual? How do you and your partners move beyond SIP and flip-SIP to develop the notion of joint work, focusing on improvement of common goals? See *Developing Mutuality in PDS Partnerships* on p. 49.

Commitment: Who Is Committed to What and for How Long?

> Several years ago, when I was introduced at a high school where my university would be developing a PDS, the first thing teachers and administrators asked about was my commitment and that of my university. "How long will you be here?" I was asked repeatedly that first September and throughout the year. "Will you and U-Mass still be here after the money [a four-year grant to start a PDS] is gone?" The following September, when I was still spending two to three days a week at the school, several teachers and administrators expressed their pleasure at my commitment: "We thought you would just be here until you had enough material to write a book about what it is like in an urban high school. Just being back the second year makes you different from the rest."

The issues of personal and institutional commitment are key, not just regarding the length of commitment, but also regarding its scope and depth. Part of the negative baggage that often exists in partnerships is the lack of commitment—a sense of being used by one of the partners (a sentiment more often expressed by schools in relationship to universities than vice versa). Some PDSs evolve out of preexisting long-term connections between a school and a university and have an indefinite end point. Some are set up to be PDSs with no discussion of end points. Others are established on a contract renewal basis—a formal commitment exists for, say, five years, at which time it will be reconsidered. Finding the balance and matching levels of commitment can be a challenge. Open-ended partnerships need to keep in mind the need for an "out" or a "sunset" provision that can be applied to a relationship that isn't meeting the needs of the partner(s) but just limps along anyway. How does it end?

The scope and depth of a partnership may also vary considerably. Some remain focused narrowly on teacher education or school improvement issues, while others use the partnership as a platform for other opportunities. See *Partnership Development Stage Theory* on p. 47, as well as *Breaking Up Is Hard to Do* on p. 48.

One partnership I've worked with used its successful work in teacher education to apply the same relationships and principles to transforming its educational administration program; another broadly expanded its PDS connections and vision to include a host of P–16 issues as well as neighborhood and community development. See *Using a Successful PDS Model to Transform a University* on p. 47.

Inclusiveness: Who Is at the Table and Who Is Not?

Caught up in the excitement and the bona fide benefits that come out of professional development schools, partners sometimes neglect to look at who is participating and who is not. Many PDSs are relationships between faculty and administrators from schools and from teacher education programs. The deepening of the relationships between these two sectors can bring about a great deal of positive energy and improvements for students and preservice and inservice educators. But they can also limit or even damage the partnership by excluding others who could and should be engaged. Arts and science faculty members are often omitted, although they provide more of the instruction of (and therefore arguably have more influence on) preservice educators than teacher education faculty do. Parents and community members, passionately interested in the education of their children and youth, may be excluded—actually shut out as the school–teacher education relationships strengthen—possibly reducing the partnership's effectiveness in addressing diversity and equity issues. Peter Murrell, who makes this argument persuasively in *Like Stone Soup* (1998) and again in *Community Teacher* (2001), suggests that PDSs may do more harm than good if their net effect is to eliminate or reduce the voices and engagement of parents and community agencies in the process of preparing teachers and improving schools.

Further, narrowly focused PDS partnerships may miss opportunities to connect with larger issues and forces in their communities. Business roundtables may have keen interests and ideas for teacher education and school improvement. P–16 councils or neighborhood revitalization task forces may provide opportunities to connect on larger and compatible sets of issues.

Issues of inclusiveness of partners and implications for diversity and equity are explored further in Chapter 5. In addition, in the toolkit section, see *Scanning the Environment for Potential Partners—Who Is Missing?* on p. 50 and *Connecting Your PDS to Larger Issues and Organizations* on p. 51.

These five broad questions shape the big picture of partnership formation. The next two sections look more closely at the challenges faced in starting and sustaining PDSs, respectively.

START-UP TASKS AND CHALLENGES

The tasks and challenges section of this chapter (and the next four) is divided into two parts. The first looks at start-up issues—what challenges are faced in the early stages of partnership development. The second addresses more mature partnerships and issues of sustaining growth and institutionalizing relationships. If you are thinking about starting a PDS or are in the early stages of initiating one, this is a good starting section. If you are past this point and are in a more mature relationship, you may want to look back to see how (or if) these start-up challenges and tasks were addressed or skip ahead to the next section.

As potential partners think about start-up challenges, it is helpful to sort them into three domains. Most people think of collaboration as something that takes place between or among partners. This makes sense and most of the tasks, challenges, and suggestions in this chapter focus on interorganizational issues. In addition, however, there are important dimensions to collaboration that apply to the internal workings of organizations and there are important aspects that refer to the larger context in which the partnership is taking place. Accordingly, this chapter is organized around the following three areas:

- Internal issues (in relationship to your own organization)
- Issues in relationship to your partner
- Larger contextual or environmental issues

If you are considering or implementing PDS partnership development, you have two major tasks to accomplish in the start-up phase. The first is *investigation*: You need to look at your own organization, possible partners, and the larger environment, and you and your organization have to decide that the benefits of working with others are worth the trouble or at least worth exploring further. As you move toward developing a partnership, you face the second major task, *initiation*: You need to find partners that your organization finds interesting enough and compatible enough to be worth investing your time with, who have a matching, mutual interest. Within these broad headings for the investigation and initiation stages, specific challenges follow.

Internal Issues

The first step is to look within. Before beginning a search for partners, think about how good a partner your own school or university would be. How open are you and your colleagues to outsiders? If change is on the agenda of a partnership, how "innovation ready" is your organization? What is the internal culture among the adults like in relationship to collegiality, experimentation, and high expectations? To help assess this, see *School Culture Audit* on p. 33 and *Assessing the Partnership Climate in Your Own Environment* on p. 34.

> At one of the first partnership workshops I led, in 1992, there were three teachers from an urban middle school sitting with their college partner. When I asked, as part of the workshop, how each partnership was formed, the teachers proudly described how for several years their school had been a model for district innovation with an extended day and Saturday classes and how the collaborative culture among the teachers had been thriving. Confident of their own readiness for a partnership, and eager to take on student teachers and grow through a relationship with a college, they sent out letters to the area colleges, looking for a partner. That had been a year a half earlier and they were pleased to find a college interested in talking to them—one which had a middle school teacher education program but wished to focus it more in urban areas. As they were getting to know one another, a small grant from the state department of education came along; they applied together and were moving forward.

As you move forward to identify a partner and start building a relationship, keep track of who is involved in the planning and commitment stage. Is it just an isolated few individuals or does the partnership have the wider support of the faculty and staff at your school or university? Does it have the support of the people in power? How will involvement with the partnership mesh with existing culture, structure, governance, and philosophy? See *Marginalization and Change in PDSs* on p. 35.

Issues in Relationship to Your Partner

The first stage of any investigation of partnership possibilities is consideration of potential partners. What do you know about the schools, universities, unions, or community organizations with whom you might collaborate? What similarities and differences exist? Is the history with potential partners good or bad? Ron Ferguson (1999) has suggested that the first step in partnership formation is development of trust—organizations want to know whether potential partners have the competence and dependability to deliver on what they promise, whether their motives can be trusted, and whether they can be counted on to act collegially. Is there a positive history of collaboration to draw on? Is there negative baggage in the history that will affect the development of trust, and if so, what can you do to overcome it? To follow up with this see *Ferguson's Five Steps to Partnership Formation* on p. 42, *Unpacking the Baggage Audit* on p. 45, and *What Do We Bring to the Mix?* on p. 46.

As the relationship develops from investigation to initiation, it makes sense to see how Ferguson's trust questions about competence, motives, dependability, and collegiality have been answered and how partners have sorted out issues of control. What degree of mutuality is expected and understood? See also *Finding a Partner: Sources* on p. 38 and *Evaluating a Potential Partner* on p. 39.

A dean of a small liberal arts college described what he did after his college and a nearby elementary school received a planning grant to develop a PDS.

"One of our faculty members and I started to go to these biweekly meetings at the school, with the steering committee they had put together. The teachers kept asking us what we were there for and what we wanted to do. We just kept listening to them, just kept coming back to them and saying it is not our agenda—it is what you want and what we can work out together. It took about three months before they stopped suspecting we were going to impose a hidden agenda on them, before they started to talk about what they wanted. Then we were able to get moving."

You also want, at this point, to think about formalizing your partnership agreement and commitments. Some partnerships, including some long-standing and very successful ones, remain based on informal "hand-shake" agreements. Many choose—sometimes right at the beginning, sometimes after they have worked together for a while—to commit to paper some sort of partnership agreement. Announcements and other ceremonies sometimes accompany these agreements. They can draw positive attention to the PDS as well as help define roles and organize structures, resource allocations, and decision-making processes. See *Making It Formal: Partnership Agreements* on p. 40.

Larger Contextual or Environmental Issues

Think for a moment about the larger context in which your organization operates. Schools are parts of districts. Departments or colleges of education are parts of universities. Unions are locals of national organizations. Looking at the larger environment helps you place your PDS development in a bigger context, something many PDS advocates miss. How conducive is the larger environment of your organization to partnership formation? Are there implicit or explicit barriers to partnership—administrators at the next level and other stakeholders who do not support and value partnership formation? Are there ways around those obstacles or ways to turn that resistance or concern to support? See *Who Cares?* on p. 218 and *What Do Stakeholders Care About?* on p. 219 in Chapter 6.

Sometimes your larger organization can provide encouragement, support, or additional resources. One of your challenges might be to align with the goals and missions of your larger organization in ways that help move the PDS forward even as they help meet a need in the larger organization. Perhaps there are individuals in positions of power and authority in your organization whose interests align and who might become allies.

A teacher education director in a large university was wondering where she would get the resources to set up a PDS. Until someone else told her, she was unaware that her university president had just become the chair of a higher education partners consortium committed to helping the neighboring city schools. When she brought the planned PDS to the president's attention, the latter was able to support it as part of the university's contribution to the consortium. In another setting, a savvy teacher seeking district support for the PDS she had helped to start prepared a briefing detailing how the PDS helped the district achieve its stated mission statement.

See *Aligning With the Larger Goals and Vision of Your Organization* on p. 50.

In addition to looking more widely within your own organization, scanning the outside environment can bring in other potential allies and help address the inclusiveness of PDSs. There are plenty of other people outside of schools and universities interested in the issues that PDSs focus on and many ways that PDSs can connect. Many of the hottest issues in the larger society—teacher quality, teacher retention, and reduction of the achievement gap—are issues that are central to professional development schools. Often educators are too unconnected, unfamiliar, or preoccupied to see and make connections to outside groups that care about similar issues. When PDS educators lift their heads up from their own work, they find other allies—partners in the community, unions, nonprofits, or political organizations who bring resources and ideas and broaden the inclusiveness and the potential impact of the PDSs.

> One PDS leader in a small city in Massachusetts has worked closely with his university, the school district, and community organizations interested in revitalizing the area around the university. Together they got grants from a variety of sources that refurbished housing stock in the area, made low-cost mortgages to homeowners who would live in the neighborhood, and built a PDS in the area, the graduates of which would be eligible for free tuition at the university.

See *Scanning the Environment for Potential Partners—Who Is Missing?* on p. 50.

ISSUES AND CHALLENGES IN SUSTAINABILITY

This section picks up where the last stopped, moving further into challenges faced in the implementation and institutionalization stages. For purposes of writing about them here and elsewhere in the book, I am treating these stages as sequential and linear in a way that, in reality, they often are not. Frequently partnerships move in and out of stages, taking some steps toward deepening their relationship and then, perhaps due to the departure of a key supporter or some other event, taking some steps back. Not only is this process less linear than it looks here, it is also powerfully affected by things that will show up in chapters on other Standards—changes in the accountability environment or new approaches to learning community.

There is also significant overlap between this chapter and the next, since much of what you are trying to do during the *implementation* phase is figure out what structures, resources, and roles you need to support the new joint PDS activities. Thus, to minimize duplication and to maintain necessary flow, there are several times where I will refer here to Toolkit ideas that are in Chapter 3, and vice versa. As you and your partners move into the institutionalization phase, I encourage you to support the changes and resolve any conflicts that may take place within your own organization, deepen and reinforce the long-term commitments with your partner, and remain ever open to inclusiveness and opportunities in the larger environment.

The following specific questions and challenges should help you think about the work of this stage.

Internal Issues

At this stage there are probably a variety of new teaching and learning activities taking place in your partnership. Perhaps you have interns clustered at the school, new forms of mentoring and coteaching, or new collaborative approaches to teaching science to preservice teachers and to children. This is a good time to look at what changes in organizational structures, roles, responsibilities, and resource allocation are taking place to support them. Many of these activities will require different sets of belief structures to fully implement. What changes in organizational culture—beliefs, approaches, and attitudes—are developing to better support these partnership activities? See *Restructuring and Reculturing* on p. 160 in Chapter 4.

As you move toward long-term sustainability, take a look to see if permanent changes are being made in governance structure, resource streams, and reward systems—in the structural supports to the work of the partnership. Is a critical mass of persons involved throughout the organization, including persons with leadership and authority? See *Achieving Critical Mass: Engaging People in PDS Work* on p. 106 and *Moving to Power* on p. 104. Are schedules and workload altered so that staff of the organization can do the work of the partnership as part of their regular jobs? See Chapter 3, *Valuing and Rewarding PDS Work* on p. 112. If these changes are not taking place, your chances for long-term sustainability are slimmer, since partnership efforts will remain individual and isolated, supported by the passion and beliefs of individuals, but not your organization.

Check on your level and readiness for change. Ask yourself and your colleagues about how big an impact your PDS work is having and should be having on your entire organization. The issues of sustainability, marginality, and depth of change are interwoven. The early PDSs typically started on the margins of their organizations as pilots and then were pulled into the core as change agents. Others remain as pockets of change, with very little impact on the rest. Partnerships not satisfied with being pockets of change need to address issues of critical mass referred to above, as well as look at the *Mechanisms for Transfer of Ideas and Approaches*, on p. 98 in Chapter 3.

> Not all PDSs strive for, or are successful at, moving from being a pilot to shaping the core of their organization. One partnership I work with is going into its fifth year with a strong and vibrant PDS program going on at the school. Yet there is little to no impact back at the university. The faculty member who leads the effort is in residence at the school. She likes it that way, preferring to work with school-based adults and kids and since she spends little time on campus and there are no real transfer mechanisms, her program has very little influence or effect on the campus. I have also seen the comparable marginalization in schools. In some schools, especially departmentalized high schools or other large schools, a relatively small subset of the teaching faculty works with the PDS. Others may have little or no knowledge about its existence.

See *ACE Depth Versus Pervasiveness Grid* on p. 37.

There are plenty of other examples where the opposite has taken place—where PDSs begun as pilots have replaced traditional teacher education programs. Also, some schools, districts, or universities have become involved in PDSs as part of a wholesale renewal strategy. Rather than starting small with individual pilots on the margins and then bringing the change to the rest of the organization, in those settings the communication patterns, use of data and other information on impacts, and mechanisms for sharing ideas are structured and organized to scale up change immediately. We will come back to these differences in approach in Chapter 3.

Issues in Relationship to Your Partner

As you begin to implement activities, what connecting mechanisms between you and your partner are being put into place to coordinate, plan, and link the activities? Here again, the structural details of this will be explored in Chapter 3 (see, for instance, in the Toolkit section of Chapter 3, *Liaison Scope, Advantages, and Disadvantages* on p. 90, and *Steering Committees Source, Advantages, and Disadvantages* on p. 92), but use the opportunity in this chapter to explore what is happening in the deepening of your relationship with your partner. How have you thought about and discussed what changes, if any, you and your partners are involved in, in each other's organizations? See *How Muscular Is Your PDS Partnership?* on p. 46 Ron Ferguson suggests that after the trust and control issues are addressed, partners need to reach agreement on agendas, secure commitments, and earnestly begin common projects. See *Ferguson's Five Steps to Partnership Formation* on p. 42.

Take a look at your decision-making processes. The PDS Collaboration Standard suggests that "Deeper levels of collaboration blur the boundaries between and among partner institutions. Fully integrated decision making for the PDS partnership exists in areas that were formerly the sole domain of one of the partner institutions." An example of this might be making decisions about admissions of preservice teachers. In many settings this task, formerly the sole purview of the university, has become a joint PDS responsibility. Some decisions might be considered relatively low stakes, such as the assignment of an intern to a cooperating mentor; others might be seen as higher stakes, such as deciding to drop an intern from the program because he or she is not effective in the classroom and does not seem to be able to learn. Use the *Ladder of Decision Making* on p. 95 in Chapter 3 to help you and your partnership assess where you are on developing joint decision-making processes.

As you move toward sustainability and institutionalization, how well have your connections and processes been put into place? If you are working well together, you may be overcoming prior negative baggage and laying the basis for further and deeper collaboration. Have you been communicating your success so that others within your partner organizations and other external stakeholders know about them? See *Celebrating Joint Work* on p. 42. Are agreements in place at all the appropriate levels to continue the work? See *Making It Formal: Partnership Agreements* on p. 40. You may need to revisit agreements and make sure that they are up-to-date with the growth of the partnership and that the right people and levels of the organization are involved. See *Renewing and Deepening Commitments* on p. 42.

Part of any renewal and deepening process assumes that the partnership pay-off is high enough to want to continue. It is a good idea to periodically check in to make sure that the relationship still makes sense to continue. Check to see if your needs as well as your partner's are being met and figure out ways to have conversations with each other about this. In some of my consulting and documentation work, I have come across some sad examples of trapped partners, where the relationship was no longer meeting the needs of the partners, but they felt compelled to stay together. See *Breaking Up Is Hard to Do* on p. 48.

Larger Contextual or Environmental Issues

Check again as your partnership grows and develops to make sure all possible partners are involved. If you did not think to add unions, parents, community agencies, or nonprofits to the partnership at the outset, explore the advantages and disadvantages of doing so now. If you do, you will need to be attentive to the ways the addition of new partners will affect the dynamics—how decision making will be shared and how new individuals and groups will be caught up on what is happening and also have their new and different ideas welcomed. See *Adding Partners Later On* on p. 44.

At this point, within your own larger organization (district, university) you will probably be getting more attention. As partnerships move from pilot or experimental status into the mainstream, they typically come under greater scrutiny in the organization. You may find that others in the larger organization, who had nothing to do with your work, have more questions, or even become resistant, as they wonder about whether this PDS-type work is a direction they will have to follow. (See Chapter 3, *Pulling in to the Core* on p. 106.) As you try to get enough resources to shift the burden of the work from individualized voluntary overload contributions to becoming part of the regular work of the PDS participants, the real costs of PDS work will become more apparent. See the cluster of ideas under Resources in Chapter 3. This may have implications in the larger organization and may pose more questions for you on how you know what you are doing in the PDS is worthwhile. (See *What Do Stakeholders Care About?* on p. 219 in Chapter 6.)

Finally, in the larger environmental context outside the school and university, what role does the partnership have in meeting the larger needs and challenges? The developmental rubric on the Collaboration Standard has a category for "Leading." This is reserved for those partnerships that exceed the Standard and play key roles not only in "systemic changes in policy and practices in the partner institutions," but in having an "impact on policy at the district, state and national levels." How, for instance, does your PDS's work fit into the challenges of getting and retaining high-quality teachers for your local area's schools? What kind of voice does it have?

One PDS collaborative I work with has parleyed its success in transforming its teacher education program through its PDS partnerships into a statewide role in the teacher quality discussion. The largest teacher education program in a small, mostly rural state, the collaborative has been able to document, in a variety of ways, impacts on student learning in its PDSs. Impressed, state legislators and the governor have allocated state monies to support the model and to encourage other state colleges and universities to develop professional development schools.

Focusing on Student Learning

Sitting as it does at the base of the PDS Standards Student Learning Pyramid, the Collaboration Standard considered in this chapter is graphically the furthest from Student Learning, at the apex. This graphical fact mirrors the reality that, in many PDSs, the issues and challenges of collaboration seem to be less about the students and their learning and more about the adults and how to best build relationships among them. As we close this section of the chapter, I want to revisit the fundamental premise of this book and of PDSs—that each of the Standards can and should connect to improving the learning of children and adolescents.

Collaboration is about joint ownership of student learning. "PDSs only really work," said Marsha Levine, director of the PDS Standards Project, "when university folks care as much about the learning of school students as school folks do." When relationships are built well, when communication about important things takes place, this joint ownership can and does take place.

Collaboration draws on the strengths and special skills of each partner to help students. Partnerships that work well to focus on student learning tap the expertise of all participants, whether by having the staff of a community-based organization involve high school students in an oral history of the school's neighborhood; trying out a new approach to inclusion from a special education teacher; testing out a different way to do dismissal developed by a joint committee of students, parents, and teachers; or drawing on the knowledge of language acquisition from a university professor.

The diversity of input stretches partners' views of how to work with students. When parents and community members work with school and university personnel, including arts and science faculty, the perspectives of all involved are expanded.

Collaboration can bring coherence and reduce fragmentation to better focus on students. When PDSs align with school improvement plans and offer consistent, coordinated directions for teaching and learning, the impact is powerful. For example, when a PDS aligns its approach to teaching of reading so interns learn the same approach that teachers use, interns can be major assets in the classroom.

ASSESSMENT

The first part of this section is a Quick-Check self-assessment framework (see p. 26)—a series of questions that you can use to quickly identify where your partnership is located, developmentally, for each of the key areas related to the Collaboration Standard. This can be used as a diagnostic tool for yourself or it can be used by a planning group as a way to check in on the understandings of the different perceptions of progress. The second part of this section includes some detailed suggestions on how best to document your findings on this Standard for internal and external stakeholders, followed by a detailed example from the Urban Teacher Training Collaborative.

Assessment Framework

Because the Collaboration Standard serves as the foundation for the partnership, the main documentation task on this Standard is descriptive. Unlike some of the other Standards, where you will be interested in showing impacts on students, experienced educators, and so forth, here you are describing the basic underpinnings of the partnership. This is the place to describe the school and university partners as well as, where applicable, families and communities, arts and science faculties, unions, museums, and other nonprofit organizations. In this section, documentation should include some background on partners and what brought them into the PDS, how it got initiated, and any key aspects of how it has grown. When you are able to, weave into this section your thoughts on how the five questions that undergird this chapter about collaboration are being addressed in the partnership:

- History: Are past relationships assets or obstacles to overcome?
- Change agenda: Is the partnership about minor coordination or transformative change?
- Reciprocity and power: Who is in charge and who is fixing whom?
- Commitment: Who is committed to what and for how long?
- Inclusiveness: Who is at the table and who is not?

Documentation of the extent and depth of the partnership should be part of this section, including data on intern placement and the depth and breadth of involvement of university and school faculty and administrators

Form 2.1   Quick-Check Self-Assessment Framework

For each statement below, assess the response that best describes your partnership, using a scale ranging from Strongly Disagree (SD), to Disagree (D), to Agree (A), to Strongly Agree (SA). Use NA for items that are not applicable in your context. Use the space below each item to list a few indicators that give evidence to support your assessment and to explain any questions you felt were not applicable.

1. Our partnership includes all   SD   D   A   SA   NA
   relevant stakeholders.
   Indicators:

2. Our partnership is fully reciprocal.   SD   D   A   SA   NA
   Indicators:

3. All of our partners are clear about the   SD   D   A   SA   NA
   nature and purpose of the partnership.
   Indicators:

4. No individual or partner dominates   SD   D   A   SA   NA
   the partnership—there is a strong
   sense of parity.
   Indicators:

5. Our partnership is not dependent   SD   D   A   SA   NA
   on any one person.
   Indicators:

6. Our change agenda has depth and we   SD   D   A   SA   NA
   are clear about what it is.
   Indicators:

7. We share a clear vision for the   SD   D   A   SA   NA
   partnership direction.
   Indicators:

8. We have unpacked and explored   SD   D   A   SA   NA
   our partnership baggage and history.
   Indicators:

9. We have a clear focus on the joint   SD   D   A   SA   NA
   work we do together.
   Indicators:

10. There are formal and informal tangible   SD   D   A   SA   NA
    commitments to the partnership.
    Indicators:

11. We celebrate our joint work and   SD   D   A   SA   NA
    accomplishments.
    Indicators:

and of any other partners. Other examples of data that could be collected to document collaboration include grant proposals, minutes of meetings, collaborative agreements, histories, calendar of partnership events, surveys of stakeholders, press clippings and copies of newsletters, and yearly progress reports (adapted from Sirotnik, 1988).

Collaboration Assessment Template

Use this brief template as a way to start organizing and gathering data related to collaboration. It is followed by a draft example from the Urban Teacher Training Collaborative in Boston.

Introduction

Collaboration is the key underpinning of the [name of partnership]. Formed in _____ between _____, the partnership has since expanded to include _____.

In addition to the educational institutions involved, partners include _____ [families and communities, arts and science faculties, unions, museums, and other nonprofit organizations].

Descriptions of Partners: Background, Philosophy, History

[This is the place to insert documents that describe the partners, as well as the philosophy behind the partnership for the school, the university, and the other partners.]

Roots and Stages of the Partnership Development

[This is the place to tell the story of setting up the partnership, including the focus on engaging in joint work and how it evolved, as well as the development of joint governance. Document your growth from independence to interdependence on issues relating to the PDS mission. The section might include a vision of where you plan to go with it. Some possible points might include the following:]

- Prior partnership history
- Engagement in joint work
- Intern placement (including numbers and any other details)

- Philosophy
- Involvement of university faculty in the PDS
- School faculty involvement at university
- Roles and engagement of other partners
- Development of collaborative governance
- Types of decisions that get made jointly (and how this may have changed over time)
- Future plans for the collaborative

Systematic Recognition and Celebration of Joint Work and Contribution of Each Partner

How has this evolved and what does it look like?

Documentation Example

What follows is the first of five excerpts from the Urban Teacher Training Collaborative (UTTC) in Boston, a partnership among the Fenway High School, the Boston Arts Academy, Mission Hill Elementary School, three pilot schools in the Boston Public Schools, and Tufts University. (Pilot schools are in-district charter schools—public schools with increased levels of flexibility and autonomy.) This is a draft document—a work in progress prepared by Linda Beardsley of Tufts, used here solely for illustrative purposes and edited and excerpted by me for those purposes. [My notes will are brackets.]

[The documentation begins with several paragraphs of overview of the need, including sections on "The Crisis in Urban Teacher Preparation," how the Traditional Teacher Training Model does not meet the needs for preparing teachers for urban schools, and how the Professional Development School Model helps address these shortcomings. Due to space concerns, these are not duplicated here. The documentation goes on to address the partners that make up the UTTC and its formation as a collaborative. Note how the document tracks the deepening commitment of the institutions over time and lays a basis, in its list of implementation goals, for assessing its impacts. The excerpt concludes with the future plans of the collaborative, so it serves as a planning document as well as a reporting device.]

THE URBAN TEACHER
TRAINING COLLABORATIVE (UTTC)

In urban teaching, my sense is we [teacher and student] have to look each other in the eye, to figure out as soon as we can what we mean to each other. Whether it is going to be a respectful relationship. Where are you going to take me? What can I learn from you? Once we figure all that out, the human-to-human stuff, then we can get to the calculus. If we don't do the relationship building first, then we can never get to the calculus.

—Director, Fenway High School

TWO URBAN HIGH SCHOOLS
COMMITTED TO TEACHER TRAINING

Fenway High School and the Boston Arts Academy are two small public high schools, located at 174 Ipswich Street in Boston, that embrace the mission of training the next generation of excellent urban high school teachers. Fenway has taken teaching interns from a number of local universities for eight years; Boston Arts Academy has had interns since it opened in 1998. The interns come from several teacher preparation programs in the Boston area including Tufts, Harvard, Simmons, UMass Boston, Wellesley, and Boston College. The Boston Arts Academy has also been a site placement for interns from the Pro-Arts Consortium schools including Massachusetts College of Art, Emerson College, Berklee College of Music, and the New England Conservatory. During the 2000–2001 school year there were nineteen interns training at Ipswich Street, ten of whom were full-time. The interns included those who were training to become teachers of mathematics and science, humanities, visual arts, music, and drama. The Ipswich Street schools have been particularly eager to help develop teachers of color and have worked closely with Tufts and Harvard to recruit minority teacher candidates.

Although the two schools are administered separately, they share science labs, a library, cafeteria, auditorium, and various services in the renovated school building at 174 Ipswich Street. Each school has its own staff, separate classes, and unique character and atmosphere. However, the schools share similar pedagogical philosophies, similar orientation toward students, parents, and teachers, and similar commitments to urban teacher training.

The Ipswich Street schools provide the kind of collaborative environment needed to prepare new teachers to be leaders for change in urban schools. The schools are structured in small clusters of teachers and students, so teachers and students can get to know one another well and form trusting relationships that make the culture of achievement possible in the urban high school setting. Teachers, administrators, specialists, and university staff continually challenge one another to consider new situations, different approaches, and progressive ideas. They confer spontaneously in corridors and offices and at the copy machine. They also confer in scheduled staff meetings. Content teams meet weekly to plan curriculum and consult on student work. Cross-content teams meet weekly to discuss individual student progress from the perspective of different disciplines and teachers. The whole staff meets weekly to discuss the larger issues of running an urban school and remaining true to its mission.

The Tufts Professional Development School

In 1999, the Tufts University Teacher Education Program was looking for an internship site for its teacher candidates who were pursuing a Master of Arts in Teaching (MAT) degree, with a focus on urban education. The Director of Teacher Education, Linda Beardsley, convened senior faculty from the two high schools and the Tufts Education Department, as well as Dean Rob Hollister and Vice President Mel Bernstein, to consider a proposal for an Urban Teacher Training Collaborative (UTTC). The primary goal of the Collaborative would be "to prepare teachers to teach effectively in urban high schools" and to "develop a model . . . in which certification candidates have a year-long experience working in and studying the context of the urban high school."

In the 1999–2000 academic year, Tufts demonstrated its commitment to the Collaborative by providing $327,000 in professional and administrative staffing, candidate recruitment, tuition-waiver costs, stipends and course vouchers for mentor teachers, and stipends for interns. In the fall of the following year,

Ms. Beardsley also secured a three-year commitment from the Boston Public Schools' Center for Leader- ship Development (CLD) to give each of the ten teaching interns in the 2000–2003 school years a stipend of $10,000.

[Editor's note: Additional documentation that UTTC might add here would be on the other partners, Pro-Arts, the importance of the arts to the collaborative, etc.]

Development of Collaborative Governance

A Steering Committee meets monthly throughout the academic year to discuss the evolution of the PDS partnership. Included on the steering committee are administrators from Boston Arts Academy, Fenway High School, and Mission Hill School; faculty from Tufts University; Intern Coordinator of the Ipswich Street Site; and support staff for the grant. In addition, an evaluator has been meeting with these key stakeholders to design an evaluation that allows the partners to see themselves reflected in the work and learn how the roles, support systems, and resources are being used to improve the preparation of urban teachers.

SHORT- AND LONG-TERM GOALS

Four Implementation Goals

The Collaborative defined four implementation goals for the first phase of the PDS program. At the end of this second year of the Collaborative, the program goals have proven to be eminently reachable. [Editor's note: For space considerations these goals are listed, but the elaboration and explanation of them has been removed.]

1. Attract a talented and diverse pool of interns to work in the Boston Arts Academy and Fenway Pilot High School.

2. Establish a Year-Long Teaching Internship Experience.

3. Create a seminar in which interns can reflect on the issues of urban education and learn from experienced teachers.

4. Develop content and strategies within the Tufts Teacher Preparation Program that will reflect the issues of urban education.

Future Plans for the Collaborative

• 2002–2003: Continue to develop the PDS model at the Mission Hill School by creating the Site Coordinator position, a Tufts University faculty liaison to the site to work with both interns and mentor teachers.

• Continue to hold the ED 102 seminar on the Ipswich Street site cofacilitated by a member of Tufts faculty and the Intern Coordinator.

• Introduce another course on site, ED 142: Education of Exceptional Students, taught by Tufts faculty. This course will be open to Tufts interns, other MAT students, and Ipswich mentor teachers. The course will include classroom observation and research on best practices to ensure that all students achieve at high levels.

• Explore additional resources from Tufts to enhance the math curriculum at Ipswich Street.

• Begin conversations with Pro-Arts Consortium Schools regarding bringing in interns in the arts to the PDS program and establishing the support system necessary . . . including representatives on the Steering Committee.

• 2003–2004: Include interns from Pro-Arts Consortium Schools.

[Editor's note: The following is specific documentation that UTTC could add in this section:]

• Engagement of Tufts faculty and administration (education and arts and sciences) in the schools, including year-to-year trends
• Engagement of Fenway, Boston Arts Academy, and Mission Hill faculty and administrators in Tufts courses, planning, and so forth, including year-to-year trends
• Systematic recognition and celebration of joint work and contributions of each partner. How has this evolved? What does it look like?

Toolkit

This section includes specific examples and suggestions for helping you address issues and questions that came up while reading the chapter. If the Quick-Check and the earlier sections of the chapter have highlighted some challenges faced in your partnership, these tools should help you get where you want to go. It includes worksheets, inventories, ideas, and small summaries of relevant theories, reflective writing prompts, and planning sheets that can be used for focusing discussions in partnership steering committee meetings. It is organized in the same fashion as the earlier part of the chapter, with the bulk of it focused on partnership development issues, bracketed by sections on the internal issues (in relationship to your own organization) and the larger contextual or environmental issues.

Internal Issues (In Relationship to Your Own Organization)

2.1 School Culture Audit

How strong is the culture in your school or university? One measure of how ready your organization is for the innovations that might come from being part of a PDS is to conduct some sort of school culture audit. You can use a variety of frameworks to measure this, including developing your own. Jon Saphier and Matt King (1985) identified 12 norms that support strong school cultures; in my own work, I have found they apply equally well to universities.

1. Collegiality
2. Experimentation
3. High expectations
4. Trust and confidence
5. Tangible support
6. Reaching out to the knowledge bases
7. Appreciation and recognition
8. Caring, celebration, and humor
9. Involvement in decision making
10. Protection of what is important
11. Traditions
12. Honest, open communication

To conduct a school culture audit, introduce the concepts at a meeting (you, and preferably others, will need to read Saphier and King's short article to get a fuller understanding of the norms) and review each one, with examples, so there is clarity on the definition of each. Once people understand the norms, you can turn the list into a self-assessment tool by asking them to rate, on a scale of 1 to 5, where your organization is, providing one or two indicators explaining each rating. If you want to take the experience further, you might choose to focus on one or two norms that the majority thinks are lacking and develop some strategies as a group for changing this. You might also share your results with your PDS partner and work jointly on improving some of each other's norms.

2.2 Assessing the Partnership Climate in Your Own Environment

How open is your school or university to outsiders? Some organizations are more open than others, more comfortable sharing information on what is really going on inside, and more willing to listen to the voices and opinions of others: Organizations that are more open to outsiders will generally form partnerships more readily. To assess your organization, generate some questions to ask yourself and your colleagues about how you respond to outsiders. I've included a few to get you started:

• When faculty transfer into your organization and have some different ideas about how to do things, do they run into a strong wall of "that's not the way we do it here" comments?

• When someone from outside—a parent, community member, central administrator, or school or university partner—asks for information, does he or she get a straightforward and honest answer or something that is carefully sanitized for external consumption?

• Do people in your organization feel damaged or battered by outsiders who "don't understand what it is like to work here"? (See *Unpacking the Baggage Audit* on p. 44 as well if you want to answer this in reference to a specific partner.)

Add other questions that pertain to your setting and turn it into a simple survey, or use it to spark a discussion in your organization. If you identify one or more areas in which you are not as open to outsiders as you would like, work with your colleagues to devise strategies to change your culture.

2.3 *Marginalization and Change in PDSs*

Your partnership, like all interorganizational relationships, has to wrestle with issues of marginality and change. It is much easier to set up partnerships on the fringes of organizations and, at the same time, it is much harder for marginalized partnerships to bring about change at either institution. Consider bringing the following quote, from Linda Darling-Hammond (1994), to one of your steering committee meetings. She sums up the implications marginalization has for PDSs as change mechanisms:

> The usual dilemma of school reform is magnified here. Because new ideas and projects threaten the "behavioral and programmatic regularities" of schools (Sarason, 1982), they frequently need to be created at the margins of the institution so they can be ignored long enough to take root. The dilemma, of course, is that if such initiatives continue to live at the periphery of the organization, they fail at their overall mission. In the case of the PDS, the difficulties are doubled, since it is the core of two previously separate institutions, which must be infiltrated, connected, and simultaneously transformed. These case studies [in the book that this is an introduction to] demonstrate that all of these innovations have grown up on the margins and only a few are making progress at working their way toward the center of either the school or the university. (p. 22)

This was written almost 10 years ago, about early PDSs. Discuss with your colleagues and partners how it applies to yours. If you find it intriguing, read on.

Many aspects of the way your PDS is organized, including the governance structures you have set up—who is involved in them and how they are woven into the organizational structure of each partner—help determine how marginal you will be. These aspects will be explored more fully in Chapter 3, but for now, where does your PDS partnership sit in relation to your school or university? Is it on the margins and working its way toward the center? Perhaps it is on the margins and pleased to stay there. Maybe it is more central to one organization, but on the periphery of the other. Use the scale on page 36 as a quick and dirty survey, applying it to the school, the university, and to any other partnering organization.

On the scale indicate with an "R" where you think your partnership really is, and indicate with an "I" where you would like the partnership to be ideally.

Low				High
Marginalized				Central
1	2	3	4	5

1. Most people in our organization don't know or care much about the PDS.

2. Most people know about the PDS, but don't see how it affects them.

3. Some people are engaged in the PDS; others are interested.

4. A critical mass of people from our organization is involved; everyone knows about it.

5. The PDS is central to the mission and strategic plan of our organization.

Where on the continuum are you in each partnering organization? Where do you want to be? Share your perceptions and those of your colleagues. If there are discrepancies between your views of the real and the ideal, discuss how important they seem to you and set some priorities for follow-up action.

2.4 Concerns-Based Adoption Model

Do you find that some members of your organization are less enthusiastic than others about embracing the changes brought about by the PDS—that some seem reluctant and others downright resistant? Based on extensive research in the 1980s on the diffusion of innovations, the Concerns-Based Adoption Model (CBAM) is a useful tool for understanding what change looks like to the individuals who are being asked to adopt a new approach into their practice. The CBAM model suggests that individuals go through a predictable set of responses to a new innovation, illustrated in the following graphic (Hord, Rutherford, Huling-Austin, & Hall, 1987).

You can use this framework to better understand reluctance or resistance shown by members of your organization to any given innovation. To make this work, think of one or two types of changes your PDS is asking individuals to make. They could be changes in their classroom practice or in their approaches to supervising student teachers. They could be in their roles in the organization or in the way they need to develop more collaborative forms of leadership. For each one, use CBAM to give you and your colleagues insights into what those changes mean for those individuals. The resulting insights may enable you to ease the transition for some of

Stages of Concern: Typical Expressions of Concern about the Innovation	
Stage of Concern	**Expression of Concern**
I M P A C T 6 Refocusing	I have some ideas about something that would work even better.
5 Collaboration	How can I relate what I am doing to what others are doing?
4 Consequence	How is my use affecting learners? How can I refine it to have more impact?
T A S K 3 Management	I seem to be spending all my time getting materials ready.
S E L F 2 Personal	How will using it affect me?
1 Informational	I would like to know more about it.
0 Awareness	I am not concerned about it.

SOURCE: From Hord, Shirley, William L. Rutherford, Leslie Huling-Austin, and Gene E. Hall, 1987. *Taking Charge of Change*. Austin, TX: Southwest Educational Development Laboratory (SEDL), p. 31. Reprinted with permission.

the more reluctant members of your PDS, or at least ease your frustrations since you will have a better understanding of what is going on. CBAM also has some powerful implications for thinking about staff development and tailoring development plans to meet these predictable concerns. (See Hord et al., 1987 for some more suggestions on this.)

2.5 ACE Depth Versus Pervasiveness Grid

Another framework for thinking about the kinds of changes your organization is considering as it becomes or matures as a PDS focuses on the choices between depth and pervasiveness. Think for a minute about your organization as having numerous subunits. A school might have clusters, grade levels, teams, or departments. A university might have departments, programs, or even separate colleges for different aspects of teacher education, foundations, curriculum, special education, arts and sciences, or separate units that focus on fieldwork supervision. When you think about change in your organization being brought about by the PDS, do you picture deep change in one subunit involved with the PDS? Do you imagine broad (but shallow) changes that affect the entire organization? Or do you envisage deep, pervasive change throughout the partnering

Typology of Change

	Low Depth	High Depth
Low Pervasiveness	Adjustment	Isolated Change
High Pervasiveness	Pervasive Change	Transformational Change

organization? In their work at looking at transformation of universities, the American Council on Education developed a simple two-by-two grid that you might find helpful in thinking about your own situation (Eckel, Green, & Hill, 2001, p. 6).

Adjustment implies modifications to existing practice and is not deep-seated or pervasive. *Isolated change* is deep but limited to one or two areas of the institutions involved. *Pervasive change* is broad but shallow. *Transformational change* gets to the core of the institutions and is both deep and pervasive.

How would you categorize the changes that are coming out of your PDS? How would you like it to be? If there is a discrepancy, use this as a discussion starter with your colleagues and partners.

Issues in Relationship to Your Partner

2.6 Finding a Partner: Sources

If you are interested in starting a PDS, you will need to consider sources for potential partners. Here is a partial list to stimulate your thinking (do some additional brainstorming with your colleagues):

- Personal contacts
- Local and regional conferences
- Preexisting relationships of other kinds (e.g., schools where your student teachers are already placed or universities where many of your teachers already go for graduate degrees, or where many of them trained)
- Local or state PDS networks
- State departments of education
- Existing larger PDS collaboratives that might be looking for new members
- Umbrella groups—if you are in an area with a number of colleges and universities, you may have an organization that links them and connects them with schools
- Community groups
- Community-based organizations

- Faith-based organizations
- Unions or teacher associations—all might be sources of contacts or interested themselves
- Public education fund organizations for school reform and improvement
- Schools district offices
- School board associations
- School superintendent associations
- P–16 networks
- Other

2.7 Evaluating a Potential Partner

When you have identified one or more potential partners, you will need to formally or informally evaluate whether it makes sense to proceed. Some questions you might ask are listed below. You can use them informally and holistically, or you might use them in a more formal way, assigning points for each potential partner in each category and doing numerical tallies. The questions listed are only suggestions—there will probably be others you wish to add:

1. Philosophy: Does [potential partner] share matching or at least compatible approaches to teaching and learning with us?

2. Proximity: Are we close enough to [potential partner] for easy connections and travel?

3. Historical relationship: Has our experience with [potential partner] been positive, or at least neutral, or is there some organizational baggage that may get in the way? (See *Unpacking the Baggage Audit* on p. 45.)

4. Interpersonal connections: Are there people-to-people connections already in place with [potential partner] or will we have to start from the beginning?

5. Supportive environment: Does [potential partner] have clear support in its own organization to form a PDS, or might it get pulled out due to larger forces?

6. Trust: Do we have positive answers to Ferguson's trust questions about competence, dependability, collegiality, and motives of this potential partner? (See *Ferguson's Five Steps to Partnership Formation* on p. 42.)

There are two final notes on this process. Although many school–university partnerships find partners in private and fairly informal ways, there are times when a more public and formal process is called for. In some situations where there is only one university, or a few universities in an area with many potential school partners, a public process often is initiated in the name of fairness and access for all. (Occasionally the reverse is true, and a school is choosing among a number of potential university partners.) If this is your situation, you might consider setting up a selection committee that draws on the school and school districts and the university (or universities) as well as members of the community, parents, public officials, and so forth. Having an open application process can be helpful in avoiding the have/have not syndrome, or the sense of backdoor deals being made. These suggestions about a public process might also apply if you are part of a network of PDSs that seeks to expand.

While most of the focus here has been on finding a school or university partner, since these are often the principal members of PDSs, this is an excellent time to think more broadly about community, parent groups, unions, nonprofit organizations, and other partners. See *Scanning the Environment for Potential Partners: Who Is Missing?* on p. 50.

2.8 *Making It Formal: Partnership Agreements*

If and when you decide to formalize a partnership agreement, you and your partners should take some time to think through what the document should look like, who should sign it, and so forth. Below is a list of questions I developed when working with PDS partnerships. Use it as a springboard to add other questions that pertain to your situation.

- Do you want to have a statement of shared beliefs that underlies the agreement?
- Who should be the signatories and at what levels of the partnering organizations are they?
- What resources should be committed and by whom? Will there be any money changing hands (compensation for teachers, for example) or are the exchanges "in kind"?
- How will decisions about resources be made, and in general, what roles and organizing structures will be built in or assumed by the agreement? (See Chapter 3 for a fuller grounding in these issues.)
- Do you think the agreement should be open-ended, have a fixed number of years for its duration, or have a point at which it is reviewed and possibly renewed?
- How explicit do you want to be about issues of mutual renewal and change?
- Do you want to build in any kind of assessment and if so, what kind, prepared by whom, and for whose review?

- How should any new organizing structures put into place in the agreement interact with existing structures?

To get a look at some sample agreements, and get some more ideas on what might go into a partnership contract, see Teitel (1998a).

2.9 Who Is Depending on Whom: Joint Work Inventory

For partnerships to be mutual, and to be sustained, there has to be some sense of mutual interdependence. Take some time with your steering committee to look at what each partner does that the collaborative depends on and then take it to the next step to look at what you do best together.

What are your areas of symbiosis with your partner? For what kinds of work do you rely on your partner? And for what do they rely on you? What are you doing that is truly joint work?

The grid below is a start of this process. Fill in specifics under each area, fill it out (perhaps separately at first), and then discuss it together. You may find that as your PDS matures, more work moves from individual to joint work.

Areas of Work	Areas We Rely on the School for	Areas We Rely on the University for	Areas We Rely on [Other Partner(s)] for	Areas of Joint Work
PreK–12 student learning				
Inquiry into best practice				
Preservice educator preparation				
Experienced educator professional development				

2.10 Ferguson's Five Steps to Partnership Formation

Adapting the work of Erik Erikson, Ron Ferguson has identified five stages in the road to partnership formation. In the grid on page 43, key factors such as "trust" are critical to getting to the next stage (on the row below). The trust factor changes as the partnership matures and deepens (goes down the grid), but is ever present, reminding us that a breakdown or betrayal of trust at any point in a partnership can set it back significantly.

At first glance, Ferguson's framework can be daunting, but once you figure out how the rows and columns interact, it can be a very useful way to look at the development of your own partnership. Once you understand it, distribute it to your steering committee at a meeting you have set aside for reflection and self-assessment and start thinking about where you are and where you are trying to go. Have you met the trust requirements needed to go from the first to the second stages? Have you sorted out the issues of control that let you move on to stage III? If yours is a mature partnership, have you reach stages IV and V? Use the conversation started by reviewing the framework to generate ideas and develop strategies for deepening your partnership's commitment and development.

2.11 Renewing and Deepening Commitments

Some partnerships prefer not to make open-ended, long-term commitments and instead choose to structure in a renewal date—usually five years. Partners then can choose to recommit for another five years, usually after some discussion, sometimes after some sort of evaluation.

What do you think about that idea for your partnership? Do you worry at all about being trapped in a relationship that no one wants to break (see *Breaking Up Is Hard to Do*, p. 48)? Or would you rather be in a long-term committed relationship that has nothing tentative about it and no time limits? If you are in the early stages of PDS development, discuss this within your own organization and with your partners. If you are already in a committed relationship, you may wish to bring this up at whatever meetings you have set aside for reflection on the progress of the partnership.

2.12 Celebrating Joint Work

Whether it is due to lack of time or some sense that it is too frivolous or self-indulgent, celebrations are often an undernourished aspect of PDSs. What is your partnership doing to celebrate its joint work? There is both an internal and external dimension to this. Do you celebrate among the insiders—the folks doing the PDS work? Is evidence of it on the walls (at the university as well as the school), written up in internal newsletters,

Tasks and Stages of Alliances (Upside and downside of each task)

TASKS ————————▶

STAGES (↓)

Initiators find enough trust and interest among potential allies to justify proceeding		*Stages (rows)*[1] — I. Trust & Interest vs. Mistrust & Disinterest; II. Compromise vs. Conflict or Exit; III. Commitment vs. Ambivalence; IV. Industriousness vs. Discouragement; V. Transition vs. Stagnation		
Trust among participants becomes focused increasingly on one another's motives, competence, dependability, and collegiality	Struggle with and compromise on initial conflicts about power, turf, or priorities, while trying to agree about and initiate activities			
Trust increases the degree to which participants commit earnestly to support alliance goals and projects and remain involved	Power relationships are less contentious as growing consensus fosters progress on the agreed-upon priorities	Reach agreement on agendas, secure commitments, and earnestly begin projects		
Trusted alliance partners collaborate to overcome any failures or setbacks; relationships grow more personal	Power relationships are stable or they evolve without the types of conflict that would destabilize the alliance	Specific aims and commitments keep participants on task for particular roles and projects	Strive industriously toward success on the agenda to which alliance is committed	
Trusted alliance partners affirm one another, are willing to recommend one another and offer to collaborate again on future projects	Achieved patterns of empowerment tend to carry forward into similar patterns in new activities	New projects and commitments evolve based on capacities and relationship developed in alliance	Industriousness produces many benefits, including enhanced capacities and new relations among allies	Reputations are updated and members move to new projects and sometimes new alliances

SOURCE: From Ferguson (1999).

Note: Columns are tasks and rows are stages. Progress is neither smooth nor irreversible, so early stages are often revisited. Participants include both people and organizations, and context matters.

or shared in celebration at various parties and public events? In addition, do stakeholders outside know of your work? Does a banner fly over the school proclaiming its PDS status and connection to the university? Do the schools and school district have a comparable place of visibility and celebration at the university or at any other partners? Are the joint accomplishments shared and celebrated at the central office of the district or in the upper echelons of the university?

Venue	What We Are Doing	What We Could Be Doing	Who Will Follow This Up
Internal celebrations • Visible evidence (walls, etc.) • Internal newsletter • Parties, appreciation • Other			
Outside stakeholders • At university • At school district • At other partner(s) • For general public • Other			

After you have assessed what you are doing and could be doing, figure out the best follow-up.

2.13 Adding Partners Later On

As your partnership matures, it may grow—to include other schools, maybe even other universities, as well as parent groups, community agencies, unions, or other organizations. Perhaps as your partnership has grown, it has needed to expand as a matter of capacity, or perhaps you scanned the environment for potential additional partners and added one or more. If you find yourself adding partners after the PDS has had a time to gel and connect with the original set, you may find it useful to think about how the new partners will experience joining your PDS and how the group dynamics are likely to be affected. Here are a few observations I have noticed; once you start thinking about this, I am sure you will observe some others.

• The expanded PDS probably will not be the same as it was with just your original partner(s). Just as a group of individuals always changes when new members are added, this is also true with partnerships.

• You might expect that the issues of trust, control, and so forth addressed in *Ferguson's Five Steps to Partnership Formation* on p. 42 will need to get replayed and reestablished.

• You might anticipate that there may be more competition or in-group/out-group issues.

• If you add parents or community partners, you might expect that there may be some issues around voice and role in what some people will see as primarily a professional educator-oriented partnership.

This is not an exhaustive list, nor does it suggest that adding a partner after your PDS has been running for a while is not a good idea. Any of these issues that do arise can be addressed, but you need to be alert for them. If you are in, or anticipating, a stage of expansion, you might use the following grid to spark discussion.

New Groups, Partners, Individuals, Organizations to Be Added	New Opportunities Offered by New Partners	Potential Changes or Challenges to the PDS With the Expansion	Strategies and Next Steps to Make the Most of the Expansion
[List new addition here]			
[List new addition here]			
[List new addition here]			

2.14 Unpacking the Baggage Audit

The history of school–university partnerships is filled with unpacked baggage—broken promises, missed opportunities, disappointments, miscommunications, or casual statements made by one party that are hurtful to another. Make a list of the baggage that your partners bring to your PDS. This can be done by partners separately and then shared or can be explored together. At whatever point you work together on this, if you think the trust level is not yet high enough, or the baggage may be particularly unpleasant, you may want to bring in an outside facilitator and think carefully about your process. Think about providing enough context and time and "glue" so that bringing up the tough stuff doesn't set you back, but rather helps you move forward.

2.15 What Do We Bring to the Mix?

The companion to *Unpacking the Baggage* is a look at the positive partnership perceptions that PDS participants bring with them. Develop and publicize lists of what each partner brings. Try going beyond the most obvious ones (such that universities offer interns and professional development opportunities, while schools offer real-world experience for the interns). Build on the obvious items to consider the deeper contributions each partner can make to the other. Consider special sources of expertise that might be available in the people or the programs. Use this not only as a way to celebrate and acknowledge each other for what you bring to the mix, but also as a way for you and your partner to be open about what you need and what you can offer one another; you may be able to reach a deeper symbiosis.

2.16 How Muscular Is Your Partnership?

Where is your PDS on the continuum between a low level of cooperation (mutual adjustment) and a high level of collaboration and change? In PDSs, an example of mutual adjustment might be a university placing a cluster of student teachers in one school without making any changes in the approach to supervision or to any other aspects of the experience the student teachers have, or a university agreeing to allow an interested faculty member to voluntarily teach an existing course on site at the school to a group of interested teachers. These changes (although they can be hard to come by) represent minor mutual adjustments that do not challenge the status quo in either institution (although sometimes they lead to other changes that do). In more "muscular" partnerships—closer to the collaborative end of the spectrum—the school and the university might be meeting to jointly plan common activities with the understanding and expectation that these activities would be different from business as usual because they were being done jointly. PDS partnerships that are more muscular—more fully developed and further along the continuum toward collaboration—can take seriously their mission in the simultaneous renewal of schools, the preparation of teachers, and the improvement of student learning.

Low			*High*	
Mutual Adjustment			*Strong Collaboration/Change*	
1	2	3	4	5

Use the continuum line above to assess the "muscularity" of your partnership. Indicate with an "R" where you think your partnership really is, and explain why. Also indicate with an "I" where you would like the partnership to be ideally.

Reasons for Your Self-Assessment. After doing this as an individual, talk to your colleagues and ultimately compare notes with your partners. If there are discrepancies between your views of the real and your views of the ideal, discuss how important they seem to you and set some priorities for follow-up action.

2.17 Using a Successful PDS Model to Transform a University

Take a moment to reflect on the brief example mentioned on page 14 of the text of how the approaches and model of the PDS that had changed teacher education were being used to transform the educational administration program at the same university. Here's a bit more information about this powerful example of the larger ripple effects of professional development schools.

A combination of several factors helped: There was a strong, externally funded collaborative with active involvement from a large number of teachers, along with a steering committee that included principals and superintendents. When a major redesign of the teacher education program was launched in the mid-1990s, the collaborative played a huge role in it. More recently, when shrinking resources suggested the need for a review of the educational administration program, the same forces, already aligned and in use, were brought to bear on the situation, allowing school-based practitioners a substantial voice in the redesign.

Has your PDS had sufficient success and positive momentum to be a force in shaping other programs or subunits within any of the partners? Combine this question with the ones associated with the *ACE Depth Versus Pervasiveness Grid* (p. 37) and think about how the collaborative approach you are using in your PDS might be a model for broader change.

2.18 Partnership Development Stage Theory

There are several stage theories available to use for PDS development. In the text here, I use the I's: investigation, initiation, implementation, and institutionalization. Dixon and Ishler (1992b) describe six stages of evolution for PDSs: formation, conceptualization, development, implementation, evaluation, and termination/reformation. The Michigan Partnership describes four stages, which use different names, but fairly closely match mine:

1 initiation/exploration: the phase in which PDS participants get to know each other, establish working relationships, educate each other, and agree on how to define the problems they are up against;

2 design: the phase in which PDS participants develop initial approaches and theories about problems they have defined;

3 pilot: the phase in which PDS participants try out the approaches they have designed and assess and revise the approaches (as well as the theories on which they are based) and

4 stabilization/refinement: the phase in which PDS participants use the capacity they have built and engage in continuous refinement over long periods of time. (quoted in Torres, 1992, pp. 2-3)

Stage theories suggest there are predictable steps that PDSs are likely to go through in their formation. Is this a helpful construct for you? If so, take some time at a partnership steering committee meeting to discuss at which stage your partnership is now. Then discuss the "so what?" question and share whatever insights you get from thinking about your location on a development stage continuum.

2.19 Breaking Up Is Hard to Do

Are you in a relationship that is no longer meeting your needs? Have you tried to address your concerns or disappointment? Is getting out the best strategy? What would it take to leave? If this might pertain to you, read the following vignette from an article I wrote several years ago called "Separations, Divorces and Open Marriages in PDS Partnerships" (Teitel, 1998c).

This vignette is about a partnership I documented over several years in the early 1990s. The teacher education program of a major university joined with a neighboring middle school as part of a grant sponsored by a state department of education. Although they barely had a middle school teacher education program at the outset (involving only one or two students a year from their secondary program), the university hoped to build one. Two years into it, there was no growth in middle school teacher education enrollments at the university. Although the partners did some neat things with their grant money (like having university professors in the school for professional development), there was no spark in the relationship. In confidential interviews, the principal expressed her disappointment with the university's failure to deliver on what she expected at the outset and noted that she had given up asking for more engagement. The university liaison told me she was content with the relationship, expecting that if the school wanted anything they would ask. Neither would pull out, even though not much was happening, since it looked bad at the district or the university to withdraw from an initiative like this. The partners drifted along until the department of education provided a graceful way out by winding down the grant program and inviting those who were interested to reapply for continued funding.

If you see some of yourself in this story, discuss it with your colleagues or read the full article to get some ideas for other difficult PDS relationships and to learn how participants improved them or got out of them.

2.20 Developing Mutuality in PDS Partnerships

Another pattern that emerged in the middle school–university partnerships in the "Separations, Divorces" study (Teitel, 1998b; see *Breaking Up Is Hard to Do*) is the lack of mutuality. The partnerships, which were supposed to be reciprocal, ended up centering on the university's helping the school "do" middle school reform, even though in most cases the higher education partner had no real expertise or capacity in middle grades education. This led to several problems: school people came to expect resources from the universities that often were not there, leading to disappointments, and teachers were sensitive to any perceived arrogance on the part of the university faculty trying to "fix" their middle schools. What's more, even though most of the participants interviewed acknowledged the clear needs at the universities for middle school expertise, there was little sustained involvement of the middle school partners in providing that expertise or in bringing about change in the higher education institution. The lack of reciprocity, coupled in many cases with the unhappiness with what the university was (or was not) providing, led to considerable frustration on the part of the school partners—frustrations which in many cases were not easy to discuss, contributing to the breakdown of several partnerships.

Does this apply to you? In what ways is yours a one-way partnership? If it is, is that acceptable to all partners? If not, how is it discussed?

Larger Contextual or Environmental Issues

2.21 Scanning the Environment for Potential Partners: Who Is Missing?

How do you respond to the argument, raised by Peter Murrell, the dyadic nature of most PDS relationships may serve to exclude other voices and other partners that could and should be at the table? If that resonates with you, take a moment to scan your environment for potential partners. Look at church groups, community-based organizations, and other organizations that care about the students you serve. Look at unions and non-profits that have common interests or focal areas with your PDS. This could be done as a wide-open brainstorm with your steering committee. Come back to it after a time and apply the suggestions in *Evaluating a Potential Partner* on p. 39, keeping an open mind to the benefits that someone you might not at first think of as a good partner brings. If you do decide to invite other individuals and groups to join you, keep in mind the lessons from *Adding Partners Later On* on p. 44.

2.22 Aligning With the Larger Goals and Vision of Your Organization

Do you sometimes feel isolated within your larger organization? I occasionally hear PDS advocates say, "We're in our own little world here." Perhaps that is exactly the way you want it, but if you are interested in making broader connections and developing friends in high places, read on. With a little effort, you can figure out ways to align your PDS work with the larger goals and vision of your organization. This can be helpful in securing resources, making changes, and, more generally, developing allies in powerful positions.

An excellent example of this was done a few years ago by Vivian Troen, then a teacher in the Brookline (MA) Public Schools. She took the mission statement of the school district and after providing a few paragraphs of background on the PDS's collaborative, she listed the system's four core values—high academic achievement, excellence in teaching, collaborative relationships, and respect for human differences—and then detailed how the PDS contributed to each. She went on to describe the major components of the collaborative and then to detail how each component has led to benefits to the school system, to the school involved, to the classroom, and to the students. This effort was highly successful in bringing information and consciousness about the PDS to top decision makers on the school board and in the central office, and helped considerably in subsequent resource allocations. You can find the document in Teitel, Reed, and

O'Connor (1998, pp. 57-61) but more important than looking at Troen's document is my recommendation that you develop your own.

Start with copies of the school improvement plans, mission statements, and core values of each your partnering organizations. Have small groups develop comparable documents for each (there will be some sections that will be common to all) and then bring them back to the steering committee to polish. Develop a strategy to get the finished products in the right hands at the school board, central office, in the upper echelons of the university, and so on.

2.23 Connecting Your PDS to Larger Issues and Organizations

This suggestion is similar to the last one on *Aligning With the Larger Goals and Vision of Your Organization*, but on a different scale. Look outside the boundaries of your organization to see key issues and areas in the larger society and community that the PDS contributes to: teacher quality, student achievement, professional development, and community development, for example.

Issue of Broad Interest	*Other Organizations Involved*	*Key Actions and Approaches of Other Organizations*	*What Your PDS Does in This Area*	*What Connections Your PDS Might Make With Others*
Teacher quality				
Teacher professional development				
Community development				
Student achievement				
Other issues				

Pick an issue and brainstorm a list of others in the larger community who care about and are active in relationship to it. Use the preceding grid to get started.

After brainstorming the list, use the final column to identify action steps you might take to connect your PDS with other organizations in a broader coalition.

CHAPTER RESOURCES

This section includes a brief annotated bibliography of text and Web resources. The full citations for the text references are in the back of the book.

For more on school culture, see the classic piece "Good Seeds Grow in Strong Cultures" by Saphier and King (1985).

If you are interested in change and want to follow up on the issues of individual responses to change and the Concerns-Based Adoption Model, see Hord et al. (1987) or www.nas.edu/rise/backg4a.htm. If you would like to consider the implications of this model for staff development, see Horsley and Loucks-Horsley (1998).

To explore some of the issues of organizational change, particularly concerning depth versus pervasiveness, see Eckel et al. (2001), or find the article at www.acenet.edu/bookstore/descriptions/On_Change/.

To follow up on challenges and opportunities in long-term PDS partnerships, see "Separations, Divorces and Open Marriages" (Teitel, 1998c).

If you would like more information about who is engaged in partnerships and who is not, see Murrell's excellent *Like Stone Soup* (1998).

For some thoughtful reflections on the challenges of collaboration from the director of a PDS consortium that includes multiple universities and several school districts, see "Collaboration: The Faint of Heart Need Not Apply" (Walker, 1999).

For an excellent primer on the basics of collaboration between schools and other organizations, including families and communities, see the collaborative work of the North Central Regional Education Lab and the Department of Education, *Putting the Pieces Together: Comprehensive School-Linked Strategies for Children and Families.* The entire document can be found at www.ncrel.org/sdrs/areas/issues/envrnmnt/css/ppt/putting. htm. The first chapter focuses on building collaborative partnerships, how collaborative efforts get started, and how a collaborative partnership plans for action. A subsequent chapter, Chapter 6, "Maintaining Momentum in

Collaboration" (at www.ncrel.org/sdrs/areas/issues/envrnmnt/css/ppt/ chap6.htm) specifically addresses sustainability questions with practical suggestions for surviving during leadership turnover and responding to community controversy.

Other ideas and how-to suggestions for partnership formation with schools and communities are available in "Investing in Partnerships for Student Success: A Basic Tool for Community Stakeholders to Guide Educational Partnership, Development, and Management." Prepared for the U.S. Department of Education by Susan D. Otterbourg, this is available on the Web at www.ed.gov/pubs/investpartner/title.html.

For an interesting look at some of the parallels and differences between partnerships that universities form with schools and with their business partners, see *Strategic Alliances: Building Strong Ones and Making Them Last* by Mary Alice Ball and Shirley C. Payne at www.educause.edu/ ir/library/html/cnc9818/cnc9818.html.

For updates on text and Web sources related to this Standard, see http://pds.edrcform.net/home/ and click on Collaboration.

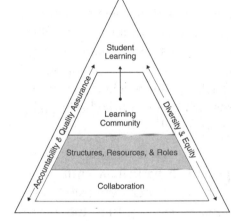

3

Structures, Resources, and Roles

Supporting Changes in the Learning Environment

P icture, for the moment, the PDS as a building where the activities related to the learning community—the improved approaches to teaching learning and leadership—take place. In Chapter 2, I described the Collaboration Standard as the foundation of the PDS. Think of the Structures, Resources, and Roles Standard as the building that sits on that foundation—along with all its inhabitants—in which the learning activities take place. The Structures, Resources, and Roles Standard addresses not just the four walls and roof that house the learning community, but also the people themselves and the resources needed to pay them, as well as to build and maintain the building.

Just as the Collaboration Standard focuses on the development of the relationship between or among partnering organizations, the Structures, Resources, and Roles Standard describes the matching organizational development that takes place—mostly internal, but some of it going on between the partners. The two Standards are closely linked, and both are organically connected to Learning Community. Any changes in the teaching and learning that might result from the formation of a PDS partnership will have implications for, and be supported by, changes in structures, resources, and roles.

For example, three years ago, a partnership I work with formed a PDS and decided to use an immersion model, in which the preservice teachers would be full-time interns at the school. To get the most out of what might seem like a relatively simple adaptation of the learning environment, a number of other changes had to take place.

New roles and expectations for school-based mentors emerged, since working with an intern for a year was a very different experience and commitment than the much shorter student teaching had been. The school-based mentors ended up meeting periodically, sorting through what it meant to be a mentor, and ultimately developing a job description and short training process. Some of them began to play roles as coteachers of university courses; others began to push back on the teacher education faculty to make sure those interns, who would now be in their classes all year, were adequately prepared.

The interns' roles changed from those of traditional student teaching. Interns were now expected to participate in faculty and team meetings, take on a range of teacher responsibilities, other leadership tasks in the school, and so on. They, too, have had developed for them an orientation and training to clarify the partnership's expectations of them; an intern job description has been prepared.

Coordinating this effort took the creation and adaptation of new roles for others. A teacher took on the part-time role of field-site coordinator, gradually reducing her teaching to half time as the role grew. University faculty members started spending significantly more time than usual (or than what was allotted for student teaching) in the school, involved with the interns, and then gradually with more and more of the other aspects of a school. The principal's role changed as he began to spend more time on teacher education issues and working with others to take fuller advantage of the time the interns could give, as after-school tutors, teachers of electives, role models for students, and so forth.

New structures have emerged to help coordinate these activities, to make decisions about intern placements, to handle questions that arise about the day-to-day work, and to help assess the big picture of where the partnership is going.

Different and new decisions about resources were made about allocation of the time of interns, mentors, faculty, and administrators, as well as apportionment of money. New, outside money was sought to help address an important equity issue: Since so much more time is required of interns in a yearlong commitment, without some form of stipends only affluent teacher education candidates would be able to participate. Funding was secured, and the partnership was able to recruit a diverse group of interns, using stipends and tuition waivers.

I could go on, but I am sure you get the idea. Becoming partners (forming a PDS) is, by itself, meaningless without developing and implementing improved approaches to teaching, learning, and leadership. The process of connecting partnership formation to changes in learning environments (like moving to yearlong internships) has profound implications for the rest of the system. Put another way, if there are changes in learning approaches that do not affect the structures, resources, and roles of the partner institutions, then chances are good that the changes are isolated and will not last or be supported.

OVERVIEW AND HISTORY

The challenges of providing structure, resources, and roles to support the learning community is spelled out in the PDS Standards:

> The PDS partnership uses its authority and resources to articulate its mission and establish governing structures that support the learning and development of P-12 students, [teacher education] candidates, faculty, and other professionals. The partner institutions ensure that structures, programs, and resource decisions support the partnership's mission. They create new roles and modify existing roles for P-12 students, candidates, faculty, and other professionals to achieve the PDS mission. The partnership effectively uses communication for coordination and linkage with the school district, university, and other constituencies and to inform the public, policymakers, and provisional audiences of its work. (NCATE, 2001b, p. 17)

Before looking, in the rest of this chapter, at the variety of ways PDSs structure their relationships, address the roles of the people involved, and manage their resources, let me flag some of the broad challenges addressed by PDSs as they navigate these paths (adapted from Teitel, 1997b).

Figuring out how to best address the structures, resources, and roles issues is a challenge for several reasons. PDSs are interorganizational collaborations and none of us have as much experience with them as we do with governance of single organizations. Even in the best of circumstances, relationships between two separate organizations can have more problems and be prone to breakdowns in communication, disagreement over resource allocations, differences in role expectations, and so on. But PDS partnerships like the one you are engaged in add several overlays to the usual challenges of collaboration, since you have at least two institutions engaged in mutual renewal that are simultaneously trying to expand professional development opportunities at both institutions, engage in research and development, and improve the education of children, adolescents, and prospective teachers. In addition, to the extent that your PDS is trying to bring about change, it challenges the status quo and brings into question entire sets of assumptions about who is responsible for teacher education and student learning. To be effective, your PDS not only has to change two institutions (each of which is strongly resistant to change in its own right), but you have to change the nature of the ways those institutions work with each other—how you make decisions together and how you grow together to take a shared responsibility for teacher education and student learning. In facing these challenges, here are four broad questions that may be helpful for you to consider:

- Structure: How much is enough? How much is too much?
- Priorities: Building bridges or putting in roots?
- Systems: How best to blend the old with the new?
- Overall: How centralized or autonomous should the PDSs be?

Overstructuring Versus Understructuring

Miller and Silvernail (1994) affectionately describe the governance structures of professional development schools as "systematic adhocracies." Perhaps you, like many others in PDSs, attribute your partnership's innovative spirit to its spontaneous, bottom-up roots. Often started on the margins of organizations by outward-looking entrepreneurial types who welcome the lack of structure and oversight, many PDSs risk being permanently on the periphery. With little attention to structure, role definition, or resource acquisition and allocation, PDSs may be highly susceptible to staff turnover, changes in leadership, or institutional priorities. They may be unable to promote institutional renewal or be otherwise woven into the fabric of their institutions. On the other hand, some PDS advocates fear that added structure, rules, regulations, and job descriptions lead to negative aspects of accountability and overly rigid policies that would sap the joy, creativity, and lifeblood out of the emerging PDS. Many PDSs add structure and formality over time and then sometimes wonder how to maintain the vitality that got them started in the first place. The tension you and others involved in PDSs face between over- and understructuring has important implications for how you think about structures, resources, and roles.

Building Bridges Versus Developing Roots

As a school–university partnership designed to simultaneously renew both institutions, your PDS faces a powerful set of contradictory pulls. To form and sustain your partnership, you need to build bridges between the organizations, yet to pursue institutional renewal requires deep roots in each organization, creating a second inherent tension. On one hand, your partnership is easier to start on the margins of organizations, where the bending of rules necessary for innovation may be unnoticed or overlooked; on the other hand, for any changes developed in the partnership to be systemic, they need to be integrated with and woven into the fabric of the entire institution. Because partnerships (especially between dissimilar institutions such as schools and universities) are hard to build, most people in your situation have placed their emphasis on building bridges to the other organization, frequently neglecting the roots that the change efforts need to have in each organization.

Aligning and Blending With the Old Versus Developing the New

As you and others in your PDS try to develop deep roots in each partnering organization, you need to figure out ways to blend existing structures, resources, and roles with those that you are developing for the PDS. For example, teachers taking on new responsibilities and leadership roles may find reluctance, resistance, and even opposition from other teachers or building administrators. New decision-making structures and new revenue streams and resource allocation processes set up for the PDS have to coexist, align with, or replace older sources, structures, and processes.

Centralization Versus Autonomy

Classic theories on organizational change tell us that a common way for organizations to innovate and to respond to their environments is to use periods of loose coupling (autonomy) followed by a more tightly coupled stage (Cameron, 1984). During the loosely coupled, autonomous stage, subunits of the organization may form new partnerships with outside groups and try new approaches, free from tight regulation and oversight. This is actually an accurate description of how most professional development schools started. In the early days (1985–1995), schools and universities were experimenting with an idea; not much was known about the structures, resources, and roles best suited for making a PDS work. Loosely configured, often out of the spotlight of the mainstream of either school or university, these pilot PDS start-ups were alternative and often peripheral projects with considerable autonomy. Then, according to the organizational change theorists, after a period of experimentation and innovation, there is usually a difficult struggle as those innovative ideas, structures, and approaches are pulled in to the core of the organization and institutionalized in a more centralized fashion. And, in fact, over time, some of those pilot start-ups have led the way to broader change at their universities as the PDS approaches they developed became the dominant or only teacher education model. Similarly, some have become effective in transforming the governance and approaches of their schools. Others have gone on to coexist with traditional programs (and may still be struggling to bring about change), and still others have faded away.

There are also PDSs that have been developed without going through the loose–tight process. After more became known about PDSs and their benefits, some universities began to start them as part of a larger, more systemic approach—not setting up semi-autonomous pilot projects, but trying to ramp up 8 or 10 or 12 PDSs simultaneously to meet the needs of the teacher education program. (Although it is more unusual, I also know of a small school district whose new superintendent decided, in a similar, systemwide way, that each of the five schools would enter PDS partnerships with the local university.) Even in these systemic or mass start-ups the issues of centralization versus autonomy come into play. Unless there is an expectation that one size fits all, there is usually some level of customization and local autonomy to take into account differences in individual school or district histories or personal relationships. Systemic PDS start-ups must address their own balance between standardization and individualization—between loose coupling, so a variety of different models may blossom, and a more uniform model and approach that is expected to be used by all.

As you move through the rest of this chapter, it will be useful to sort out where on the start-up continuum your PDS is (or, if you are reading this well into your PDS development, where it was when it was begun). Was your PDS started in the pilot project mode or as part of a larger-scale movement to establish PDSs by one or both of your partner institutions? Chances are you, like most PDSs, find yourself somewhere on the continuum between these two extremes. If so, how much uniformity is expected in your PDS? Is there a detailed set of common beliefs, structures, roles, resources, and programs used in each of the PDSs or is there a looser arrangement, with a more general set of guiding principles accompanied by substantial local discretion? Thinking this through will help, since the issues that frame this chapter—under- versus overstructuring, building bridges and putting in roots, meshing new models with the old, and overall decisions about centrality versus autonomy—play out somewhat differently depending on where your partnership is on the continuum. These distinctions often change over time—many PDSs that started as pilot projects have come to be mainstream; more on that will be discussed later when we move into issues of sustaining PDSs.

START-UP TASKS AND CHALLENGES

Structure

Pilot start-up PDSs tend to have the barest minimum of set structures and resources and only the loosest of role descriptions. This was particularly true in the early days of PDS start-ups, since there was very little knowledge base about what structures should be in place and little commitment of time or money to them. But even now, I work with a number of partnerships that are quite consciously choosing to let form follow function and deliberately not using preset models to determine the way they organize themselves. Their focus is usually on the PDS work—the learning community changes being put into place—with just enough structure, power, legitimacy, and access to resources to make those efforts work. Often teachers and teacher educators work together in these efforts, operating "under the radar" of others at one or both of their respective institutions and only adding formal structures when they run into the need.

> One partnership between a university and three urban secondary schools uses the phrase "the burden of emerging structures" to characterize organizational challenges they face when they bump into a problem. But, typical of many start-ups, they have chosen to bring in structure only as needed. Getting people to a meeting can be a challenge, and there is often confusion over what meeting is for what purpose. It is only after a few years, for instance, that they have developed a job description for the school site liaison, in part as documentation for a grant requirement and

in part because they are expanding and making similar positions in other schools.

On the other hand, higher levels of structuring are more likely in larger, systemic efforts, although these elements may emerge over time.

In 1989, a university made a focused decision to move to PDSs as the core of its revamped teacher education program. Working with six partner schools, the emerging collaborative developed a set of core beliefs that would undergird its work. In the beginning, except for the belief statements, there was considerable autonomy and flexibility around structure, with local teachers serving as key decision makers on what the PDS looked like in their school and collaboratively shaping the direction of the revamped teacher education program. Ideas and practices generated at the sites—an approach to strategic planning developed in one, for example; a cohort model for teacher interns in another—were eventually shared and spread to all. Since those start-up years, the collaborative has expanded in waves, adding about six to eight new PDSs every few years. Each new wave of additions has joined a collaborative that is steadily getting more and more structured. Although there is still some local autonomy in terms of how to spent certain funds, there are a number of givens—accepted, agreed-on practices and policies—a formal governance structure, formulas for distribution of money to schools, a clear liaison model, written expectations of mentor teachers and intern roles, and, of course, the initial belief statements that have guided the work.

I find it helpful to think of four sets of start-up tasks that PDS governance structures must address (from Teitel, 1998a). They need to manage day-to-day tasks, build bridges between the partnering organizations, support mutual renewal, and assess and plan for the long term. Some of the challenges and choices in establishing organizational structure follow, also adapted from Teitel, 1998a.

Manage Day-to-Day Tasks

Governance bodies need to manage the immediate, short-term needs of the collaborative, including the securing and allocation of resources (time and money).

There are four basic organizing structures used for connecting partners in a PDS. The first three—liaisons, steering committees, and multisite coordinating committees—work between and around existing governance structures and often are used in various combinations. The fourth, a more transformative approach, requires more substantial institutional reorganization. Which of these (or what combinations) is your partnership using (or does it plan to use)? For each model of interest, see the follow-up summary of the scope, advantages, and disadvantages in the Toolkit section of this chapter and consider which combination will serve best to manage your day-to-day tasks.

Liaisons. For many start-ups the most common day-to-day governance structure is the use of liaisons, who provide person-to-person contact as well as institutional linkages. From the university side, this is typically a faculty member with a quarter- or half-time commitment, who usually spends one day or two half-days a week at a site, sometimes augmenting the facilitating role by conducting research in the PDS or by participating in a study group or some other sort of staff development activity. If a school liaison exists, he or she is typically a classroom teacher (occasionally an administrator) who coordinates the placement of student teachers or interns, takes responsibility for arranging on-site seminars, and often works on faculty professional development. School liaisons usually do this work on top of their regular teaching load, although in some PDSs they have part-time or (more rarely) full-time releases. See *Liaison Scope, Advantages, and Disadvantages* on p. 90.

Steering Committee. Many PDS partnerships start with some form of liaison structure and evolve into the use of a steering committee. Others establish steering committees from the outset as ways of broadening input and involvement, gaining legitimacy, and helping to ease transitions if one of the liaisons leaves. At the simplest level of a partnership between one school and one college or university, steering committees are typically comprised of the school and university liaisons (if those positions exist), several school-based faculty members, sometimes one or more other university faculty, and possibly the principal or another building administrator. PDSs that are more developed may have an increased university presence on the committee—graduate students and faculty members from arts and sciences or the health professions, for instance. Other variations include parents and representatives of external organizations involved in the partnership. See *Steering Committee Scope, Advantages, and Disadvantages* on p. 92.

Multisite Coordinating Council. A common feature in larger and more systemic PDS initiatives is some sort of multisite coordinating council comprised of representatives from each PDS site, the university, and other partners. Although occasionally these are district-based or multisite, multicollege collaboratives, most of the networks are centered around universities, as schools and colleges of education have established multiple PDS sites to ensure sufficient placement opportunities for their preservice teachers. Many large PDS networks combine liaison, local-level steering committees with a broader coordinating council to shape collaborative-wide policy and recommend some parameters for school-site decision making. See *Multisite Coordinating Council Scope, Advantages, and Disadvantages* on p. 93.

Transformative Models. A fourth model of organization would only apply to a systemic initiative; it is a more radical organizational transformation. The liaisons, steering committees, and multisite coordinating councils described so far leave existing school and university structures intact and try to find the best way to link them. A few approaches to PDS governance suggest that substantial redesign of existing organizational structures is necessary for real collaboration and simultaneous renewal to take place. To some extent this has taken place on the school side, where it is common for schools to move from a hierarchical principal-driven structure to more of a shared decision-making approach. Many PDS networks require evidence of a shared governance system as a prerequisite for the participation of a school. John Goodlad and the National Network for Educational Renewal have called for establishing "Centers of Pedagogy" at the university level that specifically focus on the simultaneous renewal agenda. The creation of centers of pedagogy calls for major structural reorganization, with profound implications for governance, personnel, and resource issues. Several of the universities participating in the National Network for Educational Renewal have made these structural changes. Representatives of arts and science faculty members and their department chairs, along with faculty from the teacher education program and partnership school faculty comprise a professional education council. See *Transformative Models Scope, Advantages, and Disadvantages* on p. 94.

> I once visited a college of education that had reorganized with what I am calling the transformative model. All the language was about the "triad"—the involvement of school-based personnel, arts and sciences faculty, and teacher education faculty in a manner of decision making related to education. It was refreshing to see principals sitting on standing committees of the college, clearly stakeholders in what was going on. The organizing structure was called the COP—the Center of

Pedagogy—and it was remarkable how the language and decision-making process changed things.

Build Bridges

Because PDSs are formed between and among dissimilar organizations (schools, universities, and other partners), governance has to provide opportunities to air philosophical differences, sort out the different goals and turf issues, and establish what activities are common and what are primarily the domain of one institution.

In your PDS, many decisions that formerly were made by you or one of your partners are now being made jointly. This is an important part of the "move from independent to interdependent practice" called for in the Standards. But this change comes with a variety of challenges, including sorting out which decisions should be joint, how they should be made and by whom, and how to resolve any underlying differences in philosophy or approach.

In addressing which decisions are joint, as PDSs start up they usually begin by collaborating on lower-stakes decisions, such as in which classrooms student teachers or interns will be placed, before they get to higher-stakes discussions such as what the teacher education curriculum should be or how the school should respond to a statewide push to increase test scores. I have found the concept of a ladder of decision making useful—establishing a hierarchy of the types of decisions that need to be made in the partnership and identifying who is making them. See *Ladder of Decision Making* on p. 95 for examples and for further discussion and application of this idea.

How decisions are made is also key. Are formal structures and votes used? Often steering committees and smaller multisite coordinating councils make decisions by consensus. Who speaks up in these settings? How much parity and mutuality are present? In addition to new organizational structures, PDSs can bring new cultures—especially around decision making. Sometimes there is a shift from hierarchical, unilateral decisions with matching cultural shifts in power, information flow, and the ownership of problems. Are you seeing any of these changes in your PDS? For more information, see *Decision-Making Processes* on p. 96.

One PDS I visited developed a very strong collaborative culture for decision making. When a problem arose at either the school or the university that could be seen as relating to the PDS, they would "form a cluster on it." A cluster was a cross between a research-based study group and a subcommittee of the PDS steering committee (which was the school governance body). Typically composed of parents, teachers, and administrators from the school and university, the cluster would thoroughly explore the presenting problem or challenge, gather research (drawing on published scholarship and practice in other settings), and then make recommendations. Topics ranged from figuring out a better way to handle the school's chaotic dismissal time to agreeing on which approach should be used to introduce reading in the first grade (which also meant which approach would be used in the classes of interns, which were taught on site and woven into the instruction of the elementary students). The cluster would remain active to monitor and support the implementation and to help assess results and fine-tune processes.

As joint decisions move from low stakes to higher ones, from decisions about school dismissal to decisions about how to teach reading, the likelihood of greater disagreement over philosophical difference increases. See *Dealing With Differences in Philosophy and Belief Structure* on p. 97.

Support Mutual Renewal

When PDS partnerships promote a simultaneous and mutual renewal agenda, their governance structures must go beyond merely linking two stable organizations; they must include roles for participants to play in each other's change processes and must figure out ways for the new, joint governance to mesh with the preexisting structures of each organization even as the joint structure grows to take on increasingly important decision-making authority.

Some of the issues discussed and the decisions made by PDS governance are self-contained and have only a limited impact on the rest of the workings of the school or university. Decisions about matching of student teachers with cooperating mentors, for instance, will not be likely to have a far-reaching impact on the school or district. Similarly, choices about what content field-based courses will have will probably cause few ripples of change back at the university. But as your PDS moves beyond these mutual adjustment-type decisions and begins to explore broader aspects of the PDS change agenda, issues addressed by governance will have greater impacts. As your partnership develops, you may begin to explore the whole scope and sequence of the teacher education curriculum or push for a greater role in the budgeting processes in your districts. As you look at this hierarchy (use the *Ladder of Decision Making* on p. 95 in the Toolkit to guide you through this), think about the roles you and your partners can play in each other's renewal. See *How to Be a Change Ally in Your Partner's Organization* on p. 97.

A critical part in school and university renewal that is often overlooked is the structure set up for information flow within the PDS and in relation to each partnering organization. The mechanisms for communication and connection of individual PDS start-ups with the rest of their own organizations are often poor or nonexistent. From a university perspective, PDSs (especially those I am calling pilot projects) are often off-campus and out of sight. There may be little coordination and impact. The same can be true within a large school where only a subset of faculty and administrators is involved with the PDS. Look at your own PDS and the communication structures that are in place. You might expect that in a systemic initiative where PDS models represent the directions the school or university is heading there would be stronger mechanisms for sharing ideas and communication. The multisite coordinating councils should do this, but not all do it well. How well are these information transfer tasks being addressed in your PDS? See *Mechanisms for Transfer of Ideas and Approaches* on p. 98.

Assess and Plan for the Long Term

Governance bodies need to think long-range in ways that facilitate the renewal process, assess progress, address the long-range needs and interests of each partner and of the collaborative, and secure stable revenue streams for the time and money needed.

In the start-up phase, while focused on meeting the day-to-day challenges of creating a PDS, this assessment is probably the last thing that is on your, or anyone else's, mind. Yet it is an important issue to think about from the outset for several reasons. From a technical perspective, it is important to collect, from the beginning, baseline data for assessing your progress and impact as a PDS. Second, long-range planning is essential for short-range day-to-day decisions—if you don't know where you are going as a partnership, it is hard to keep a focus and forward motion. Finally, it is critical as a philosophical stance. It helps you and your partners keep sight of why you got involved in the PDS in the first place. It allows you to use the organizing structure of the PDS from the beginning to provide opportunities to establish processes that keep bringing the PDS back to its initial goals. Some PDSs, especially those in a multisite network, have annual retreats that serve as assessments on the year gone by, reflections on progress toward the PDS goals, and long-range planning sessions. (See *Keeping Your Eyes on the Prize* on p. 99.)

Roles

New systems of organization, new governance structures, and new learning community activities all lead to different roles for those who work in PDSs. Some of the challenges to attend to in the start-up stages include the following:

- Emerging role definitions
- New leadership roles and potential conflicts
- Support and preparation for individuals taking on new roles and for those adapting in old ones

Emerging Role Definitions

Roles in beginning PDSs tend to be flexible, as PDS advocates feel their way into the work. In the start-up stages you rarely see job descriptions, unless the PDS is part of a more systemic multisite effort and ideas and job descriptions are being brought over from a more established PDS to help a newer one get started. Since much of the PDS work is extra in many start-ups, it is donated time—determined by passionate advocates whose approach is not shaped by formal job descriptions but by a collaborative "can-do, whatever it takes" approach.

Despite the lack of clear job definitions, there are definitely new and adapted roles. Take, for example, classroom teachers, who take on whole new sets of responsibilities in PDSs, perhaps including the following: (adapted from Teitel, 1996c)

• Expanding involvement in the preparation of preservice teachers in a PDS, including such schoolwide issues as screening and placing student teachers, as well as overseeing their introduction to the entire school (not just the classroom), operating in the larger arena of the college, serving as supervisors of interns, teaching and guest lecturing courses at the colleges, and planning curricula

• Working on the continued professional development of experienced educators at school and college through the formation of book clubs, presenting at and attending regional and national conferences, peer coaching, visiting other schools, and presenting workshops to student teachers

• Developing high-quality education for diverse students—taking on the roles of curriculum developers and curriculum interpreters

• Researching, engaging in continuous inquiry into improving practice, supporting each other in conducting research, presenting at conferences, and taking leadership in developing new models of collaborative research

• Leading, as collaborative, inclusive approaches to decision making develop within these school–university partnerships, which provide important opportunities to reinforce and enhance the new roles called for in the preceding four specific aspects of the PDS agenda

Similar lists of new roles and expectations can be made for university-based faculty, interns, administrators at both institutions, and parents and family members. See *New and Modified Roles in PDSs* on p. 100. Special note should be taken of the linking roles that get played connecting the partnering organizations. These individuals who serve as liaisons, site coordinators, on-site university faculty, and teachers in residence at the university are critical parts of the glue that hold PDSs together and make them work. See *Boundary Spanners* on p. 100.

New Leadership Roles and Potential Conflicts

These new leadership roles create new pressures on teachers—different responsibilities that can lead to potential conflicts with colleagues, administrators, and others involved in the PDS.

Here are some examples of conflicts I have seen faced by teacher leaders in PDSs (adapted from Teitel, 1996c):

• A third-grade teacher working on the partner college's curriculum committee feels frustrated about the lack of parity she sees and worries about maintaining her sense of personal efficacy as she is struggling to make change at the college.

• The teacher coordinator of a PDS notices that both of the most recent student teachers to be placed with a longtime colleague have done poorly and seemed to be failing until their placements were switched and they blossomed. The coordinator wonders how to tell the colleague that she cannot have a student teacher placed with her because she has not done a good job mentoring the last two.

• A PDS coordinator hears from a friend that several teachers in the building are talking behind her back, asking "Who does she think she is?"

• A coordinator is conflicted over the poor performance in the fourth week of a student teacher's placement. The university supervisor wants to give the novice some more time, but the cooperating teacher feels like his students are suffering whenever the student teacher takes over the class. The coordinator feels caught in the middle, torn by a growing sense of responsibility for student teachers and a desire to honor the university partner's requests and a concern for the students and teachers of the school.

Similarly, if the school in your PDS partnership is striving to meet most or all of the four common PDS goals, it will need as dramatic a shift in principal leadership behaviors as it does in teachers. Several aspects of being a PDS affect the roles and expectations of principals: the emphasis on preservice and inservice professional development means that your PDS principals are not only facilitators of their own staff members' learning, but also of their roles as mentors and guides for others. The engagement in inquiry over best practice, and taking seriously the commitment to provide quality learning experiences for all children, means your principals need to support staff members in becoming curriculum developers, researchers, and advocates for equity. The growth of teacher leadership that is such a key part of PDSs potentially creates competition with principals for leadership and authority in the school. As Peter Wilson (1993) points out, these changes add up to a fundamentally different view of the role of the principal: "Traditionally, principals have exercised control by limiting access to information in a hierarchical organization. Teachers engaged in action research, creating knowledge, and collaborating directly with university faculty will be empowered. They will require a new kind of leader, one who is empowering and enabling" (p. 229). The principals in your PDS need to build community, nurture leadership in a variety of areas, and support and negotiate the change process.

Early PDS start-ups often had very little involvement from principals or deans, let alone superintendents or provosts. Even recently, start-ups sometimes leave out or minimize connections with those in formal leadership roles to avoid the potential conflict between emerging faculty leadership roles and those of principal or dean. This approach may provide short-term reduction of potential conflicts by essentially postponing them; ultimately they need to be resolved for the long-term integration of the PDS into the organization.

"It's the second year of our PDS," the university faculty liaison told me, "but it's like we are starting over. The faculty liaison that I replaced got into some serious power struggles with the principal. There was a strong faction of teachers who were taking leadership in the PDS start-up. The principal got threatened and started to shut them down. My predecessor took sides with the teachers. I had to come in and reestablish neutrality. It was a mess that we are still [at the end of the second year] recovering from."

See *Principals, Deans, and Partnership Power Dynamics* on p. 101.

Support and Preparation for Individuals Taking on New Roles and for Those Adapting in Old Ones

To take on these tasks effectively, the school and university faculty in your PDS need skills that formerly only principals and deans had: budgeting, staff development, evaluation, and so on. But the PDS context also calls for skills that may be new for your principals and deans as well: knowledge and skills in developing partnerships, creating communities, dealing with a collaborative change process, working with diverse stakeholders, conducting research, evaluating programs, and supporting others. Further, everyone needs to develop additional skills in negotiating the fragile balance in their relationships with their counterparts in the partnering organization.

How are the emerging leaders, as well as those already in positions of authority in your PDSs, being prepared and supported for their new or changed roles? See *Approaches to Supporting New Roles in PDSs* on p. 110.

Resources

Most start-up PDSs are grant-funded (if they have any external funds at all) and survive largely on the donated labor of committed educators at the school and university. In some cases, course releases or small stipends are available for the individuals involved. Sometimes partnerships are allocated a pool of money for operating expenses—again, from external funding or from contributions from one or both partners. Occasionally, especially in larger, systemic efforts, there is significant funding from the outset. The source might be external or from one of the partners, perhaps a reallocation or redirection of funding.

Typical start-up costs for the first year of a single PDS might be on the order of $50,000, divided into roughly five equal parts, according to Clark (1997): part-time staff coordination of the project; technology (computers and telephones); furnishings and other capital space costs; workshops and meetings; and learning about PDSs through consultants, site visits, and reading materials. These setup costs, which might be needed for the first year or two, would be on top of any annual operating costs that the PDS would incur. Depending on the size, scale, context, and focus, annual costs range from $150,000 to $500,000, some of it in-kind and most of it shared between school and university. See *PDS Start-Up Estimates and Operating Cost Factors* on p. 102.

In early stages of PDS development, the money spent on these or other resources committed to a PDS are often speculative, since there are risks that the PDS may not get off the ground and the benefits may not be immediately apparent. Recipients of resources in the early stages benefit from this increased flexibility and lower expectations for accountability.

> In the mid-1990s, I was on a task force with representatives of eight PDSs from around the country. Our charge was to look at institutionalization or sustainability issues. When we got to the resource section, we started by describing the financial support our separate programs had received until then. One of us was the coordinator of a multimillion-dollar foundation grant to start and support a half-dozen professional development schools. Another had hundreds of thousands of dollars redirected from the closing of a lab school. Others had grants ranging from 5,000 to 50,000 dollars. One had several course releases her college provided, and two had no additional funds—it was all donated or exchanged. Money—and the sustaining of it was a concern to all (except for the redirected lab school), but it meant different things. The multimillion-dollar grant recipient was wondering what she would do when the grant ran out in a year. She would no longer be able to pay teachers, for instance, substantial sums for taking an intern; would they do it anyway, she wondered? Other (less well-funded) programs were concerned that the participants who were very committed to the PDS would burn out if they were not rewarded for their work.

Your PDS is a labor-intensive endeavor, which, when its true costs are calculated, can be quite expensive. Since your PDS probably does not fit neatly into the budget of the university or schools, stable funding patterns are difficult to work out. In times of scarce resources, questions about mission and purpose will be raised, especially about an activity that may at first not seem to be connected to the central work of the institution. Some PDSs have thought creatively about all the resources available to them and drawn on innovative uses of the human resource of time. See *Early Strategies for Providing Resources for Start-Ups* on p. 102.

ISSUES AND CHALLENGES IN SUSTAINABILITY

This section picks up where the last stopped, moving further into challenges faced in implementation and institutionalization. At this point, regardless of whether your PDS started out as a pilot project or as part of a more systemic move to PDSs, there is some convergence around common issues in sustainability. PDSs that started as pilots interested in sustainability and influence on the mainstream need to move organizationally from the outside toward the core. At the same time, systemic initiatives need to take ideas that are becoming core or mainstream and apply them to all the subunits. Both sets of PDSs need to address ways to transfer ideas and the issues of centrality and autonomy, building bridges and mutual renewal—all continue in this phase with implications for structures, resources, and roles.

Structure

The structural demands of start-up governance—managing day-to-day tasks, building bridges between the partnering organizations, supporting mutual renewal, and assessing and planning for the long term—take on different ramifications in the sustainability phase.

Manage Day-to-Day Tasks

How do you make sure that your governance structure engages all the PDS participants in ways that encourage ownership, continuity, communication, vitality, and commitment? How do you retain enough flexibility to avoid ossification and evolve to meet the changing needs of your PDSs? The governance model that might have worked well for you when you were a small start-up PDS may be inadequate to the tasks of managing a larger, more central partnership. How do you remain fluid in your structures, but also consistent in the visions, goals, and directions in which you are trying to move?

One challenge you face that gets more prominent in the sustainability phase is the need to mesh your PDS work with existing governance bodies. Consider the popular form of linkage: local-level steering committees. Since they are dedicated to the development of the PDS, steering committees can maintain a strong focus on those tasks. But this can also be a disadvantage, since it entails creating a parallel decision-making structure that may duplicate existing governance structures such as school improvement councils. On one hand, the steering committee can be focused on PDS-related activities exclusively and provide a new arena for discussion and decision making, especially if the existing structure is politically polarized or otherwise ineffectual. (I know of quite a few schools where a well-functioning PDS steering committee eclipsed or even became the de facto school governance body because of a weak principal or ineffective school site council.) On the other hand, separate committees add more time and meetings into the lives of busy people; schools that are restructuring can be overwhelmed with a sense of too many groups, too many projects, or too many steering committees. What is more, the work of separate PDS steering committees may be less connected to the mainstream of the school or university than if PDS work were embedded into the existing governance structures. Some partnerships have resolved the choice by changing structures over time, usually starting a separate PDS steering committee and then integrating it into regular governance, or by setting up semi-autonomous PDS steering committees as subcommittees of the school improvement council.

The challenge of interacting well with existing and evolving organizational structures is particularly important to you if yours is a pilot PDS start-up which needs to move from the margins to increase its legitimacy and power. See *Moving to Power* on p. 104. If you are in a systemic initiative, you may already have access to legitimacy and power. Challenges facing systemic, multisite partnerships include continuing to sort out the proper balance on the centralization-versus-autonomy question and the degree of connection your PDS desires to have among the sites. How much uniformity should exist among your PDS sites? Should they look the same at the activity or program level? At the organizational structure level? Should roles and resources be the same in each PDS? And how much connection do you wish there to be among your PDS sites? If your multisite PDS partnership is centered around a university (as most of them are), does the network operate like spokes of a wheel radiating out from the university, with little connection among the PDS sites, or is it a network where there is as much site-to-site connection as there is to the university? See *Multisite Networks: Wheel Versus Spokes* on p. 104.

The PDS I described above, with a strong center of pedagogy model in place, had several school sites linked by a multisite coordinating council. With about three years of history together at the time of my visit, they viewed themselves as a developing, but tightly knit PDS group. Visits to the schools involved showed that part of that was accurate—through the triad model, many teachers and administrators felt closely connected and involved with teacher education and a variety of processes at the university. What surprised me was the way all the connections radiated back to the university (spokes in the wheel) and how few school-to-school connections or transfers of ideas there were. Even the most active PDS members at one of the schools had little knowledge of any of the other partners, had never been to another of the PDSs, and did not know anyone from the other schools except their representatives to the coordinating council.

Build Bridges Between the Partnering Organizations

Communication issues become even more critical in the sustainability phase. As you have undoubtedly noticed, schools and universities are different worlds, with different goals, senses of time, reward structures, and cultures. There will inevitably be sticky issues that arise. Teachers may worry about how well prepared student teachers are or be critical of poor supervision provided by the college; student teachers may feel the cooperating teacher is rigid, with out-of-date teaching methods; university supervisors may be critical of the teaching or mentoring skills of the cooperating teacher. When these issues arise in traditional student teacher settings, most problems are seen as individual and are dealt with accordingly. Unless something is of crisis proportion (the cooperating teacher is claiming the student teacher is unfit for the profession or the student teacher is demanding a different placement), conflicts are usually minimized and, if possible, swept under the rug. If you are in a professional development school, your PDS represents an institutional commitment that is public, not the private individual arrangements that historically have characterized student teaching. Because both the school and the university have much more at stake when a PDS is established, walking away from any problems that arise in student teaching or any other aspect of the relationship is usually not an attractive option.

Further, to the extent that your PDS is more than just a cluster of traditional student teacher placements, a whole new set of problems and issues may emerge. Roles in many PDSs are deliberately blurred between campus-based and school-based faculty, which may lead to more potential conflicts about who is doing what and why. Full-fledged PDSs have comprehensive goals that go beyond the student teacher component to address the professional development needs of inservice faculty (at the school and the university) as well as the improvement of the teacher education programs and the education that goes on in the school. Higher levels of joint planning and collaborative decision making lead to greater interdependence and as your PDS takes seriously its role in the simultaneous renewal of both institutions, and begins to address critical issues of equity, conflict and resistance to change are inevitable. How you and your colleagues and partners address the conflicts that will arise in your PDS is perhaps the most important factor in determining your longevity as a partnership and the success you will have in reaching your goals. See *Honest Talk About the Undiscussable Issues in PDSs* on p. 105.

In addition to being able to talk to one another, partnerships need to address the difference in cultures between and among the partners and how they interact and affect one another. This is especially true as PDSs include more than just the school and university teacher education partners, but engage with parents and community members, unions, and arts and science faculties. As a diverse set of partners involved in PDSs works to share ideas, negotiate philosophical approaches, and collaboratively change their institutions, nothing less is required than a fundamental change in organizational culture. See *Dealing With Differences in Philosophy and Belief Structure* on p. 97.

Support Mutual Renewal

Supporting mutual renewal requires you and your partners to have clear mechanisms to support the spread of ideas from the periphery to the core (and possibly back again) and clear roles for one another to play in each other's processes. Over a decade ago, I argued that for PDS partnerships to be "pulled into the core" and thus have any real impact as a mechanism for the renewal of schools or teacher preparation institutions, three conditions must exist (Teitel, 1992):

1. Distinct approaches, techniques, or philosophies must evolve which distinguish PDS-related activities from the usual way the schools and the teacher preparation institutions conduct their affairs.

2. Mechanisms must exist for these new approaches, which are often developed in alternative programs, to influence others' mainstream approaches to teaching, learning, and teacher education.

3. For any impact to be long-lasting, there must be signs that PDS-inspired approaches, and the structures that support them, are being institutionalized.

The first condition, the distinct features of PDS partnerships, has been amply documented by now, but without influence or institutionalization, the most wonderful collaborative arrangements possible will have only limited effect, will not lead to the renewal of schools and teacher education, and, more than likely, will need to continue to struggle for resources to go on.

So pulling PDSs into the core means finding mechanisms that might be used to influence mainstream teaching as well as learning and devising ways to institutionalize those changes. See *Mechanisms for Transfer of Ideas and Approaches* on p. 98.

You can anticipate struggles with the existing policies, mechanisms, and procedures: There are many aspects of the way colleges, universities, and schools are organized and run that may mitigate against the influence of PDS-inspired ideas. University policy can discourage practitioner involvement at the university, for instance, by requiring doctorates of all instructors, at whatever level. Similarly, teacher contracts may limit or prevent teacher roles at university. Reward structures often discourage university faculty members from getting involved in PDSs because they are aware that their activities will not be valued during promotion and tenure evaluations. Teachers in K–12 institutions often find they must do all their PDS work in addition to their regular teaching responsibilities. These are the kinds of structural challenges you need to take on in order to support deep-seated change. See *Pulling in to the Core* on p. 106.

Assess and Plan for the Long Term

The sustainability phase brings on more pressure for accountability, information flow, and the use of data. Structures need to be in place to assess the impacts of specific processes of teaching and learning and leadership approaches and to communicate ideas within the PDS. Perhaps most important is making sure time and place are provided for the PDS to reflect on its progress toward its long-range goals. See Chapter 6 in general for assessment and accountability approaches. For reflection on long-term planning and goals and maintaining a focus on student learning, see *Keeping Your Eyes on the Prize* on p. 99.

I was recently invited to facilitate the annual retreat of a large PDS collaborative centered around a state university. The collaborative had been founded in 1989 with five sites committed to a set of belief statements. It has undergone two changes in leadership and has grown to more than 20 sites. For part of the retreat we posted the five original core beliefs and asked the participants to self-assess their individual partnerships in relation to them and then to assess the overall collaborative and give short notes of evidence for their assessments. The process brought up discussion of some touchy issues and served well as a way to reconnect with the underlying values that had brought people together.

Roles

As your partnership moves to address sustainability issues, the tasks you face in relationship to roles shift somewhat.

- The concept of emerging role definitions becomes solidifying and defining roles and expanding the pool of involved participants.
- The concept of new leadership roles and potential conflicts becomes expanding the range of leadership to increase organizational capacity.
- The concept of support and preparation for individuals taking on new roles and for those adapting in old ones continues as a task, but adds the notion of rewards: supporting, preparing, and rewarding those in new and altered roles.

Solidifying and Defining Roles and Expanding the Pool of Involved Participants

Part of the transition to the sustainability phase is that roles, which may have been more flexible and embedded in the individual people who performed them, become more sharply defined and institutionalized.

When you ask about role definitions in partnerships that are just starting to think about sustainability issues, you quickly get the flavor for this transition. In one PDS I work with, when I asked for job descriptions for some of the key liaisons, for instance, there were none available, although the partnership had been functioning quite well for several years. The original people were still in the positions they had played and had figured out what to do to make the place work. When I tried it a different way and asked who did a particular task, I was told, "Oh, Jane does that," but it was apparent that not everyone knew what Jane, the school-based coordinator, did. When the partnership was planning to expand to another setting, the participants talked about the need for a "Jane" over there and for the first time asked Jane to write down what she did, and that generated their first job description.

You want to think about codifying the roles not only in cases such as this one, where new PDSs are being added, but also as a strategy to minimize the impacts of turnover and as a way to bring more people on board. PDS partnerships are made by people—people who look outside the boundaries of their own organization and see that the benefits of collaboration with others outweigh the costs. Partnerships, especially in the beginning, are often based on strong personal connections between one or a few individuals from each organization. Yet as long as those relationships are personal, and are not structured into job descriptions, partnerships are highly susceptible to staff turnover. And as long as one or a few individuals from each organization are the only ones to interact with members of the other organization, these partnerships may never be fully, or more broadly, realized. PDS advocates need to be moving toward greater and greater involvement of their colleagues in all the partner organizations. They need to draw them into contact with one another and build those contacts into relationships. The boundary between the organizations should not be the narrow intersection of the liaisons and a handful of others, but the longest possible border, with multiple large and small connections. This engagement of many people from both organizations is not only important in changing the culture of the collaborating institutions, but critical to developing a web of connections and relationships that helps sustain the PDS and support the kind of flexible institutionalization that is needed. See *Achieving Critical Mass: Engaging People in PDS Work* on p. 106 and *Pulling New People In* on p. 108.

Expanding the Range of Leadership to Increase Organizational Capacity

There are a variety of leadership roles called for in PDSs. Some roles are needed for making change in an organization, others are needed for managing the day-to-day details, and still others are needed for working across the boundary—interpreting each organizational culture to the other. Take a look at the *Leadership Roles in Sustaining PDS Work Inventory* on p. 109 and see who in your partnerships is taking on these tasks. They should not all be invested in one or a few individuals; if they are, consider the suggestions in *Achieving Critical Mass* on p. 106. Pay particular attention to the compatibility of those taking leadership in the PDS with those in administrative leadership and authority. Are they the same people? Do they work well together? Check for possible conflicts between new leadership structures and traditional control in the school or university. Issues or possible tensions that might have been ignored in PDS start-up stages may get more attention (and cause more conflict) during the sustainability phase. See *Principals, Deans, and Partnership Power Dynamics* on p. 101.

A colleague at a large state university told a group of us about a difficult transition at the school for which he was the liaison. After two very successful years of making connections to parents and teachers in the school and developing some effective PDS activities—all with the active engagement and support of the principal—he was dismayed to find the principal removed from the school by the central office. Her replacement came in with a different approach to teacher leadership: He was the boss, and the collegial decision-making processes that the PDS had put into place were dismantled. Several of the teachers who were actively engaged in the PDS were unhappy with these developments and were planning to transfer to other schools and the very continuation of the PDS was threatened.

See *Surviving Leadership Transitions* on p. 109.

Supporting, Preparing, and Rewarding Those in New and Altered Roles

To be effective in these new roles, PDS faculty, administrators, parents, and others need organizational supports as well as opportunities to learn and practice new skills. Organizational supports include time, support for the role changes, and revised reward structures. See *Approaches to Supporting New Roles in PDSs* on p. 110.

If anything, principals tend to get even less support than teachers in adapting to the new roles and demands. Principals regularly face what Roland Barth calls the "burden of presumed competence," where assumptions about their knowledge and skill often hamper their acquisitions of new learning. Along with all the other leaders in PDSs, they need support. See *Suggestions for PDS Leadership Development* on p. 111.

In addition to preparation and support, having a reward system at participating institutions that reflects the importance of PDS work is key. This includes salary, incentives, promotion, and tenure as well as more symbolic signs that the work matters and is appreciated. See *Valuing and Rewarding PDS Work* on p. 112.

Resources

Sustaining PDSs requires adequate resources, including a budget line at participating institutions and a schedule that permits staffs from the respective institutions to focus on issues and work pertaining to the PDS during their regular workday. Perhaps in your PDS, as in many others, in the beginning stages a considerable amount of extra work was done by committed participants, often in addition to, and not instead of, their regular jobs. As your PDS work moves in from the margins and moves away from being done on the backs of dedicated people, schools, universities, and districts have to look at the real costs in time and money. PDSs face the challenge of finding reliable sources of money, and, moreover, freeing up staff members' time to work on the PDS. As you think about the challenges of sustaining your PDS work, your basic choices are getting additional resources or working more creatively with what you have.

Using the model of the increased costs of teaching hospitals as an analogy, some PDS advocates have been able to increase the resources available. Some states, such as North Carolina and West Virginia, will use a different funding formula for its state universities involved in PDSs. Others have used Federal Title II monies—available for the enhancement of teacher quality. Still others have secured substantial and long-term grants from public or private sources. Some of these strategies come with a higher accountability push—more documentation of impacts, or higher expectations, for, say, retention of new teachers or student learning.

A long-term solution proposed over a decade ago involves blending a variety of funding streams to fund PDSs. In 1991, Theobold suggested, "Professional development schools will necessarily wed public school districts, schools and colleges of education, teacher organizations, and state governments into an economic union, which involves a significant reallocation of resources within and among the four sets of institutions" (p. 89).

While this has not yet happened in any large-scale way, there are universities and school districts in Maine, New Mexico, and Hawaii that have collaboratively committed to shared funding approaches (Clark & Pilecki, 1997). Some districts have aligned the funds that would be used for professional development and redirected them toward their PDSs, which have become the site of that professional development. See *Funding Stream Challenges and Solutions* on p. 112.

Other approaches redirect streams of existing funds. One way is to replace the traditional teacher education program with the professional development school approach, rather than fund both at the same time. Others strategies that work within existing budgets try to weave expectations and operations of the PDS into the status quo. One approach is to redefine job descriptions so PDS work is embedded in the job. See *Redefining PDS Work Into Job Descriptions* on p. 113. Another is to use all the resources (human as well as fiscal) available in the PDS in a creative and coherent way. See *Creative Approaches to Finding PDS Resources* on p. 114. A third is to use trades between or among partners as ways to provide cost-free service to one another. See *Trading as a Resource Strategy* on p. 114.

Focusing on Student Learning

When you spend time in a variety of PDSs you quickly see how changes in structures, resources, and roles in PDSs have a direct impact on students. PDSs that have figured out how to make their partnership work for students operate with an active PDS steering committee that really marshals the resources of the partnership. This organizing structure may go by different names, and may sometimes overlap with the school improvement team or council, but when it is working well, it serves as a magnifying glass for the partnership. It focuses in on the needs and opportunities for student learning, making them visible for all participants. And just as a magnifying glass can intensify light, the steering committee focuses and amplifies the resources that can be brought to bear for students using all available time, space, money, and people to focus on student learning. Examples abound in PDSs: community service learning projects required for interns provide afterschool and academic support for students; a university faculty member's expertise in special education is brought to bear on the challenging work of including all students in a seventh-grade cluster; or the "free time" available to classroom teachers when interns are teaching goes toward working with students who need extra help.

The role changes brought about for all these educators in a high-functioning PDS generally strengthen the connections between what they are doing and student learning. For preservice teachers, being in a PDS means less observation of the teaching–learning process and more hands-on work with individual tutoring and small-group instruction. For classroom teachers, it means being able to work in smaller settings and in more focused ways with students or to serve as an inquiry facilitator, leading an organized look (with preservice teachers and colleagues) at how students learn best. For university faculty, being in a PDS takes away the "once-removed filter" that teacher educators usually have—where their impact on student learning is only through others. In PDSs, university faculty work side by side with school-based educators and prospective educators, learning from one another even as they help students learn.

ASSESSMENT

Form 3.1   Quick-Check Self-Assessment Framework

For each statement below, assess the response that best describes your partnership, using a scale ranging from Strongly Disagree (SD), to Disagree (D), to Agree (A), to Strongly Agree (SA). Use NA for items that are not applicable in your context. Use the space below the self-assessment to list a few explanations or indicators that give evidence to support your assessment and to explain any questions you felt were not applicable.

For those in the *start-up* stage, we have:

1. Sufficient administrative support or   SD   D   A   SA   NA
   enough benign neglect to get started
   Indicators:

2. Eager risk-takers willing to try out   SD   D   A   SA   NA
   new ideas and approaches
   Indicators:

3. Individuals willing to expand their   SD   D   A   SA   NA
   roles beyond job descriptions
   Indicators:

4. Enough organizational structure to   SD   D   A   SA   NA
   manage things
   Indicators:

5. An early source of money, or time,   SD   D   A   SA   NA
   to get things started
   Indicators:

For those working on, or toward, the *sustaining* stage:
   (adapted from Teitel, Reed, & O'Conner, 1998)

1. The partnership is "woven into the fabric"   SD   D   A   SA   NA
   of PDS institutions—used in job
   descriptions, course catalogs, integrated
   into the core values, culture, and attitudes
   Indicators:

2. A critical mass of persons is involved from all the PDS institutions, including those with leadership and authority, with methods in place to bring new people on board.
   Indicators:

   SD D A SA NA

3. The partnership has a governance structure that involves all participants in ways that allow for ownership, continuity, communication, vitality, and commitment.
   Indicators:

   SD D A SA NA

4. Adequate resources exist, including budget lines at participating institutions, and a schedule that permits staff to do PDS work during their regular work day.
   Indicators:

   SD D A SA NA

5. A reward system is in place, including salary, incentives, promotion and tenure, to reflect the importance of PDS work at all participating institutions.
   Indicators:

   SD D A SA NA

6. New and changed leadership roles are understood and supported.
   Indicators:

   SD D A SA NA

7. A thoughtful and effective blending of old and new structures and policies exists.
   Indicators:

   SD D A SA NA

8. The partnership is rooted in all partner organizations.
   Indicators:

   SD D A SA NA

9. The blend of centrality and autonomy in the partnership is revisited and understood.
   Indicators:

   SD D A SA NA

Assessment Framework

To be effective, the partnership has to develop new roles, responsibilities, and decision-making processes as well as new organizational structures, resources, and resource allocation processes. This is the place to describe how the collaborative is organized and the work supported. For example, included here would be descriptions of the governance council or steering committee, how joint decisions get made, and how the partnership is managed.

Types of data that would document this section include job descriptions and evidence of jointly conducted searches for personnel in new or modified jobs at the intersection of the institutions; evidence of boundary-crossing capacities; changes in reward structure (e.g., promotion and tenure language) at both institutions; operating budgets; and schedules that show how time is used—both at the school and at the college—as well as journal entries or reflections of participants. Other sources might include memos of understanding; union agreements; schedules that show PDS roles for faculty, administrators, and interns; calendars; and evidence of inclusion of interns in the life of the school and their importance in making time available for other PDS activities.

STRUCTURES, RESOURCES, AND ROLES ASSESSMENT TEMPLATE

To be effective, the partnership has had to develop new roles, responsibilities, and decision-making processes as well as new organizational structures, resources, and resource allocation processes.

Organizational Structures and Support

Describe here how the collaborative is organized and the work supported. For example,

- Governance council–steering committee membership
- How joint decisions are made
- How partnership is woven into the fabric of each institution
- Job descriptions
- Catalogs
- Publicity materials
- Critical mass of faculty engaged in all institutions
- Other

New and Changed Roles

Supporting evidence might include job or role descriptions, reflections by participants on what their roles are or how they have changed.

New and Modified Roles	Supporting Evidence (Possible Examples)
On-site coordinator/liaison	Job description, personal letter
Mentor teachers	Fall orientation notes for mentors
School administrators	Partnership agreements, grant applications
University faculty (immersed)	Annual faculty reports, partnership agreements
University faculty (nonimmersed)	Minutes of meetings on roles, divisions
Other	Project manager's job description Complete set of meeting minutes

Use of Resources

Describe how resources have been used to support the joint work. This might include grant funds or reallocation of time and money from existing resources. Sources include budgets, grant proposals, and PDS funding.

How are decisions about resources affecting the partnership made?

Communication Structures

What is in place to communicate information among the various stakeholders?

DOCUMENTATION EXAMPLE

This is the second excerpt from the assessment framework for the Urban Teacher Training Collaborative. See the Documentation Example in Chapter 2 on p. 29 for background on the Collaborative. This section, which was written by Linda Beardsley of Tufts University (with my editorial comments in brackets), is included for illustrative purposes. Note the collaborative already has assembled some documentary support; at several points I refer to these with a comment, as in "UTTC may draw on existing job description or orientation notes here."

To be effective, the UTTC has had to develop new roles, responsibilities, and decision-making processes as well as new organizational structures, resources, and resource allocation processes.

One of the most challenging and promising aspects of the UTTC is how the nature of this collaboration necessitates the development of new roles and organizational structures and the reconsideration of how resources are used throughout all aspects of the program. Historically, university teacher training programs have debated and discussed how best to balance academic study of educational history, research, and philosophy with practice in district classrooms for preservice teachers. Through a reliance on the PDS model, the UTTC has made a bold statement, moving the locus of the Tufts Teacher Preparation Program to the school site, thus underscoring the importance of the practicum placement on the development of teacher practice. By accepting as part of their mission the development of a new generation of effective urban educators, the school sites endeavor to become more articulate about their practice, more reflective about their own work and how the mission shapes the learning and teaching within the community. In the PDS model, both the university teacher education program and the practicum sites reinvent themselves to ensure that Teaching in Partnership [the philosophical approach underpinning Tufts Teacher Education program] becomes a reality in many different ways throughout the collaboration.

As currently conceived, new roles will include internship coordinator, mentor teacher, university liaison, and administrative support. New structures will include the full-year, full-time internship and the location of university courses at the school site rather than at the academic institution. New cultural concepts will include Teaching in Partnership in many different forms.

New Roles to Support Teaching in Partnership

The Site Coordinator is a .4 professional position that supports the UTTC Interns and their Mentor Teachers at the school site. He or she oversees the Tufts Interns in collaboration with the University Liaison. He or she works with the Mentor Teachers and the University Liaison to ensure that the Interns' experiences in the classroom and the broader school community are positive and lead to professional growth and teacher licensure. He or she models effective classroom practice, professional leadership, and an understanding of and commitment to successful school and classroom reforms. [To further document this, UTTC may draw here on existing job descriptions.]

The Mentor Teacher serves as a cooperating practitioner for a UTTC Intern. He or she plays a critical role in the development of the Intern's professional role and insights. He or she shares the classroom, the students, expertise, and vision in an effort to inspire and instruct new professionals. The Mentor Teacher approaches this role as an opportunity for professional growth and as a way to prepare new teachers to work effectively in urban schools. He or she demonstrates and articulates a variety of instructional and assessment strategies designed to meet the individual learning needs of students to ensure that all students are able to achieve the learning standards and habits of mind of the school and district curriculum.

In the UTTC, mentor teachers have strong input into defining the schools' mission and educational philosophy. They create curriculum in all disciplines. They establish standards and procedures for assessment of student work. They give critical feedback on teaching practices and investigate new techniques, materials, and resources. They seek out and interact with community members who bring expertise, opportunities, funding, and other forms of support to the school. They follow up with parents to create home–school links. They counsel students about academic and life goals and difficulties. They plan and execute special events, advise student government, serve on graduation panels, vote in board meetings, coordinate relationships with corporate sponsors, and represent the school in educational conferences. [To further document this, UTTC may draw here on existing Fall Orientation notes for Mentors and role descriptions.]

The University Liaison uses a team approach to oversee the Intern's progress. He or she serves as an adviser for the apprentice teachers in collaboration with the Intern/Site Coordinator, mentor teachers, and the building principal. This person also serves as a resource to the school community and support for the school site's restructuring efforts by helping the staff identify the applied research that underlies restructuring and results in successful student achievement and family involvement. He or she demonstrates and articulates a variety of instructional and assessment strategies designed to meet the individual learning needs of students and teachers. [To further document this, UTTC may draw here on existing job descriptions for liaison and for project manager.]

[Another new role UTTC still needs to document is the "professor of the practice"—a Tufts faculty member on site in the school. It will also be important for UTTC to address in the full documentation the modified roles—how involvement in UTTC brings about changes for faculty and administrators at the schools and at the university.]

New Structures to Support Teaching in Partnership

Full Year/Full-Time Internship

From almost the first day they enter the schools, interns are treated as coteachers. This means that they participate in many if not all the activities of their mentor teachers. They create curriculum, establish procedures, give critical feedback, attend staff and team meetings, and so on. Gradually, as the year proceeds, they take on more responsibility for programs affecting a broader array of students, staff, and outside contacts. For example, Fenway interns coordinate the schoolwide science fair, which requires them to interact with the many judges who come from the outside to help in assessing student exhibitions. As they become accustomed to the democratic processes within the schools, they become more and more comfortable expressing their own views and taking leadership on projects.

UTTC interns join the program first and foremost to become excellent classroom teachers. However, the example of their mentor teachers teaches them to be strong, versatile, forward-thinking teacher leaders as well. After a year in the educational environment of Fenway and Boston Arts Academy, interns carry with them the picture of what an   urban learning community can be, and they are more likely to find or create that environment in their future work life. Knowing that good schools are possible, they have the optimism and skills to push for healthy change when they see it is needed. [For further documentation, UTTC may draw on existing descriptions of expectations for interns, as well as orientation notes.]

Other specific documentation that UTTC could add in this section includes the following:

- Location of university courses on site—implications for structures, roles, and resources

- Governance council or steering committee membership, charge, bylaws, or operating procedures

• Minutes of meetings for how joint decisions get made (these exist and would need to be analyzed)

• Evidence of how UTTC is woven into the fabric of each institution

Job descriptions

Catalogs

Publicity materials

• Evidence of how two schools in one building affect the collaborative

• What the focus on the arts means from an organizational and structural perspective

• Evidence of whether a critical mass of faculty is engaged in all institutions

• Use of resources: Evidence of how resources have been used to support the joint work. This might include grant funds, as well as reallocation of time and money from existing resources. Use budgets and existing grant proposals, including proposal for Boston Public Schools PDS funding.

• Information on how decisions about resources affecting the collaborative are made, drawing on minutes and any other organizational documents or agreements

• Communication structures: What is in place to communicate information among the various stakeholders?

Toolkit

3.1 Liaison Scope, Advantages, and Disadvantages

Chances are you have one or more liaisons or site or PDS coordinators helping to link members of your partnership. The range of decisions left up to liaisons as well as their scope and authority vary from site to site. If your PDS is small, the liaisons might be operating without steering committees or broader coordinating councils. Their scope may be limited to low-stakes decisions about the details of day-to-day operation of the PDS.

They may plan workshops for experienced and student teachers, make decisions about how they choose to use the time they personally devote to the PDS, and have discretion over a small budget. For decisions that involve greater resources or other people, your liaisons will probably need to check in with deans, principals, or other decision-making bodies.

In thinking about the functioning of your liaisons, look at the list of advantages and disadvantages (adapted from Teitel, 1998a) and take some time to reflect on which of each apply to your partnership.

Advantages. Typically the strong personal connection that develops between the school and college liaison serves as the linchpin of the relationship and the connecting point of each organization. Liaisons have the tasks of involving others in their own institution and of interpreting to them the culture of the other institution. In PDSs where there is a university-based and a school-based liaison, sometimes the powerful personal link between the liaisons becomes the de facto governance structure, even if they also have a steering committee. When they are working with each other well, the liaisons can often make decisions quickly and easily. Usually operating near the fringes of each organization (especially in the start-up phase), the liaisons often have a fair amount of autonomy, unless their decisions or plans start to lead to changes that affect more people in their institutions.

Disadvantages. The personalization and informal decision making cuts both ways. The people who have the time and energy to do the day-to-day work as liaisons in PDSs often do not have much positional power within their own organizations; in some cases, there has been no real structural legitimacy given to the role. Since the PDS initiative can come to be seen as the liaison's individual project, the liaison's lack of structural legitimacy may mean that decisions that affect others may be difficult to implement. Since PDS work at the university can be "out of sight, out of mind," liaisons may find themselves isolated or ineffective back at their own institutions, unless their work is woven into university governance structures in some ways. The sheer amount of time and effort required for partnership and PDS development creates problems for structures that focus so much of the work on one or two individuals. Liaisons are often stretched with the new and seemingly endless demands of PDS formation, while still needing to meet the rest of their obligations to their own institutions and positions. Finally, partnerships that are dependent on personal connections of one or two individuals, unless they do careful succession planning, can lose significant momentum (or even fall apart) with a liaison's departure.

3.2 Steering Committee Scope, Advantages, and Disadvantages

More than likely, you also have a steering committee to help deal with the day-to-day decisions of running the PDS as well as some of the more long-range issues. Committees are usually involved with student teacher placement and the planning of professional development activities. In addition, in more developed PDSs which are embracing a simultaneous renewal agenda, committees have responsibility for the broader school or university improvement agenda, focusing, for instance, on curriculum and instruction at both institutions or on pursuing a joint action–research agenda.

In thinking about the functioning of your steering committee, look at the list of advantages and disadvantages (adapted from Teitel, 1998a) and take some time to reflect on which of each apply to your partnership.

Advantages. Steering committees can be useful mechanisms to involve others within the school or university in the PDS and will sometimes also include parents and community and business members. Steering committees offer increased legitimacy for the decisions that are made. Sometimes this is due to inclusion of those with more positional power—principals and deans—but legitimacy can also come from the fact that the committee may have been anointed by some consensus process or some higher authority. The committee has the potential (often unrealized) to be a place where issues of equity and parity are discussed. More people involved can also mean a broader division of labor and a smoother transition in case of departure.

Disadvantages. Since they are dedicated to the development of the PDS, steering committees can maintain a strong focus on those tasks. But this can also be seen as a disadvantage, since it entails creating a parallel decision-making structure that in some settings duplicates existing governance structures, such as school improvement councils. On one hand, the steering committee can be focused on PDS-related activities exclusively and provide a new arena for discussion and decision making, especially if the existing structure is politically polarized or otherwise ineffectual. But they can also add more time and meetings into the lives of busy people, and the work of separate PDS steering committees may be less connected to the mainstream of a school or college than if PDS work was embedded into the existing governance structures. Some partnerships have resolved the choice by changing structures over time, usually starting a separate PDS steering committee and then integrating it into regular governance or by setting up semi-autonomous PDS steering committees as subcommittees of the school improvement council. Steering committees can also be seen by some as adding a layer of bureaucracy that can stifle the spontaneity and bottom-up nature of PDS collaboration.

3.3 Multisite Coordinating Council
Scope, Advantages, and Disadvantages

If your PDS has several sites, it probably has some sort of planning or coordinating council. These collaborative-wide bodies are usually composed of representatives from each school site and the various stakeholders at the university and the district offices (as well as, sometimes, other community, business, or union partners). As opposed to site-based steering committees, coordinating councils will typically include those with more positional power—superintendents, or associate superintendents, principals, deans, and department chairs, as well as faculty at both sets of institutions. As a broader, more powerful board might, coordinating councils typically meet relatively infrequently—monthly or even quarterly. Some set up subcommittees for the work between meetings; sometimes after the PDSs are well established, the council may recede in importance, certainly vis-à-vis day-to-day operations. Councils typically focus on broader policy issues—such as allocation of funds—decisions that might affect all the sites or the teacher education program at the university. They might plan common activities such as a program of professional development during the summer that is open to all PDS participants. Policy implementation is usually left to the site committees, which might, for instance, decide how to compensate supervisors and cooperating teachers from the funds allotted by the council.

The decision-making scope of the coordinating councils, as well as their composition, may vary considerably. At one university, for instance, decisions about most everything are made by a group in which all the teacher coordinators participate as equal members. This group makes broad policy for the teacher education program and includes its teacher coordinators in such high-stakes decisions as promotion and tenure and the search for a new dean. Other universities more commonly restrict the scope of coordinating councils' decision making to those issues that immediately pertain to the PDS and make other decisions about university programs through an internal governance process. Similarly, district-based coordinating councils may also have limits set on their scope, often to how some or all the district's professional development monies and time for experienced teachers are allocated.

In thinking about the functioning of your coordinating council, if you have one, look at the list of advantages and disadvantages (adapted from

Teitel, 1998a) and take some time to reflect on which of each apply to your partnership.

Advantages. Coordinating councils can provide important connections for PDSs to power and resources and to the administrators who control them at school, district, and universities. These administrators often become key advocates for PDS approaches on campus and in school districts. The councils can be good places to explore issues of equity and parity and to sponsor collaborative-wide assessment and research. Some coordinating councils provide mini-grants that sites apply for in order to foster these efforts. If constituted to bring in parents, unions, or community groups, the councils can be good places to expand the influence and impact of the PDS.

Disadvantages. Councils can become too large and have difficulty making decisions, or they can get too far removed from the action of the PDS. A coordinating council could represent another layer of bureaucracy and have a stultifying effect on the spontaneity of a PDS. Policies made at a collaborative-wide level may not be sufficiently sensitive to the individual context of each PDS. Councils may offer the appearance of parity and collaboration but in reality be limited in their scope or not really model equality between schools and colleges in their decision-making process.

3.4 Transformative Models Scope, Advantages, and Disadvantages

If you are in a partnership that has created a center of pedagogy, or a similar major structural reorganization, the scope can be broad indeed. Such centers not only focus on everything that might formerly have been seen as the purview of teacher education, but they also involve arts and science faculty and school district issues.

In thinking about the functioning of your center of pedagogy or similar reorganization, look at the list of advantages and disadvantages (adapted from Teitel, 1998a) and take some time to reflect on which of each apply to your partnership.

Advantages. By broadening the stakeholders in the decision making for teacher education, the center of pedagogy approach sets the stage for a much deeper institution-wide commitment to improvement of the preparation of teachers. Fragmentation and lack of clear focus can be reduced as responsibilities for teacher education are no longer diffused over a number of disconnected departments; at the same time, wider buy-in to the guiding education postulates can be obtained. Such a change begins to transform the university into a more focused and effective partner, enabling it to renew itself even as it is working more collaboratively with schools and school districts.

Disadvantages. Moving to a center of pedagogy can lead to a variety of internal disruptions: confusion over job roles and conflicts with union contracts, disruption of communication channels (often predicated in a university on departmental structures), or thorny questions about how to evaluate faculty for promotion and tenure and how to clarify departmental responsibilities. The focus and autonomy gained by having a freestanding center sometimes comes with a certain degree of isolation—a sense of being out of the mainstream of university governance and culture.

3.5 Ladder of Decision Making

A useful tool for assessing the movement from independence to interdependence called for in the Standards is the ladder of decision making, a concept suggested by Lynne Miller of the University of Southern Maine and adapted here from Teitel (1997b). The ladder organizes the types of decisions a partnership faces in a particular area and ranks them according to how high or low stakes they are. For example, from the perspective of a university involved with teacher education, a ladder of decision making might look as follows:

(Higher Stakes—Higher Impact)

- Certification of, and accountability for, new teachers
- Continuation of teacher candidates (establishing what counts as successful completion of courses, or practica)
- Admission of teacher candidates
- Overall teacher education curriculum
- Budgeting
- Curriculum or instruction decisions about a course taught at college
- Curriculum or instruction decision about a field-based methods course
- Field placement decisions

(Lower stakes—Lower impact)

The ladder of decision making is used as an illustration of a useful concept, not as an exhaustive list of the choices facing PDSs. Within each of the broad categories above, there could be whole subsets of decisions, each with its own hierarchy. For instance, within field placement decisions, there are a number of subissues which might run (from lower to higher stakes): placement with specific teachers (and who decides); length of placements (one semester or a school year); blend of placements (mixes of urban, suburban, etc.); expectations of student teacher work during the placement; and so forth. The ladder of decision making is useful even though at different institutions (or between individuals or groups at the same institution) there may be disagreements about the relative position of items.

Try the ladder of decision making as a tool in your setting. Use it to track the different decisions your partnership makes, noting whether, over time, areas that were primarily the responsibility of one partner have moved into the joint decision-making arena. Doing this will help to track changes over time and the open discussion it can engender about who decides what can be helpful in clarifying things that may be murky and in providing opportunities to discuss parity within your relationship with your partner.

3.6 Decision-Making Processes

As partnerships, PDSs are more likely to have collaborative decision-making structures in place. What does this mean in your setting? Use the following quick and dirty inventory to check on how decisions are made in your organization, in your partner's, and in the collaborative space you have developed in your PDS, then discuss the implications for your partnership.

How Decisions Get Made	In Your Own Organization	In Your Partner's Organization	In Your PDS
Consensus			
Democratic vote			
Discussion, then authority makes decision			
Top-down decision			
Add other categories here			

3.7 Dealing With Differences in Philosophy and Belief Structure

Have there been tough decisions you and your partner have had to make? Have you noticed any changes in the comfort level with one another as you and your partner have made increasingly interdependent decisions (see the *Ladder of Decision Making* on p. 95)?

Think of a decision made by your partner that has bothered you. If you are based in a school, perhaps the university decided to require all supervision of interns to be done by university-based faculty, ending several years of successful use of school-based faculty as supervisors in your PDS. Or perhaps they made a decision about the coursework sequence that the interns have completed before they enter your school, and you feel strongly that the interns are not being prepared properly. For university-based partners, perhaps you object to the school or school district adopting a program such as Success for All, when you have a more constructivist orientation to education and thus have strong philosophical objections. These are all areas that have traditionally been in the sole purview of one of the partners, and in most cases not historically shared, yet they have important impacts on you as a partner. For parents or community-based partners, suppose there are decisions being made that you don't think are in the best interests of the children.

When these kinds of issues arise in your partnership, how do you go about expressing your views? Is there open discussion (see *Honest Talk About the Undiscussable Issues in PDSs* on p. 105)? How do members of your partnership advocate for their positions? How explicit is your discussion about the underlying philosophy and belief differences between you?

3.8 How to Be a Change Ally in Your Partner's Organization

Sometimes differences in philosophy and belief show up within one of the partnering organizations and you and your PDS counterpart are allies. Can you think of a time your counterpart (in the partnering organization) faced a struggle in his or her own organization about an issue on which you supported him or her? For example, imagine you are a university faculty member and that the PDS has been making great progress with an innovative but unconventional approach to teaching math, but due to flagging test scores in other schools, the district mandates that everyone (including those in the PDS) use a particular math series. You, along with the principal, math coach, and teachers, think adopting the district's approach would be a step back and would lose ground for student learning. Or imagine, as a school-based liaison, that your university partner has a new dean who is questioning the commitment of faculty time for the PDS and who suggests that the half-time course release of university liaisons can be eliminated. Along with your university counterparts, you are confident this will seriously undermine the progress made by the PDS.

What are some battles your partner is fighting in his or her organization and what are some ways you can (delicately) be allies for each other? Take some time to write these down and share them with your partner, paying attention to both the content (what you are supporting each other on) and the process (how you delicately support each other).

3.9 Mechanisms for Transfer of Ideas and Approaches

How do others in your organizations learn the details of what you are doing in the PDS? On college campuses, PDSs can sometimes be out of sight and out of mind, where ideas and approaches developed in the PDS are not even known (let alone adopted) by other university faculty or other programs. The same can happen in a large school, where a subset of staff is involved in the PDS, or in multisite settings, where neighboring schools end up reinventing practices that have been successful at other PDSs. Some mechanisms used to transfer ideas include the following:

• Teacher sharing sessions: These are organized within a PDS to share best practices with interns, but are sometimes extended to include novice and experienced teachers at the PDS and other PDSs in the network.

• Cross-site visits: These visits are done between PDSs within a network, sometimes as "critical friends," sometimes for a newer PDS to learn some start-up ideas, and sometimes just to see how another PDS is doing things.

• Annual best practices conferences: One or two days long, these are often sponsored by a regional or local PDS network. They can be general sharing sessions on what is working or they might have a specific focus such as literacy.

• Action research presentations: Many PDSs support inquiry teams conducting action research on the impacts in their PDS. Their findings can be reported to a variety of audiences.

• Faculty meetings (at school or university): Best practices and research results can be shared and discussed.

• Tours and open visits: In states such as Maryland, where state policy has established that all new teachers will be prepared in PDSs, an extensive schedule of PDS tours has been established, so those new to it may see PDSs in action. These have been helpful for outsiders, and a positive side effect has been that it pushes people within a PDS to learn what others are doing.

What do you do to share ideas and approaches within your PDS (and your PDS network, if it is a multisite)? Brainstorm a list of what you currently do and what you think you could do to facilitate the transfer of ideas. Bring this up at a steering committee meeting.

3.10 Keeping Your Eyes on the Prize

Have your commitments to equity and to improving student learning been lost in the busy shuffle of creating and sustaining a partnership? To help your PDS hold true to its direction and vision, you may want to figure out some strategies to reconnect it with its underlying goals and mission. What follows is a list of some approaches other PDSs have used to help do that. See which might be useful in your partnership and brainstorm others that might help in your setting.

•   Accreditation standards can help. Standards such as the National PDS Standards referred to in this book, or adaptations of them like those that have been developed and finalized in Maryland, can be powerful resources. PDSs will also be reminded about reconnecting with their core goals from other forms of accreditation, such as the teacher education standards of the National Council for Accreditation of Teacher Education.

•   Local or regional networks can provide mechanisms to help remind PDSs of what they are doing and where they are going. The St. Louis PDS Consortium, for instance, has each of its constituent PDSs share with the membership an annual report that outlines its goals for the year (tied to the National PDS Standards) and the data it has collected that show the progress toward those goals.

•   Many grant funders require some sort of reporting that might cause PDSs to reflect on these issues.

•   Annual retreats held by PDSs themselves can be opportunities for reflection and planning, at which thoughtful reconnection to underlying PDS goals can be made.

•   Sometimes this work is done by a visionary leader or a person who is the designated "nudge"—whose job it is to keep reminding colleagues that the energy and work of the PDS must benefit students.

Which of these make sense for you? What would you add to help your partnership keep its eyes on the prize of equity and student learning?

3.11 New and Modified Roles in PDSs

PDSs create new roles and modify a great many others. Use (or modify) the questionnaire below to develop an inventory of new and modified roles in your PDS. You may find that taking the few minutes to do this, and sharing it within your PDS, is useful in helping you clarify the roles that are evolving and in figuring out ways to provide appreciation, preparation, and support to people in these roles.

For those in new roles (liaisons, site coordinators, parent coordinators, directors of inquiry or action research groups):

1. Describe your new role. If a job description exists, attach it (marked up, if necessary, if the role has evolved significantly since the description was written).

2. If you are in this role part-time, how much time do you commit to it? What else do you do, and what has been taken off your plate to make room for the new work?

3. In what ways have you been prepared and supported in your new role?

4. What preparation and support would be helpful?

For those in modified roles, the comparable set of questions includes the following:

1. Describe how your role has changed due to the PDS.

2. If you have added new aspects to your job, what has been taken off your plate to make room for the new work?

3. In what ways have you been prepared and supported in your modified role?

4. What preparation and support would be helpful?

3.12 Boundary Spanners

The boundary spanners in your partnership are critical in providing the glue that holds it together. They help interpret the other organization to members of their own, look for joint opportunities, bring people together, and solve interinstitutional problems that arise. They have a variety of titles: site or PDS coordinator, PDS director, liaison, and faculty member in residence (at school or university). Their job is a challenging one, requiring leadership and interpersonal skills that transcend those needed for roles within an organization.

Who are the key boundary spanners in your partnership? What challenges do they face? What support would help them do their jobs more easily or more effectively? You might consider bringing together the boundary personnel periodically for discussion of these questions, perhaps reading some of the literature on their role, provided in the reference section.

3.13 Principals, Deans, and Partnership Power Dynamics

Are the changes in roles and expectations in your PDS leading to struggles over leadership and decision making? In many PDSs, the need to work cross-institutionally and to share power and authority with outsiders, and with leaders on the faculty of school or university, leads to adjustments and difficult dynamics with those with formal authority— principals and deans.

Take some time to look at your partnership. Who are the individuals with positional authority in your PDS and in what way are their roles being changed? Include them in an honest talk about the changes, and any challenges, and discuss options for supporting them better or otherwise relieving stress or addressing conflict.

Formal Leadership Role	Type of Challenge or Conflict (if any) as Part of Being in a PDS	Ideas for Support of Those in Formal Leadership Roles in PDS	Suggestions for Organizational Changes to Address Conflicts
Principal			
Dean			
Director			
Others			

3.14 Early Strategies for Providing Resources for Start-Ups

How are you supporting the start-up of your PDS? Sometimes PDSs get started with almost no additional money, mostly by a reallocation of time and a willingness of individuals to do the work on overload. The interns' time becomes a key element of this, helping to reduce student–teacher ratios, provide individual tutoring, and so forth. Clustering student teachers saves travel time for supervisors, so those with a critical mass in one building can spend more time there and less on the road.

At the next level of support, I have seen universities support PDSs by providing one or more course releases to faculty who are involved. Since part-time replacement costs for a faculty course are usually quite low, this can provide a part of someone's time for just a few thousand dollars. Small grants (in the $5,000–$10,000 range) can be used to provide stipends for school-based personnel who are committing some of their time. Other PDSs are well funded from the outset.

What strategies for resources has your PDS used to get itself going? Name them by creating a list, including everything you can imagine that contributes to the PDS: money, reallocated time, personally donated time (overload), space, research done by a class, and so on. Share the list widely; you will be surprised at how many different resources have been donated, aligned, or allocated. When you are done, reflect on what the future brings. Are you starting to outlive those approaches and do you need to try out different ones to sustain the work?

3.15 PDS Start-Up Estimates and Operating Cost Factors

In addition to the roughly $50,000 described for start-up costs discussed earlier in the chapter, to gain some perspective on your operating costs (and possible funding sources) use the following skeletal budget (from Clark, 1997, pp. 22-23) for comparison and discussion purposes. Keep in mind that the size, scale, scope, grade level, type of community, and focus of your PDS will affect these costs, as will your average annual costs per staff member, expectations for stipends in your area, and so on.

Note how Clark divides costs into three broad areas: preservice, professional development/inquiry/renewal, and general and indirect costs. When you figure your budget, does this make sense for you? Clark also makes some assumptions about division of costs between school and

Cost Item	Paid by School District	Paid by University
Preservice FTE • Regular faculty • Adjunct/clinical coordinator • Stipends (20 at $400 per student) • Clerical related activity • Travel • Cohort/team-building activities	 $23,000 (.5 FTE) $ 8,000 $ 2,250 (.15 FTE) $ 150 $ 200	$46,000 (1 FTE) $ 300 $ 800
Professional development/ inquiry/renewal • Adjunct faculty/clinical coordinator • Other staff costs/ released time • Stipends	 $23,000 (.5 FTE) $ 6,000 $ 6,900 (leader) $23,000 (summer)	 $ 7,900 (leader)
General and indirect costs • Classroom space • Supplies • Travel • Technology • School district administrative costs • Secretarial support • University administrative costs • Program evaluation	N/A $ 2,000 $ 4,000 $ 1,500 $ 5,300 $ 2,250 (.15 FTE) $ 500	N/A $ 2,000 $ 1,000 $ 5,000 $ 3,590 $ 2,500

university. Does this make sense in your partnership? Are there other types of expenses you anticipate (or have)? Are there other significant partners who participate and cost-share?

3.16 Moving to Power

If you are in a pilot PDS project, what is your relationship to mainstream power and authority in your organization? Do those in charge ignore you—perhaps providing you with benign neglect? If that is the case, and that is the way you want it, read no further. But if you envision yourself trying to spread ideas from your PDS to the mainstream, or you seek greater legitimacy and sustainability, think about ways to "move toward power." A few thoughts follow to stimulate your own thinking.

Since your PDS needs legitimacy within your own organization, especially for making higher stakes decisions, think about how you steadily seek recognition and legitimatization at the appropriate levels of power. In what ways are you embedding or at least integrating your work into existing structures? This will not always be possible in the beginning, but it should be the direction in which you move. You can do this through setting up a PDS subcommittee of the school- or district-based planning team, or of the appropriate body of the university or department of education. See also *Aligning With the Larger Goals and Vision of Your Organization* (on p. 50 in Chapter 2). Your direction should be toward getting sanction and high-level involvement and toward being active and present on the agenda of each institution's governance bodies.

Keep in mind, however, that the involvement of those with power and authority, while ultimately essential to institutionalization, can be a mixed blessing, especially in start-up phases. Premature high-level support for PDSs may lead to an increase in attention and possible opposition before your fledgling PDS can get rooted.

As you think about this, share your thoughts with colleagues and partners to best map your PDS's strategy in relationship to power.

3.17 Multisite Networks: Wheel Versus Spokes

When I visit or study multisite networks, I usually see them as one of two types. Some seem to work like spokes radiating out from a hub (often the university) with little contact between and among schools on the wheel; all knowledge, information, and connections flow back through the hub. Other networks function more as all-points collaboratives with as much contact school to school as there is back to the hub. Fill out the following grid to help sort out how these organizational issues play out in your partnership.

Type of Information or Process	Spokes (all connections go to go through hub)	Wheel (connections to hub and directly to other points on wheel)
Decisions about policies and procedures		
Transfer of ideas/ best practices		
Resource flow		
People-to-people contact		

Which multisite model best describes your partnership? Are you satisfied with that arrangement?

3.18 Honest Talk About the Undiscussable Issues in PDSs

The public face of PDSs is usually that of a win–win collaboration, where all partners are equal and everyone's needs get met. The reality is sometimes different. Are there some tough issues to discuss in your PDS— topics that people try to avoid or are reluctant to bring up? With more at stake than in the traditional student teaching model, and with a broader array of potential conflicts due to a more comprehensive purpose, you and your PDS partners need to talk with each other honestly about your goals, your concerns, and the problems that are arising. Perhaps your PDS is fortunate enough to be in relationships that allow for this level of honest dialogue. Many are not. Citing several examples of dysfunctional or struggling PDSs in the literature (and noting that many more cases never get reported), Muchmore and Knowles (1993) conclude, "These stories also evidence a brutal reality: school-university partnerships are likely to suffer from instances of very personal conflicts and hurt that exist within schools and teacher groups unless these issues are brought to the fore" (p. 19).

Try sharing that quote with members of your PDS community, taking the time to do this in an environment where individuals can answer honestly. You might construct a simple survey asking PDS participants to agree (strongly or otherwise) or disagree with a statement such as "I feel like I can always communicate honestly with anyone in the PDS about anything that arises within it." You could also put certain topics out and check the comfort level with honest talk more specifically. Once you have seen to what extent your PDS could benefit from some honest talk, refer to cases in the Appendix for some more specific strategies for how to promote this important form of communication.

3.19 Pulling in to the Core

If your PDS is (or started as) a pilot project and you and your partners are interested in seeing it become more of a mainstream part of your organizations, consider and discuss the quote below. (See also *Moving to Power* on p. 104.) The action of trying to bring PDS approaches and ideas to the mainstream may create its own reaction: Gold and Charner (1986, p. 26), writing about other forms of organizational collaboration in ways that are applicable here, point out that

> The very fact of top-level support may arouse sources of hidden opposition. People who might have ignored a project operating modestly under the direction of a junior professor or manager will pay close attention to the same project if it appears to have the blessing and interest of the top executives. Is the project a harbinger of things to come? If it were expanded, what would be the implications for the standard ways of doing things? If made permanent, who stands to gain, and who to lose?

You might consider sharing this quotation with your steering committee and asking if your PDS is successful in moving to the core of your schools and university, who stands to gain, who to lose, and what the sources of support and opposition you anticipate are. In an honest conversation among the steering committee, you may wish to be specific, naming names or departments and using this discussion as a springboard to help you move to where you want to go.

3.20 Achieving Critical Mass:
Engaging People in PDS Work

In PDSs, personal relationships matter, and matter a great deal. The more individuals in each of the partnering organizations who are involved with the PDS and with each other, the deeper the impact of the PDS and the more likely it is to be sustained. The challenge is to reach out and engage people in all the partnering organizations, to pull people in and create ownership in the PDS and what it stands for. Listed below are a few approaches to this that I have seen successfully used:

• List the tasks and the people who perform them in your PDS. You can combine this with the *Leadership Roles in Sustaining PDS Work Inventory* on p. 109 and then identify the people who perform those roles. To get you started, I included the list from *Leadership Roles*. Cross out those that do not make sense for you, and add others that do. If you find (as many of you will) that frequently much of the work is being done by the same small group of individuals, use that as a springboard for reaching out to others.

Task	Who is doing it now?	Who could be doing it?	What would it take to engage him/her in it?
Liaison			
Resource finder			
Sponsor/ buffer			
Mirror/ assessor			
Champion/ inventor			
Partnership personnel director			
Manager of nuts and bolts of partnership			
Coach/ facilitator			
Other			
Other			

•   Develop a menu of options to make it easier for colleagues to get involved. To get arts and sciences faculty engaged in the PDS, a colleague in Massachusetts, Debra Pallatto-Fontaine, developed a "menu" of choices—ranging from "finger foods," such as coming once to speak to a class at the school, to fuller "appetizers" such as observing teaching practice through participating in rounds, to "entrees" such as getting involved in codeveloping or coteaching a course. Adapt this idea for your partnership, stressing the key idea of choice and of offering differing levels of engagement tailored to the individual needs of your colleagues.

•   Reach out to new hires (see *Pulling New People In* below).

3.21 Pulling New People In

How does your PDS reach out and engage new people? A continuing challenge in developing and maintaining a critical mass is the ongoing need to draw in new people, many of whom will not have been involved in the discussions and excitement back at the start-up of the PDS. Have you figured out how to involve new participants in ways that draw on their ideas and visions for the partnership at the same time as you make it known to them what the PDS is all about and what its core commitments are? Here are a few ideas to spark your own:

•   Include the PDS in job descriptions, applications, interviews, hiring, and orientation so new hires know throughout the process that they are entering a PDS and what that means.

•   Reach out to include new people in PDS activities.

•   Engage new teachers in PDS activities that support their work. You can invite them to seminars for interns on, for instance, classroom management or on how your school teaches mathematics.

•   If you have experienced teachers conducting classroom inquiry, you might pair new teachers with them and their interns, focusing on helping them develop and test teaching strategies in their classrooms.

•   New administrators and university faculty can be matched with counterparts in your PDS network to orient them to the new and changed roles they have.

What are you doing to bring new people in? What can you be doing?

3.22 Leadership Roles in Sustaining PDS Work Inventory

Develop a list of the tasks and roles in your partnership. Here is one list started by Jed Lippard (then a student in a partnership course I taught at Harvard) and subsequently augmented by participants of a PDS collaborative at their annual retreat. It is not an exhaustive list; use it as a springboard to defining more clearly what needs to be done in your partnership. Combine it with *Achieving Critical Mass: Engaging People in PDS Work* on p. 106 to figure out how to spread the work and pull more people in.

- Liaison: Connects the partnering institutions and looks for opportunities and challenges on the border between and among partners
- Manager of nuts and bolts of partnership: Takes care of the myriad details—budget, scheduling, and so on
- Partnership personnel director: Works on matching and supporting the individuals who take on the various roles of the partnership
- Resource finder: Identifies and goes after additional resources inside and outside of partnering organizations
- Sponsor/buffer: Is high enough in each organization to protect the PDS efforts, especially if it runs into conflicts with existing policies and procedures
- Coach/facilitator: Helps and supports those in other roles
- Mirror/assessor: Reflects back to the partnership in informal and formal ways; helps keep a focus on what matters for the partnership
- Champion/inventor: Innovator who sees partnership opportunities or new learning opportunities within the PDS

3.23 Surviving Leadership Transitions

One of the toughest challenges your PDS may ever face is when one or more key leaders leave and new ones take their places. If leaders come in without an understanding of and commitment to the existence of the PDS, they may not be supportive of the time and commitment needed to make the PDS work. New principals and deans can be especially critical, since their support is essential. Here are some ideas that help in the transition:

- Put the PDS into job descriptions, promotional materials at the school and university, and every step of the hiring and interview process.

- Develop an agreement or a memo of understanding that commits the partnership at the highest levels and in the most specific terms. (So if a principal leaves, there is a still a superintendent or district commitment to the PDS.)

• Have a widespread publicity campaign about the PDS so it is a known and supported part of the school and university. You might weave the word PDS into the name of the school, for instance.

• Collect and have available data on the impacts of the PDS on students, new teacher retention, and so on. See Chapter 6 on Data, and see *Aligning With the Larger Goals and Vision of Your Organization* (on p. 50 in Chapter 2).

What is your history in surviving leadership transition? What is your transition plan?

3.24 *Approaches to Supporting New Roles in PDSs*

Some specific strategies that have been used to support teachers in their new and modified PDS roles include the following (adapted from Teitel, 1996c):

• Time: Teachers need time outside of class for other leadership work in the PDS. Some PDSs juggle time to create blocks, like a 75-minute lunch once a week to permit the discussion of issues necessary to develop a PDS. Others use interns to free up teachers for as much as a day a week for alternative professional time.

• Support for role change: For teachers this means changing the expectations and definitions of the teacher's job, so it is not solely a direct service to students. This may involve educating parents, colleagues, and other administrators that involvement in leadership activities is a legitimate part of a teacher's role. For administrators, this may mean developing parental support to avoid any concerns over the increased exposure of students to student teachers or an alternative arrangement while teachers are involved in leadership work. It also means that central offices acknowledge the legitimacy of a shared governance and a shared responsibility approach, which might mean waiving requirements or providing extra resources.

• Revised reward structures: For teachers, the intrinsic rewards of PDS work include increased expertise, efficacy, collegiality, and self-renewal, while the extrinsic rewards are power (through involvement in decision making), status (through presenting at conferences and being recognized as resources by the university, for instance), and extra pay (for meetings held after school). Although the increased pay is not always significant, it has high symbolic value.

Which of these (and other) psychological and financial supports is your PDS providing for teachers? How would you expand this list to apply to other partners—university faculty and administrators, parents, and community partners? What are you doing and what could you be doing?

3.25 Suggestions for PDS Leadership Development

Formal and informal leaders in PDSs need opportunities to learn and practice new skills. Despite the pressures of these transformed roles and the myriad things teachers and administrators need to know and do to be effective in them, there is usually little to no formal preparation or support for teachers or principals taking on new leadership roles. Virtually all the learning is on the job.

List the new skills needed for principals, deans, teachers, university faculty, and parents, using the grid below. You may find it helpful to draw on the survey questionnaires used in *New and Modified Roles in PDSs* on p. 100.

Role	Skills Needed for New or Modified Position	Skills Provided by Partnership
School-based teachers		
University-based teachers		
Parents		
Deans		
Community members		
Arts and science faculty members		
Interns		
Principals		
Others		

Think about the sources of support. Many PDSs make the presumption that teachers, administrators, and university personnel have the needed knowledge and skills to take on these roles. Do you? If you were to take seriously the needs for skill development, what could you do?

3.26 Valuing and Rewarding PDS Work

Take a look at the hard work that PDS participants perform—in many cases over and above their current jobs—and look at the ways in which your partnership and its partnering organizations value and reward the work. To get started on this, below are three broad areas of possible reward. They certainly overlap, and you may wish to add to them:

Recognition. What kind of recognition and appreciation do participants get? Are there awards, ceremonies, mentions in newsletters and publications of the partnering organizations, thank-you's from presidents, provosts, deans, superintendents, principals, nonprofit directors, and so on?

Feedback on Impacts. How are data collected and shared that show the impact the PDS is having (on students, on adults, on the community), so participants know that what they are doing matters and is impactive?

Financial Rewards, Promotion, Tenure. Does extra work in the PDS lead to extra pay or other compensation (time, other resources)? Does it count for promotion? Have you revamped your university's promotion and tenure guidelines (as several universities engaged in PDS now have) to give weight to PDS work? Are PDS participants able to perform their PDS work as part of their job, not as overload?

Take an inventory of what you do and what you could do to convey the clear sense of PDS work being valued.

3.27 Funding Stream Challenges and Solutions

Unless you are fortunate enough to live in a state where there are major changes in the PDS funding environment (such as having a different funding formula for state universities that are also PDSs, similar to the differential funding used for teaching hospitals), most of what you do about funding streams will happen at a local level—with your university, your school district, your community, and its partners. To help get a handle on addressing your resource needs, look at the flow of resources in your PDS by filling in the grid below. It helps if you think of resources as more than money—as time, space, and people (human resources).

Resources	School School District	University	Grant Funders	Community or Other Partners
Money				
People				
Space				
Time				

Does seeing the sources of your support laid out help you see any discrepancies, inequities, or other potential sources?

3.28 Redefining PDS Work Into Job Descriptions

If PDS work is not to be a continued add-on, it must be woven into the work and expectations of the PDS participants' lives. To see how far you have come (and move yourself along on this), take a look at the list of tasks you generated on *Achieving Critical Mass: Engaging People in PDS Work* on p. 106. In that exercise I suggested you use the list as a way of tracking how you could engage others in the PDS work. Now, take the same list and check on the extent to which you have embedded those tasks in someone's—anyone's—job description. Make a two-column grid with the tasks in one column and the second column showing in whose job description the task appears. If you find column 2 repeatedly blank, think about ways to embed the work.

Tasks needed for PDS	*In whose job description does this task appear?*
	[Names of individuals or job titles]

3.29 Creative Approaches to Finding PDS Resources

When he looked at resources and support for PDS activities in four high-performing, mature partnerships, Jon Snyder (1998) found a complex interaction between the groups of educators doing the PDS work and the structures and resource supports that worked best to sustain them. The sites Snyder visited did not simply let loose the educators and expect them to transform the support structures; nor did they set up the structures and realign their funding streams without attending to what the educators were doing and the relationships they were forming. The processes went hand in hand and were shaped by three factors:

- Partnerships depended on three sets of resources—school-based educators, university-based educators, and prospective educators (with the latter as a key resource for virtually everything else).

- Clustering resources in numbers (e.g., groups of interns at one site) and over time (e.g., yearlong internships and university commitments at the school) were key.

- Clustering only worked when structures and processes were in place that supported those professional educators so real learning opportunities come out of it.

To make this all work, Snyder suggests that effective support structures for each of the three categories or people are essential—for school-based, university-based, and prospective educators. For instance, for one of those groups, the university-based educators, Snyder offers examples of typical schedules that allow them to meet their university obligations as well as do their PDS work, of faculty scholarship incentives that let them sign up for specific work in the PDS in lieu of a portion of their teaching load, of commitments and supports from the presidents of the universities, as well as of promotion and tenure policies that encourage all faculty—including those from arts and sciences—to work in the PDS.

Apply these ideas to your PDS, checking to see to what extent you are using the maximum resources available to you from these three sets of educators and to what extent you have aligned your resources and support structures to sustain them.

3.30 Trading as a Resource Strategy

Some PDSs have made the exchange of services the backbone of their resource strategy. Case, Norlander, and Reagan (1993) argue that PDS initiatives should not be funded with grant money—that the core of what is done should be based on reallocation of existing resources and time. You may or may not agree with their argument that too many projects disappear once the soft money stops flowing, but you may be intrigued by their approach: by changing job descriptions and curriculum approaches and by seeking economies of scale in student teaching and alignment of research, service, and teaching, they describe how their PDS partnerships use existing resources for core activities and get external jointly written grants to augment their activities. Harris and Harris (1995) describe how several of the partnerships in the National Network for Educational Renewal address the challenge of finding time and money through creative exchanges. In one instance, the PDS uses money the university would ordinarily pay to part-time student teacher supervisors to hire preservice teachers to work as half-time interns, thereby freeing capable cooperating teachers to supervise other preservice teachers. In another setting, cooperating teachers whose classes are being taught by capable preservice teachers replace other teachers for professional development workshops, and so on. Harris and Harris note that when dollar values are assigned to these activities, one PDS network (with 23 partner schools) had an operating cost of three quarters of a million dollars that was all exchanged in-kind, with no money transferred at all.

Services, Expertise, or Other Resources	Provided by School	Provided by School District	Purchased From Outside Collaborative	Provided by University	Provided by Community or Other partner

Use the preceding grid to see what you are currently exchanging and what you are purchasing from outside.

Have you ever tried to put a dollar value on the services exchanged among partners? If you think it would be helpful for yourself or any of your stakeholders, set up an exchange table, including some calculations for rates. Have you been as resourceful as you could in developing these exchanges?

CHAPTER RESOURCES

This section includes a brief annotated bibliography of text and Web resources. The full citations for the text references are in the back of the book.

Structures

For specifics on governance models, including sample partnership agreements, see Teitel (1998a). Additional partnership agreements are available online at the Clinical Schools Clearinghouse Web site: www.aacte.org/Eric/pro_dev_schools.htm.

Maryland's (2001) PDS implementation manual (http://cte.jhu.edu/pds/about.cfm) has guidelines for structuring coordinating councils, for developing memoranda of understanding, and for a strategic planning process.

One of the best pieces on the challenges of mixing institutional authority that come about in PDSs was written more than a decade ago by Barbara Neufeld (1992).

Roles

For more on boundary spanners see the aptly named "Walking the Fault Line: Boundary Spanning in Professional Development Schools" by Sue Walters (1998) and also "Creating Common Ground: The Facilitator's Role in Initiating School-University Partnerships" (Collay, 1995).

See a special double issue on PDSs of the *Peabody Journal of Education* (1999) for articles on role changes for university administrators (Stroble & Luka, 1999), teacher education students (Kimball, 1999), mentor teachers (Kyle, Moore, & Sanders, 1999), university faculty (Hovda, 1999), and liaisons (Schack, 1999).

See Maryland (2001) or http://cte.jhu.edu/pds/about.cfm. The online "Implementation Manual" has several pages of suggestions outlining specific roles and responsibilities for site coordinators, higher education liaisons, mentors, principals, and so on. The Benedum Collaborative in West Virginia includes similar information on its Web site www.wvu. edu/~benedum/noframe/nfabout.html.

Resources

For more models for costs of PDSs, see Clark (1997) and Clark and Pilecki (1997).

For a host of excellent ideas for roles and resource effectiveness from some of the best-established PDSs in the country, see Snyder (1998).

For details of other examples of how partnerships handle their resource needs and exchanges, see Case et al. (1993) and Harris and Harris (1995).

The third chapter of the *Putting the Pieces Together* report of North Central Regional Education Labs (at www.ncrel.org/sdrs/areas/issues/ envrnmnt/css/ppt/putting.htm) has some good suggestions for finding and developing financial resources for school-linked comprehensive strategies, and for using financial and human resources effectively and seamlessly.

For updates on text and Web sources related to this Standard, see http://pds.edreform.net/home/ and click on Structures, Resources, and Roles.

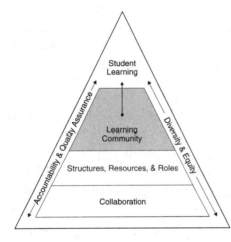

4

Learning Community

*Improving Approaches
to Teaching, Learning,
and Leadership*

The Learning Community Standard and the ideas that it represents are at the heart of the professional development school. The Standard represents the improved approaches to teaching, learning, and leadership that make professional development schools important innovations in schooling and teacher preparation. This chapter focuses on the development of the PDS as an inclusive learning community, as well as on the teaching, learning, and leadership approaches that are developed and sustained in it.

When I come in to give a talk or provide a keynote for a PDS conference, I often start by putting on the overhead the four functions of PDSs: the improvement of student learning, the preparation of educators, the professional development of educators, and inquiry into best practice. I then ask members of the audience to tell us what they are doing in each category. I do this for several reasons. For newcomers to PDSs, it is a good way to learn what

PDSs do. It is an interactive warm-up that is also a sharing mechanism—participants often get some good ideas for programs and activities during this part of the session. It also focuses all of us on what the PDSs are actually doing—for kids, for teachers, and so on—and it is a subtle way to focus attention on gaps such as a PDS that only works on issues of teacher education, for instance, but does no inquiry or professional development. The discussions usually generate long lists that are quite impressive and provide a good warm-up and introduction into the focus of my talk.

The lists, impressive as they are, can at first seem like a string of unconnected activities. As I listen and sort through these lists of the activities that are the substance of the Learning Community Standard, I ask myself six questions:

- Connection: What is the valued added to this activity by the fact that it is part of a PDS?
- Philosophy: What does this activity say about the PDS's philosophy of teaching, learning, and leadership?
- Learners: Who are the participants and who are the learners in this PDS?
- Assessment: How do you know that the new PDS activities and approaches are better than the ones they replaced?
- Sustainability: If this is a better approach to teaching and learning, can it be sustained?
- Depth: Do the approaches or activities lead to core changes in teaching, learning, and leadership?

OVERVIEW AND HISTORY

Here is the language of the Standard, followed by an elaboration of the six questions noted above, along with suggestions on how you might apply them to the activities that are at the heart of the learning community of your PDS.

The PDS is a learning-centered community that supports the integrated learning and development of PreK–12 students, teacher candidates, and PDS partners through inquiry-based practice. PDS partners share a common vision of teaching and learning grounded in research and practitioner knowledge. They believe that adults and children learn best in the context of practice.

Learning supported by this community results in changes and improvement in individual practice and in the policies and practices of the partnering institutions. (NCATE, 2001b, p. 11)

Connection: What Is the Valued Added to This Activity by the Fact That It Is Part of a PDS?

The Standards call for the "integrated learning and development of PreK–12 students, candidates, and PDS partners." When I hear of the many interesting-sounding activities and approaches used in PDSs, I wonder which of them might be taking place regardless of the partnership—in other words, what does "integrated" mean? If a fourth-grade teacher is trying out a new approach to teaching mathematics, is that a "learning community innovation" under the PDS? What if it shows connections to others in the learning community—such as other partners at the university or in the community—or is supported by other collaborative structures?

When the PDS Standards were released in 2001, they were accompanied by a *Handbook for the Assessment of Professional Development Schools* (NCATE, 2001a), which provides concrete examples of how the Standards can be applied through a self-study and visit process. The *Handbook* provides examples of PDS work:

- Concerted and systematic efforts to reduce the achievement gap among PreK–12 students of various groups
- Collaborative initiatives to improve continuity of instruction across learning environments to improve children's reading skills
- Collaborative research initiatives to create a "new and improved" reading program offered in a bilingual literacy program
- Professional development programs to support continuous development of the P–16 community of learners through a systemic approach that combines candidate preparation and professional growth for both university and school faculty
- Restructuring efforts for preservice education leading to collaboration between special education, general education, and related services faculty at the university and school site in offering and delivering integrated coursework and field–clinical experiences for candidates
- Implementing the study of university and school partnerships to examine multiple features such as

   Initial entry of a cohort in a partner school

   Observation skills of a new cohort

Collaboration among partners

Quality settings for the placement of teacher candidates

Site coordinators and site professor roles in the partner school setting

According to the *Handbook*,

What makes an initiative PDS work is that it is undertaken by PDS partners and candidates and it simultaneously focuses on meeting PreK–12 students' needs and supporting the learning of faculty and [teacher education] candidates. Such work is characterized by collaboration, inquiry, accountability, and learning in the context of practice. (NCATE, 2001a, pp. 6-7)

Last February, rather than hire a substitute teacher for the 10th-grade English teacher when she had to be out for a month for surgery, a PDS I work with arranged to have one of the yearlong interns teach the class. The whole community launched into action to support the intern, with substantial learning for all. An intern who was placed in another classroom shifted some of her load to help out and coteach some portions of the class. The experienced teacher who serves as the on-site coordinator adjusted her schedule to help. A month before the intern was to take over, the weekly on-site seminar for all the interns shifted into gear, helping her plan her lessons, debating different strategies for teaching the content and assessing student progress. The English methods class back at the university was affected, with the professor using the classroom challenge faced by the intern as a focus of three classes. During the month-long teaching experience, these support groups continued to help and to learn from the intern's experience. At a reflection and documentation session in June, it was apparent that the "ripples" caused by this one change in the normal order of things were extensive. Preservice teachers who were not involved in the PDS reported in their final evaluations for their English methods class how helpful the sessions focused on the intern's practice were; the seminar coleaders felt it was the best thing that could have happened to focus the seminar for everyone. The on-site coordinator reported on how other teachers in the building had been impressed by the unit the intern (with all of her support) had put together, and they were hoping to be able to use some of it in their own classes.

The PDS Standards Student Learning Pyramid graphic that frames this book shows the main connections for how the three target groups (interns, experienced educators, and PreK–12 students) interact in the learning community in ways that ultimately contribute to increased student learning. The story of the absent teacher shows how any number of side effects and unanticipated impacts can ripple out from the learning that goes on in a professional development school. The story highlights the importance of collaborative structures in the PDS and a community where everyone learns. What are the connections and integration of the learning in your PDS?

Philosophy: What Does This Activity Say About the PDS's Philosophy of Teaching, Learning, and Leadership?

Is there a pedagogical philosophy embedded in your PDS, and to what extent do all partners share it? Much has been written, especially in the early days of PDSs, about the goals and vision PDSs have for learning. In the early 1990s the National Center for Restructuring Education, Schools, and Teaching at Teachers College, Columbia brought together representatives of all the major groups promoting PDSs and developed a vision statement that calls for "centering schools on learners and learning" in a long list of ways that include the following:

- An unalterable commitment that all children can and do learn
- Commitment to inclusive, adaptive approaches to children and their learning and the full participation of all learners in expanded educational opportunities, with respectful consideration of gender, class, race and culture
- Continual practical and reflective work in developing curriculum and alternative teaching strategies
- Classrooms and schools based on the realization that teaching and learning are reciprocal processes demanding active work on genuine tasks that are meaningfully assessed
- Curriculum and teaching that support multiple learning strategies, appropriate and varied assessment, and genuine accountability for student growth, development and learning (NCREST, 1993, pp. 3-4)

According to one of the architects of the Holmes Group approach, "Apart from the PDS design itself, the Holmes Group and others are not advocating a particular pedagogical model or curriculum scope and sequence" (Murray, 1993, p. 62). Nonetheless, the clearly expressed beliefs that all children can learn, and their commitment to "teaching and learning for understanding," suggest the possibility that this "may well require a radical revision of the school's curriculum and instruction" (Holmes Group, 1990, p. 7). For many scholars and activists in PDSs, the calls for interactive teaching with a real push for higher order thinking skills for all children lead inevitably to a constructivist approach. But others have argued that approaches that may work well for some children may not for children from low socioeconomic backgrounds or students of color (Murrell, 1998).

This question does not just apply to approaches to student learning. The same questions apply to approaches to preservice and experienced educator development—mentoring, decision-making approaches, teacher empowerment, models for supervision of interns, and professional development.

What are the philosophical underpinnings of your PDS? Do you and your colleagues and partners see your PDS as simply a partnership mechanism, devoid of any philosophical underpinnings? If you have a philosophical approach, is it shared? How has it been arrived at? Does it have to be uniform for you to work effectively together? How much tension is good? PDS advocates use the phrase "creative tension" to describe how, in PDSs, the world of theory rubs against the world of practice. The Standards call for a commitment to "learn from practice"—what does this mean and how is it done in your PDS?

Learners: Who Are the Participants and Who Are the Learners in This PDS?

For me, this triggers two questions: Who is included in the partnership to be part of the learning community and who is doing the learning in the partnership? The language of the Standard is explicit about the inclusiveness of the PDS learning community:

> The PDS partnership includes principal and supporting institutions and individuals. The principal PDS partners are members of the PreK–12 schools and professional preparation program who agree to collaborate. The supporting PDS partner institutions include the university, the school district, the teacher union or professional education association(s). Arts and Sciences faculty, other interested school and university faculty, family members, community members, and other affiliated schools are important PDS participants in the extended learning community.

In addition to exploring who is included (and who is not) in your PDS partnership, the second question asks who is actually learning. Is it just the

PreK–12 students, just the preservice teachers, or just the classroom teachers? To what extent are all the members of your PDS community—university faculty, administrators, parents, and community members—learning?

Assessment: How Do You Know That the New PDS Activities and Approaches Are Better Than the Ones They Replaced?

Since PDSs are not about making change for the sake of change, it is important that all the experimentation and new approaches encouraged as part of the learning community undergo careful assessment at some point in the process. More on this in Chapter 6, but it is a key framing concept as you look at any and all learning community activities: "Is this approach better? How do we know it, and how do we show it?"

> I saw a wonderful example of experimentation tied to assessment in a PDS I visited as part of the Standards Project. A partnership for more than seven years at the time of my visit, the PDS had developed a strong collaborative culture of problem solving and integrated teaching and learning. Parents and school and university faculty and administrators formed a "cluster" to develop the reading approach for the school jointly. A key aspect of the reading instruction program was the use of small groups and one-to-one instruction by the university students. To make this work, the alignment was complete—the preservice teachers would be learning the same reading approach the PDS classroom teachers used. The program the group adopted was tried for two years, with the cluster checking periodically to assess whether the implementation of the plan was complete and to support the work of the people making the changes. The cluster also kept track of the student achievement data, broken out to see how students from different racial groups were doing. When the results after two years were disappointing, the planning group reconvened to explore other options together.

Sustainability: If This Is a Better Approach to Teaching and Learning, Can It Be Sustained?

I have seen some innovative learning strategies tried in PDSs—such as one-to-one tutoring of struggling children by master teachers—that were effective but not sustainable. If approaches are so labor-intensive, expensive, or inefficient that they cannot be continued, they will have no lasting impacts. When approaches are effective and efficient, they are more likely to be scaled up and sustained. It helps if an approach has many ripples (the same activity or approach helps PreK–12 students, preservice teachers, and experienced teachers at the same time) or other efficiencies make it possible to sustain (e.g., clusters of preservice teachers reduce travel time for supervisors).

What are the practical sustainability issues for your PDS?

Depth: Do the Approaches or Activities Lead to Core Changes in Teaching, Learning, and Leadership?

This, of course, is a recurrent theme in this book. Are the changes in teaching, learning, and leadership in your PDS minor adjustments or changes closer to the core?

START-UP TASKS AND CHALLENGES

The concrete examples of the challenges faced on this Standard can be best examined by looking at the three target groups for PDSs: PreK–12 students, preservice educators, and experienced educators.

Supporting Student Learning

Students in professional development schools have enhanced learning experiences in at least three ways:

- *In the classroom*, by the presence of additional adults—preservice teacher interns, university faculty, and community partners complementing the classroom teachers—students also benefit from improvements in curriculum, instruction, and assessment from enhanced learning and collaboration of all the above-mentioned adults, as shown in the PDS Standards Student Learning Pyramid

- *In the school setting*, from extracurricular offerings, after school and before school study, informal counseling, relationship building, mentoring, and other contact with interns and other partnering adults

- *In the community setting*, from connections to the university through tours, access to facilities and labs, contact with mentors, and community partner connections

Finally, the collaborative aspects of the PDS provide a framework and platform for all manner of innovation in subject area, development of interdisciplinary curricula, and imaginative use of time for instruction and working in different configurations with children. See *Enhancing Impacts on Students in PDSs* on p. 147.

Challenges in the start-up stage include keeping track of the various initiatives and balancing the needs for coherence and focus with flexibility and openness to new ideas. Start-up problems to be avoided include the following:

• Fragmentation: All educational institutions, especially schools, are inundated with often-competing pulls and initiatives for new programs. The challenge is for PDSs not to be just another pull, which might mean from the school perspective that, on top of everything else, the school now works with student teachers. Rather, make the PDS an umbrella or structural mechanism for the rest to fall under. See *Avoiding Fragmentation Frazzle* on p. 149.

• Missed opportunities (for collaboration): Even though adopting a "let many flowers bloom approach" makes sense for many start-ups, PDSs need some level of information sharing and coordination so participants are not missing opportunities for collaboration. See *Information Coordination Mechanisms* on p. 150.

• Lack of documentation: Although getting baseline data for assessment purposes is very important, it can be seen as onerous (and in many cases simply not get done) by people engaged in trying to get programs going. See *Assessment Template* on p. 138 in this chapter as well as Chapter 6.

• Lack of equity: Patterns of student organization such as tracking are sometimes ignored in PDSs. Occasionally, enrichment programs or other PDS enhancements for students actually reinforce the greater privileged access that some students have in schools. See Chapter 5.

• Competing directions coming from poor alignment of school, university, and community partners: In one partnership I work with, there are competing approaches to the teaching of reading coming from within one of the partners—from different units within the university. This became a problem when different faculty members were working at cross-purposes in the partner schools. Resolving these differences, or at least acknowledging them so work can be done constructively, is necessary. See *Finding (or Developing) Philosophical Coherence* on p. 150.

- Complacency: PDSs need to make sure improved teaching and learning are on the agenda. Because it is often seen as an honor for a school to be asked to be a PDS, sometimes people in the school see themselves as model teachers and then don't think of their own learning and growth as part of the process. This often also applies to university personnel. See *Change Is Always for Someone Else* on p. 151.

Teacher Education

Some sort of enhanced experience for preservice educators is at the heart of all PDSs. Philosophically, this difference represents an important part of the professionalization of teaching, where teachers are being socialized into a different conception of teaching and of schools. These philosophical beliefs lead to a number of organizational and structural changes in the field-based portion of student teaching: clusters of preservice teachers working together as a cohort, placed in a school community, rather than with one individual teacher, and often for longer or more intensive internships. Supervision is usually much more frequent, often done by, or in collaboration with, school-based educators. Interns are typically welcomed as part of their school community, engaging with other teachers, administrators, and parents in ways that more closely resemble that of beginning teachers. Often there are big changes in the campus-based portion of the preservice teacher experience: University coursework is often on-site or more closely integrated with the experience, with faculty members involved in the school in far more collaborative ways—ways that respect the knowledge of school-based or community-based folks. See *Enhancing the Preservice Teacher Experience Through PDSs* on p. 151.

Challenges during the start-up stage include addressing all aspects of the preservice teacher's experience—at the school, on the campus, and in the community. There are several potential pitfalls to be avoided:

- Poor philosophical alignment within the program: PDSs need to make sure all aspects of the teacher preparation program are coherent and consistent. In some, for example, the regularly assigned university supervisors of student teaching take a very traditional approach to their job, not understanding that the context and expectations are different in a PDS. See *Getting Your Programmatic Ducks in a Row* on p. 152.

- One-way "fixes": PDSs need to make sure mutuality and reciprocity are reflected in the redesign of teacher preparation. Are school-based faculty equal partners? Is as much change going on in campus-based aspects of the preparation program as at the school? See *Redesigning the Components of Teacher Education* on p. 153.

- Lack of attention to equity: Even as they are improving the preparation of preservice teachers, PDSs may do little or nothing to better prepare teachers to meet the equity challenges of schools. See Chapter 5.

- Out of sight, out of mind: Some PDSs are totally disconnected from the university. Preservice teachers never set foot on campus. While this strengthens their connection to the world of practice, it is useful to explore what is lost in this. See *Total Immersion: Advantages and Disadvantages* on p. 153.

- No community ties: PDSs need to look for involvement with community partners in ways that break down the dominance of teacher education and school faculty as the only sources of knowledge and legitimacy on teacher preparation and student learning. If teachers are to be better prepared to work with parents and community, these wider connections need to be made during their preparation. See *Making the Community Part of Teacher Education* on p. 154.

- Complacency: Make sure that new approaches to preservice teaching are not the start and end of PDS. For example, PDS cooperating teachers in Shen (1994) expressed the view that being a PDS meant yearlong student teaching, more cooperating teacher involvement, greater attention to matching, and on-site supervision assignment to a team. They did not mention any of the other goals of PDSs: their own growth as teachers, improved student learning, or research of inquiry into practice. See *Is Everyone Learning in the PDS?* on p. 159.

Professional Development for Experienced Educators

The philosophical roots of teacher professional development in the PDS are the twin beliefs that teachers are the key to educational renewal and that continuous inquiry into practice is the key to successful teacher development and growth. Much of the professional development for experienced educators is tied to, and a natural outgrowth of, the three other areas associated with PDSs—working to improve student learning, expanded roles in teacher education, and research and inquiry. For school-based faculty, professional development follows from a great expansion of roles, a stretching in new teaching methods, and a broader conceptualization of the role and definition of teachers. Successful involvement with preservice teachers can expand the possibilities for teacher leadership, growth, and professionalism. It requires teachers to crystallize what they know and articulate it to novices, but it also has other farther-reaching effects. See *Experienced Teacher Development in PDSs* on p. 154.

An important subset of the experienced educator group is the group of novice teachers, those with less than three years of experience. As the numbers of new teachers hired grow, more and more PDSs have sizable groups of new teachers, some of whom may be graduates of the PDS. They can benefit from being inducted into a professional development environment.

> For the past few years, in the urban high school partnered with my university, there have been 10 year-long interns "immersed" in the school. For each of those years there have also been 6–10 new teachers. We found that much of the orientation, discussion time, and support that we arranged for the interns was extremely useful to the new teachers. We began to invite the new teachers to the intern seminar held on-site, after school; many of them came and that helped them even as it enriched the discussion for the interns. Each year from three to seven interns went on to become new teachers in the school; one of them has now completed the cycle by becoming a cooperating mentor.

See *New Teachers' Benefits in a PDS* on p. 155.

As with experienced teachers, for university teacher education faculty, growth is often a result of the new roles they play in PDSs. In a PDS, their relationships change with all the other PDS partners—interns, teachers, school and district administrators, arts and science faculty at their own universities, parents, and other community partners. Sharing authority for teacher education, learning from other partners, and even rethinking what the knowledge base for teacher education is, and who owns it, are powerful transformative activities with the potential to lead to professional growth and development. In addition, university faculty find that the presence of PDS interns in their classrooms can change the dynamics and lead to additional growth as teachers.

> I recently facilitated a meeting for just the teacher education faculty for a PDS partnership I was working with. Over the

previous three years, the university was shifting from a traditional teacher education program, with most placements in suburban schools, to one with expanded year-long urban PDS placements. When I asked what were the gains and the losses of the shift, there was considerable honest talk about pluses and minuses of the change. One fascinating response (listed by most of the faculty present as a positive change) was the change brought about in their classrooms by the presence of the year-long interns. "They challenge me," said one long-time professor. "While the others [noninterns] nod and write down what I say, the [PDS interns] question me. Since they are fully immersed in a school all year long, they try out what I suggest immediately, and come back the next week, and tell me it didn't work. It has been great, but it pushes me."

See *University Faculty Development* on p. 157.

For those individuals who are the liaisons or who otherwise take leadership on the boundary of both (or all) partnering organizations, there is a particular set of challenges in a PDS: making the partnership work, representing your own organization to the partners, interpreting the partners' organizations for your own colleagues, and figuring out how to be change agents in one another's settings. All these provide a tremendous push to leadership and growth. See *Boundary-Spanner Challenges and Growth* on p. 157.

In theory, professional development in the PDS applies not only to school- and university-based faculty, but also to administrators at both sets of institutions and to all other partners. Administrators are left out or have minimal roles in some PDSs. Even when they are more deeply involved, they are often seen as supporters or leaders, but not necessarily as individuals who are learning and growing as a result of their involvement. See *Is Everyone Learning in the PDS?* on p. 159.

Start-up issues include bringing all parts of the system into alignment and not forgetting that everyone is a learner in PDS. Here are some potential traps to avoid:

• Poor professional development policy alignment: Sometimes when it comes time to plan inservice workshops or other forms of professional development, even well-established PDSs get ignored, as administrators bring in outside speakers for one-shot workshops. Schools, school districts, and universities with PDSs need to tap into the professional development talent, energy, and planning capacity of those PDSs, and those in the PDSs need to figure out how to shape the larger professional development (PD) agenda. See *Taking Control of Your Professional Development* on p. 158.

• The inner circle of PDSs: In some PDSs, a subset of faculty, staff, administrators, and parents are engaged and benefiting. Those outside the inner circle may be left out, or feel excluded or otherwise removed. PDSs need to attend to issues of equity and access to see who participates and who benefits in PDS enhancement and growth. See *Who Benefits From PDS Professional Development and Who Doesn't?* on p. 159.

• Lack of attention to issues of equity: Sometimes even PDSs that are working to restructure schools for increased equity for students, and possibly even making changes in their preservice teacher programs to better prepare teachers for equity, neglect the professional development needs of their experienced faculty and administrators on this score. See *Developing Strategies to Address Diversity and Equity* in Chapter 5 and use the suggestions from *Is Everyone Learning in the PDS?* (p. 159) to ensure that the approaches your partnership is using to address issues of diversity are being learned and used by all.

• The learners and the learned: Most of what is reported in the literature about PDS professional development focuses on PreK–12 teachers, with less attention paid to the professional development of university faculty and even less to that of administrators at either institution. This imbalance suggests the possibility that there are differing perceptions of the need for and importance of continuing professional development for all participants in the PDS. See *Is Everyone Learning in the PDS?* on p. 159.

• Omission of unions, parents, and community agencies: If professional development is seen as something that only goes on between school-based and university-based educators, PDSs will be missing much of their potential. Just as it is important for preservice teachers to understand and connect to the communities their students come from, so is it for the experienced educators. See *Including All PDS Partners in Professional Development* on p. 160.

ISSUES AND CHALLENGES IN SUSTAINABILITY

Many wonderful, creative, and innovative ideas have been developed and implemented in PDSs. For these ideas to have long-term impacts and help in the simultaneous renewal of schools and teacher education, they have to show that they work by sufficiently improving processes and impacts so that others in the PDS think it is worthwhile to scale them up. As you think about scaling up and issues of sustainability and institutionalization in your PDS, it helps to sort innovations into what Larry Cuban (1988) calls first- and second-order changes.

First-order changes increase the efficiency of operations without changing the outcomes or questioning the underlying beliefs and values that characterized it. In PDSs, simply clustering student teachers in a building might be a first-order change—less travel time for the supervisors—but presumably everything else about the content and processes of student teaching might remain the same.

Second-order changes restructure the organization by "fundamentally alter[ing] existing authority, roles, and uses of time and space" (Cuban, 1988, p. 342). Or, to connect the idea to other scholars on educational change, they bump into the "regularities of schooling" that Seymour Sarason (1982) talks about—in both sets of educational partners. They require, in Michael Fullan's language, restructuring and reculturing. See *Restructuring and Reculturing* on p. 161.

> "It was fine when we went to a system of clustering student teachers in the partner schools," a director of teacher education at a large state university told me. "But it got real interesting when the Collaborative Steering Committee changed the supervision model to give a much bigger role to the classroom teachers. At first it seemed no one liked it. Lots of the teachers didn't understand what their new roles were, and the university folks who used to do this on their own weren't crazy about adjusting. Loads changed, there was some opposition (mostly at the university) but we got over it. It took a few years to make it happen; now it is regular, and an important part of the changes that have taken place."

When second-order changes are taking place (or proposed), opposition can come out of the woodwork. People who may have ignored PDSs (or any of the philosophies and approaches associated with them) when they were on the fringes of the organization will give much closer scrutiny as they come into the mainstream. Any changes in "authority, roles, and uses of time and space," will, absent thoughtful discussion and change management, very likely trigger a backlash and response. See *Bumping Into the Regularities of Schooling* on p. 161.

On the other hand, PDSs can operate without getting to those second-order changes. At the other extreme, they can, for instance, operate with what looks like a great deal of organizational change with little or no change in approaches to student learning. Kimball, Swap, LaRosa, and Howick (1995), writing about the National Network for Educational Renewal partner schools, warn that:

> The means to effective partnership can easily become ends in themselves. For example, the energy for change in schools may become focused only on improving working conditions for teachers, establishing more collaborative decision making structures, or creating more flexible schedules, all of which can be means to the end of the learning but should not be ends in themselves. Administrative practice can change without passing the advantage to the classroom. (p. 24)

The same point can easily be made about teacher preparation or professional development. There are strong forces in schools and universities in defense of the status quo; a great deal of activity can be implemented without actually having any impact.

The conflicts created by second-order change and the friction between the old and the new put pressure on PDSs to have the following:

- Good assessment practices that are seen as credible by all stakeholders
- Strong professional development for all participants for new and changed roles
- Excellent communication—honest talk where issues can be aired
- Efficient sharing mechanisms so there is opportunity to share ideas and approaches
- Savvy leadership that understands the change process and is not afraid of conflict
- Clear core values and commitment to equity since tough choices will need to be made

If your PDS addresses these areas well, you have a good chance of reaching your potential in sustaining the improvements in teaching, learning, and leadership that emerge in your learning community.

You and your PDS partners and colleagues will face some tough choices, since conflict between the old and the new is inevitable. Oversimplifying somewhat, your choices when faced with opposition are quitting, working through the messy discord to reach your goals, or doing something in between—some level of compromising or settling.

An option that exists in partnerships, like in marriage, is divorce or separation. Ron Ferguson, in his stages of partnership development (see *Ferguson's Five Steps to of Partnership Formation* on p. 42 in Chapter 2) points out that, in the second stage, if partners cannot resolve the underlying trust issues or conflicts over control and direction of the partnership, they may choose to leave. Sometimes these departures are not clean or easy, due to other political factors. There may be a cost in publicly leaving a PDS that has been announced to the press and the community by the superintendent and university president, for instance. This can lead to dwindled-down separations that remain partnerships in name only. See *Breaking Up Is Hard to Do* on p. 48 in Chapter 2. On a more positive note, some partnerships that choose to break up can be much more successful the second time around. See *Second "Marriages"—Learning From Partnering Mistakes* on p. 162.

The hardest choice, the one I am clearly in favor of, is the difficult, messy path of simultaneous renewal. This puts the partner organizations in creative tension with one another and creates internal discords within each partner between old and new approaches. This requires a close look at what brought each partner in, what your core values are, and how much you are willing to put on the table with one another. I am not suggesting that you rigidly adhere to every plan you started with or that any deviation is a sign of compromise to be avoided. Plans change and goals evolve as partnerships develop. What I am suggesting is that you look closely at goals that are being abandoned that you still care about or at topics for discussion that keep getting deferred. If you and others in your PDS are backing away from what you care about because it is too hard, or too messy, I encourage you to hang on and keep your eyes on that prize. This book is focused on supporting you in figuring out how to do this.

There is a vast middle ground between quitting the relationship and always staying true to what brought you into the partnership in the first place. It is in that middle ground that I think most PDSs operate. I quote here at length from the first long-term study I did on PDS implementation and institutionalization. That study (Teitel, 1997a) raised questions and concerns that worry me even today and shape the way I look at sustainability of PDSs.

As someone who believes in the value of PDSs, I am pleased by these findings. I am impressed with the gains that have been made at these institutions, and filled with admiration for the dedicated faculty and administrators at the schools and colleges and universities for their perseverance, often in the face of opposition, and limited resources, to make these PDSs work. I have no doubt that their work is improving the lives of preservice teachers, students, and experienced educators.

At the same time, I am left with a nagging thought about exactly what is getting institutionalized in these partnerships. When I frame the successes of these partnerships with the view that professional development schools should serve as mechanisms for simultaneous and mutual renewal of schools and teacher education programs, these achievements start to look less substantial. What seems to have gotten institutionalized here are better methods of conducting the field experience portion of preservice education, by using approaches that not only benefit the preservice teachers, but have many excellent spinoffs for the experienced teachers at the school and college. These positive interactions between the worlds of school and college are starting to get institutionalized in these PDSs, and are leading to some benefits and some modest changes in both places, but I worry that the core enterprise at each place is not being touched. What is worse, I worry that that core may never be touched, that the relationships have reached (or will soon reach) a plateau, and will stay there, because the participants are basically satisfied with the very real successes they have attained. Deeply ingrained issues like the way students of color are treated at the school, or fundamental considerations of how teachers are prepared at the college are much harder to tackle. (p. 331)

This concern about the plateau—the notion that this is as good as it gets (and that that is sufficient)—is supported by Ismat Abdal-Haqq (1999), who makes a similar point about equity:

The prevailing PDS model, the view of equity enshrined in the model, and the widespread acceptance of the sufficiency of surface approaches to addressing equity have acquired a formidable momentum that may obscure, trample, or render stillborn alternate, and possibly more productive, attempts to craft working alliances between schools and universities. (p. 154)

Writing about education change in other contexts, Tyack and Cuban (1995) suggest that most innovations that get successfully institutionalized do so by being adapted (some may say "perverted") to match institutional needs. Is that what is going on here?

The plateau concept does not make me despondent, or leave me without hope, but it does makes me wary. It emphasizes for me the importance not just of working toward sustainability, but of constantly checking to see if what we are sustaining is what we want. See *How Inevitable Is the Plateau Effect?* on p. 163.

Focusing on Student Learning

Of all the Standards, probably Learning Community is the one with the most obvious connections to student learning. Students are, after all, the key element in that community, participants in shaping it, and also direct beneficiaries of improved approaches to teaching and learning used by teachers and prospective teachers. A recent presentation I saw by a PDS underscored for me the way successful learning community approaches could have impacts on students, as well as powerful ripples out to other members of the learning community. Working in a rural school where significant numbers of children were lagging in their reading abilities, the PDS steering committee decided to try a particular reading fluency approach. Preservice teachers were trained in the method and then matched with individual struggling readers to observe and help them in this reading process. The direct method, and the one-to-one attention provided by the teacher education students, had phenomenal results for the children, raising their enthusiasm for reading as well as their test scores. But the learning was just as powerful for the preservice teachers. By working (and succeeding) with students struggling with their reading, they learned more about teaching reading than they would have by observing someone teaching a whole-class lesson or by working with a group of more successful readers. It was clear from the interns that the ripples of this experience will shape their teaching and have positive impacts on a great many more students.

ASSESSMENT

Form 4.1   Quick-Check Self-Assessment Framework

For each statement below, assess the response that best describes your partnership, using a scale ranging from Strongly Disagree (SD), to Disagree (D), to Agree (A) to Strongly Agree (SA). Use NA for items that are not applicable in your context. Use the space below each item to list a few explanations or indicators that give evidence to support your assessment and to explain any questions you felt were not applicable.

1. The culture encourages innovation and provides incentives.   *SD   D   A   SA   NA*
   Indicators:

2. Learning and ongoing professional development for all PDS participants draw on new collaborative structures in mutually beneficial and reciprocal ways.   *SD   D   A   SA   NA*
   Indicators:

3. Good use is made of partner roles in "integrated learning and development."   *SD   D   A   SA   NA*
   Indicators:

4. The PDS scans for missed opportunities and takes advantage of possible connections.   *SD   D   A   SA   NA*
   Indicators:

5. Strong and consistent attention is paid to equity issues for students, preservice, and experienced educators.   *SD   D   A   SA   NA*
   Indicators:

6. All participants demonstrate learning.   *SD   D   A   SA   NA*
   Indicators:

7. Joint processes are in place to assess new approaches to teaching and learning and leadership, and scale up goods ones.   *SD   D   A   SA   NA*
   Indicators:

8. Excellent communication is in place so   *SD   D   A   SA   NA*
   that partners talk honestly with
   one another.
   Indicators:

9. The PDS has efficient mechanisms   *SD   D   A   SA   NA*
   and opportunities to share ideas
   and approaches.
   Indicators:

10. PDS leadership understands the change   *SD   D   A   SA   NA*
    process and is not afraid of conflict.
    Indicators:

11. The PDS has a clear set of core values and   *SD   D   A   SA   NA*
    commitment to equity.
    Indicators:

Assessment Framework

At the heart of the partnership are the improvements in its learning community—the experiences of students and adults working together focusing on improving student learning. Consequently, at the heart of any PDS assessment is the documentation of these improvements and of their impacts on students and on preservice and experienced educators.

As the PDS Standards Student Learning Pyramid shows, student learning is enhanced in at least three ways in a PDS partnership:

• Through better preparation of interns and their enhanced roles inside and outside the classroom with school students

• Through professional development and other experiences that the faculty, staff, and administrators at the schools and the college have, engaging and focusing them on student learning

• Directly for the PreK–12 students through an improved learning environment—improvements in curriculum and instruction, enhanced relationships inside and out of class with interns, teachers, and other adults

These strands are often intertwined and may include or lead to other learning community outcomes that affect student learning, such as engagement with families and communities. For example, a family literacy program or a program to engage community members as guest speakers or coteachers in a PDS may have positive and important impacts on student learning and influence each of the three major strands above.

Data to be collected include syllabi and course sequencing (for PreK–12 students as well as preservice teachers), evidence of effective strategies for working with diverse students, professional development opportunities and plans for experienced educators, evidence of the beliefs underlying the practices, and documentation of what experienced teachers do with out-of-classroom time provided by interns.

Data ideally would incorporate multiple measures— for example, for one outcome, improved learning for preservice teachers, data might include perspectives of hiring principals, classroom observations of graduating teachers, and student test scores (Stallings, 1991), as well as questionnaires on preservice teacher preparedness drawing on views of preservice teachers, school-based mentors, and college faculty (Loving, Wiseman, Cooner, Sterbin, & Seidel, 1997), along with archival data on graduates—where they applied to work, where they were hired, and what follow-up assessments of their preparedness and teaching skill over time show. Other sources of evidence might include notes of meetings and seminars; structures and forums for creation and dissemination of knowledge (e.g., action research, study groups, critical friends groups) and samples of their work; plans for and records of actions taken to share work with colleagues within school and other schools; activities that include the families of children as learners; and data collected systematically on teaching and learning and made available to everybody (NCATE, 2001a).

LEARNING COMMUNITY ASSESSMENT TEMPLATE

To make the strongest linkages between learning community activities and desired outcomes, each of these three learning community strands should be documented in two ways. The first part should identify and document the kinds of *experiences* PDS participants in that category are having (with an emphasis on what aspects of those experiences are unusual or particular to the PDS). The second part should identify and document the *impacts* those experiences are having on the PDS participants.

There is a template for these on page 142 with one example partially filled in for illustrative purposes. Note, however, that although they are broken out in three groups, there are important links between and among them. This is followed by a more detailed example from the Urban Teacher Training Collaborative.

Better Preparation of Interns and Their Enhanced Roles Inside and Outside the Classroom With School Students

To get started, think of the innovative features of your PDS and how they are changing the experience of preservice teachers. How, for instance, does your partnership provide opportunities for interns to develop their skills and knowledge in working with diverse students? Are the interns treated as junior faculty members and included in most or all school faculty events? See *Enhancing the Preservice Teacher Experience Through PDSs* in the Toolkit section, page 151 for other prompts and examples.

Once you have identified ways to finish the template prompt "Interns are . . . " look for examples of supporting evidence, which might be schedules, course syllabi, and assignment rosters, and place these in the second column. Next think through the impacts you think are plausibly linked to the experiences the interns are having and place them, and their supporting evidence, in the impacts and evidence columns, respectively. For example, perhaps the interns in your PDS do a four-week rotation in a special education class, which you think has impacts on their abilities and dispositions about working with diverse learners. See partially filled in template on page 142 for an example of this.

This portion of the documentation sets up a plausible link between the activities that interns are experiencing and the impacts they are reporting.

The same template would be used for the other two target populations:

• Professional development and other experiences of the other faculty, staff, and administrators at the schools and the college engage and focus them on student learning

• High school students have an improved learning environment—better curriculum and instruction, enhanced relationships inside and out of class with interns, teachers, and other adults

Further, rather than see these as three disconnected process–product charts, look for linkages between and among the interns,

Interns Are:	Supporting Evidence	Impacts on Interns	Supporting Evidence
• Immersed in a four-week rotation in a special education class • Developing adaptations in curriculum and instruction for diverse learners • Working one to one and in small groups with special education students • Teaming with experienced teachers and other interns to develop and teach a content area unit • Reflecting on issues of exceptionality in their seminar	*Assignment rotation schedule* *Intern handbook that outlines expected tasks during this rotation* *Description or sample of the unit(s) developed* *Syllabi and/or teaching notes for the intern seminar*	• Better able to diagnose exceptional students • Increased teaching repertoire • More confidence in teaching diverse learners • Better dispositions regarding high quality learning for all students	*Exit interviews with interns* *Reflections, work products for on-site courses/ seminars* *Observations of mentor teachers and university supervisors during the rotation and after it* *Feedback from students*

the experienced educators, and the PreK–12 students. To follow this example, you would then document the impacts that working with interns in the rotation had on the experienced special education teachers, and further, the ripples out to the regular education teachers that the interns worked with subsequently. Demonstrating how approaches and dispositions picked up during the rotation have impacts on the school- and university-based faculty that the interns go on to work with adds a powerful dimension to the connectedness of a PDS. The documentation could continue, showing how these experiences for interns also have important impacts on PreK–12 students. Look at the impacts on the special education students of having the interns in for four weeks, as well as the impacts in the classes the interns go on to work with, as a result of their increased skill and understanding of exceptionality in learners.

DOCUMENTATION EXAMPLE

We continue here with an example from the assessment framework of the Urban Teacher Training Collaborative. See Chapter 2 for background on the partnership. The sample included here is different from those in Chapters 2 and 3, which were draft responses to the assessment prompts. This excerpt is a detailed elaboration of the Learning Community Assessment Template, based on input from the UTTC Assessment Group about what activities and impacts make sense to document for the collaborative. This is outlined for all three participant populations and like all the other draft excerpts, it is not necessary complete or final, but is included here to be illustrative. Note that sources listed by name in italics already exist, while those with a double asterisk still need to be developed. A refresher on abbreviations: the schools involved are the Fenway, Boston Arts Academy (BAA), and Mission Hill (MH). HBCU are historically black colleges and universities. MetLife refers to a grant which requires the Collaborative to follow its graduates into their first years of teaching.

Better Preparation of Interns and Their Enhanced Roles Inside and Outside the Classroom With Fenway/BAA/MH Students

Interns Are:	Supporting Evidence	Impacts: Interns Gain	Supporting Evidence
• Fully experiencing range of what teachers do e.g. • coteaching 2 core courses, co-advising Advisory group, performing duties of staff, meeting with parents, etc • Developing inter-disciplinary units; e.g. Facing History • Gaining a context for applying theory in real practice • Working with kids inside and outside of class	*Brochure and outline of intern activities* *ED101 syllabus* *Intern orientation* *Interdisciplinary unit products* *Intern assignment calendar*	• Realistic preparation • Content area knowledge and relationship to inter-disciplinary learning • Teaching skills • Critical thinking skills • Strong commitment to urban schools through the development of deep relationships with students and community	*Evaluation for Boston Public Schools PDS Program (2001, 2002)* *Curriculum product* *Closing survey by site coordinator* *Exit interviews with interns (2001, 2002)*

Interns Are:	Supporting Evidence	Impacts: Interns Gain	Supporting Evidence
• Tied to community (early stages of this) • Working in a diverse environment • Integrating curriculum with the arts (BAA/MH) • Getting high-quality and intense mentoring • Working in a cohort • Members of a professional community that is emotionally supportive and focused on improving teaching and learning	Other documents and evidence to support these**	• Strong sense of importance and possibilities of professional culture • Sense of teaching in relationship to families and communities	Reflections, work products for on-site courses/ seminars Course evaluations by interns Intern hiring and retention numbers** Follow-up data on first and second year teaching experience of interns (connect with MetLIfe)** Other sources** including follow-up with non-interns at Tufts for impacts on them of being in classes at PDS and with interns

Professional Development and Other Experiences of the Other Faculty, Staff, and Administrators at the Schools and the College, Engaging and Focusing Them on Student

Adults Are:	Supporting Evidence	Impacts	Supporting Evidence
BAA/Fenway/MH faculty and Administrators are: • Mentors/coaches • Coteaching with interns	Charts, schedules Numbers, rosters Examples, plans, & syllabi	• Translating coach model for interns to work with student portfolios	Administrator or supervisor observations** Brief comments or reflections by teachers on

Adults Are:	Supporting Evidence	Impacts	Supporting Evidence
• Coteaching with Tufts faculty • Reflecting on practice (having interns as mirrors) • Getting personal benefits— intrinsic (giving back, sharing expertise) and extrinsic (stipends, vouchers, flexible scheduling) • Engaged in other professional development related to being in partnership • Supporting personal and emotional issues in intern development	Anecdotal comments to site coordinator Intrinsic— reflections** Extrinsic—name them** "Good teaching" and "Teaching together" workshops	• Gaining enhanced professional growth and practice • Being professionally renewed, recharged, and more deeply fulfilled	practice, recorded by site coordinator** Professional conference presentations/ papers, other scholarly activity (list **) Changed classroom practices, as reported by?** Changed interactions with students (e.g., portfolios) **
Tufts faculty are: Immersed: • Engaged in day-to-day realities of school in a sustained and personal way • Coteaching with school-based faculty	"Team Approach" document describing roles and types of engagement Other education faculty involved who teach interns; and other roles they play (judges, etc.), rosters and schedules	• Thinking of how to improve schools and Tufts program • Pushed in thinking about theory/ practice by interns • Reexamining own values, refocusing on realistic urban challenges	Changes in teacher education curriculum (ED 101 syllabus, outline, questions, portfolio, ED 102) Changes in policy (minutes of teacher education meetings)

Adults Are:	Supporting Evidence	Impacts	Supporting Evidence
Non-immersed: • Teaching mixed classes of interns and traditional student teachers Both groups: • Working with an increasingly diverse intern pool with clear focus on urban issues	Arts and Science faculty rosters and schedules **		Increased involvement of Tufts education faculty in school (trend analysis and reflections **) Increased engagement of arts and science faculty (numbers, roles, policy implications, reflections **) Impacts on non-PDS Tufts students **

Secondary School Students Have an Improved Learning Environment—Better Curriculum and Instruction, Enhanced Relationships Inside and Outside of Class With Interns, Teachers, and Other Adults

Secondary School Students Have:	Supporting Evidence	Impacts: Secondary Students:	Supporting Evidence
• More adults in the classroom • Collaborative approach of teaching team leads to better problem solving • More availability of outside help • Increased number and variety of electives	Intern hours served (for this and several others in this column, the information is available; it needs to be tabulated)	• Develop a greater sense of self-worth (coming from more attention from adults) • Are more empowered	Administrator observations and comments** Intern-student connections • Reflective writing by students (e.g., after participation in intern-led activity, like play**)

Secondary School Students Have:	Supporting Evidence	Impacts: Secondary Students:	Supporting Evidence
• Relationships with adults closer in age to them • Knowledge, skills and experiences of the interns affects teaching techniques in use, curriculum (e.g., hip hop, poetry), college advising (e.g., HBCUs) • "Fresh air" of outside adults' experiences • Increased accountability with outsider involvement and assessment • Benefits of BAA/Fenway teacher impacts • Benefits of Tufts faculty impacts [If there are specific impacts at each of the three schools that might be different, they would be added here.]	Electives, extracurricular offerings Afterschool help Tuft faculty and intern roles in exhibitions, through rosters, schedules See impacts of involvement in UTTC on faculty and administrators and track how that affects students (this includes direct impact of Tufts faculty on secondary students)** See impacts of involvement in UTTC on interns and track how that affects students **	• Have greater academic skills • Get bigger boosts in basic skills from more individualized attention • Are less alienated and more connected • Have greater identification with adult intellectual role models • Are more accountable	• Reflections by interns (some already exist; need to be more systematic**) Attitudes, frequency of coming for extra help, etc. (compare classes with and without interns?**) Performance assessments or test scores** Student reflections, surveys on alienation, connection, tracked over time** Interview questions for interns, about contributions**

Learning

In addition to what is suggested in the tables above, data to be collected might include syllabi and course sequencing (for secondary school students as well as preservice teachers), evidence of effective strategies for working with diverse students, professional development opportunities and plans for experienced educators, evidence of the beliefs underlying the practices, and documentation of what experienced teachers do with out-of-classroom time provided by interns.

Toolkit

4.1 Enhancing Impacts on Students in PDSs

One of the most important questions you will answer for yourself and others concerns the impacts of your PDS on students. Use the following (adapted from Kimball et al., 1995, and supplemented with examples from my own consulting and research) as a springboard for looking at how each of the following contributes to the improved learning experiences students in your PDS are having:

- *Preservice teachers:* These include the individual learning experiences students have with interns, for example, the effects of units or special community-service learning projects set up by the interns, tutoring or small group work, mentoring, or other aspects of role modeling or relationship building.

- *Classroom teaching teams:* When interns and classroom teachers collaboratively teach, the mix of perspectives and approaches can improve the teaching of both and create an enhanced learning environment for students. The involvement of university faculty can deepen this.

- *Additional partners:* Working in close partnerships with community agencies provides other perspectives and adult role models for students, as well as opportunities and access to a much wider range of facilities and organizations. Broader collaborations with arts and science faculty in the university can also affect students through direct contact, as well as improvements in curriculum and instruction.

- *Meaningful assessment and inquiry:* Many PDS efforts improve assessment of student work and lead to increased opportunities for students. Teacher inquiry groups that conduct action research can help identify student learning issues and help share best practices.

- *Equity focus:* PDSs that take their equity agenda seriously often work student by student, using a case management style to identify what each one needs to increase learning.

The assessment portion of this chapter makes some suggestions about how to document this, but for now, just list the experiences your students are having in the PDS that are helping their learning. Use the list for discussion purposes and as a way to think about documentation, as well as for public relations (it will be helpful for you to have a clear answer to the question about the benefits the PDS provides for students).

4.2 Avoiding Fragmentation Frazzle

Take a look at the list of initiatives your school or university is engaged in. According to Hess (1999), the typical urban school district pursues more than 11 "significant initiatives" in curriculum, scheduling, assessment, or professional development. Since many of these contradict or are incompatible with one another, you need to see if your innovations are overloading or pulling you and your colleagues apart. Think about how your focused work in the PDS helps provide coherence and possibly a structural umbrella for organizational changes going on in your partnership.

Take a few minutes to list the significant innovations going on in your school or university department, as well as those in your larger environment (district or university) that affect you. Use the following grid to get discussion and action on reducing fragmentation frazzle.

Initiative	Who or what is the impetus behind it?	How compatible is it with the direction of PDS?	What can you do to increase alignment and reduce fragmentation?

4.3 Information Coordination Mechanisms

I have seen PDSs miss opportunities for coherence and collaboration because different parts of the partnership quite literally did not know what others were doing in it. In a partnership between a large university and a high school, for example, there was an ongoing relationship between the math departments of the high school and the university for an entire year before the staff at both institutions involved in the PDS even knew about it and could capitalize on it to align it with other PDS efforts.

What is the status of the coordination of PDS-related efforts in your partnership? Does some body (person or steering committee) keep track of everything? Some PDSs like to put a process in place to, in effect, "register" connections between the university and the school; others prefer to grow organically and let many flowers bloom with the lowest possible regulation or paperwork. What do you do and how well is it meeting your needs?

4.4 Finding (or Developing) Philosophical Coherence

The Toolkit section of Chapter 3 included some ideas of *Dealing With Differences in Philosophy and Belief Structure* (p. 96) between or among partners. It is also important to figure out how much coherence exists and how much is wanted within the subunits of any one partner. Does it matter to you if one unit of the university takes a constructivist approach to the teaching of math, while another takes a more traditional approach? What might be accepted—or even welcomed—as an example of intellectual diversity at the university can become very confusing for partners in the PDS to understand or make sense of. The following are some ideas about addressing philosophical (in)coherence:

• *Think about the end users and the impact on them.* If interns are taught in their math methods classes to teach one way and then are evaluated by their arts and sciences math supervisor on another, it can be messy for the interns, the students, and the cooperating faculty at the school.

• *Detect it.* Do some scanning in your partnership for inconsistencies in approaches by asking students, interns, faculty, parents, community partners, and administrators.

• *Resolve the contradictions, or acknowledge them and live with them.* Your PDS may decide the price of the tradeoffs for resolution and coherence in some cases may be too high, but having a forum for the discussion and a process to make those decisions is important.

Is philosophical coherence (or the lack thereof) an issue for your partnership? If so, try using the three-step process to work your way through the issue.

4.5 *Change Is Always for Someone Else*

In the history of school–university partnerships (as with other relationships), it seems that partners are all for change, but it is usually their partners that they see changing, not themselves. Does this apply to your partnership and, if so, how? To move the discussion forward on this, take some time at your steering committee, or at a PDS retreat, to "name the change."

- Put up chart paper that lists each of the organizational partners including any relevant subunits (such as teacher education and arts and sciences, or perhaps a different department at a high school).

- Give the participants yellow sticky notes and have them jot down some key ways in which each of the partners is changing or has changed in the course of the PDS partnership.

- After individuals have placed their stickies (in a large group, it helps to have teams or participants organize and summarize the stickies on a particular chart), use the ensuing discussion to look at who is changing and how and who is not.

(A bonus of this activity at a retreat is that it offers a chance to reflect on the gains and impacts of the PDS on the partners.)

4.6 *Enhancing the Preservice Teacher Experience Through PDSs*

Use the following list—developed by a PDS consortium I worked with a few years ago—as a springboard for looking at the ways in which your PDS helps improve preservice teachers. The list is organized into changes in the school- or field-based components of teacher preparation and changes in the campus-based portions (usually courses). Although it is important that coursework and fieldwork are intertwined, the distinction (suggested by Zeichner & Miller, 1997) is a useful one when looking for changes and improvements in teacher education programs. Taken collectively, the consortium partnerships developed significant innovative practices in the preparation of teachers in the following areas.

Impacts on field-based components:

1. Preservice teachers spend more time in the school.

2. Preservice teachers learn and connect with the entire school in a planned and purposive way.

3. Teachers and peers collaborate with preservice teachers and each other.

4. University supervisors are more accessible at the school and support for mentoring student teachers is available to school staff.

5. Respect for teacher knowledge is evident in involvement in decision making by school staff.

6. Innovative approaches are used to assess and understand the development of teaching.

7. A cohort of preservice teachers develops a strong sense of support and a professional community.

Changes in courses and other traditionally campus-based teacher preparation activities:

8. Coursework is physically placed in the school.

9. There is increased use of real observation and involvement in the classrooms.

10. School-based faculty and administrators take increased roles as teachers, coteachers, and guest speakers of campus-based courses.

11. School-based faculty and administrators are giving feedback on and shaping college courses and overall preparation programs.

12. Attitudes and approaches of campus-based faculty members change through involvement in the PDS: Sum up these differences.

Which of these changes are taking place in your PDS and what else is going on that is not on the list? Which would you want to add?

4.7 *Getting Your Programmatic Ducks in a Row*

Do you find that, putting it bluntly, the left hand doesn't always know what the right hand is doing? I have seen some PDSs that were so well planned that everything worked in synchronicity from the outset, but this is rare. In one partnership's planning year, staff systematically thought through every point of contact a preservice teacher would have at the school and university. The PDS founders included staff from offices often neglected in PDS planning and brought them onto the planning team—admissions, financial aid, the registrar, and university supervisors, as well as the usual PDS teacher educators and school-based personnel. Working together, they ironed out dozens of details before any students were admitted to the program.

But this level of planning is the exception, not the rule. Who is attending to these alignment issues in your PDS? One simple but powerful way to see if the needed components of a teacher education program are aligned is to ask the end users—the interns. Through surveys during and after their program, PDSs can learn about what has worked and what has not. How are you learning about these issues? Are you listening and taking action? Several PDSs I have worked with use follow-up questionnaires or, even better, pull graduates a year or two into their teaching together to debrief their preparation experience. What are you doing (or planning) for this gathering of information?

4.8 Redesigning the Components of Teacher Education

Is there an imbalance in what is being changed or redesigned in your program? You can use the distinction between field-based and campus-based aspects of teacher preparation made by Zeichner and Miller (1997) (and referred to above in *Enhancing the Preservice Teacher Experience Through PDSs* on p. 151) to look at the balance.

Do you find, as many of the early PDSs did, that most of the change in teacher education was in the field-based portions, with the university-based changes much slower to come? Use the list in that toolkit, or a comparable one that you develop, as a way to do a quick check for balance on this issue and bring it to the steering committee for discussion and action.

4.9 Total Immersion: Advantages and Disadvantages

If your PDS is organized around the total immersion model, or you are thinking about it, take some time to list some of the advantages and disadvantages. Most immersion programs place interns full-time in the school for the entire school year. In some cases, all classes are delivered at the site, so students never return to the university and never interact with other preservice teachers. Here are a few advantages; you may wish to add more.

- Intern learning is in context, all the time.
- Interns do not miss any of the important phases of the school year (as opposed to many teacher education programs that have student teaching start a few weeks after the start of school, so preservice teachers miss the way an experienced teacher sets up a classroom and develops behavioral norms).
- A strong cohort of interns is developed, all in each other's classes and tightly tied to the life of the school.

A partial list of disadvantages includes the following:

- Disconnection and lack of affiliation with the university
- A loss of intellectual diversity, with little contact with other students or teachers from the university
- Lower impacts of the PDS on the rest of the university, since it is out sight and thus out of mind

Use this partially completed framework of pros and cons to get discussion started in your PDS about how much immersion is good and how much is too much.

4.10 Making the Community Part of Teacher Education

All too frequently, educators do not know much about their students' home life and their communities. This is particularly true in urban or rural schools, where preservice teachers may have grown up in different environments themselves. How much do the experienced educators at your schools and university know about the background and environment of their students? If your PDS includes parents and community members, how much is their voice heard among the professional educators in the PDS? What strategies do you have in place to provide opportunities for preservice teachers to understand and engage with the schools' community? Here are a few ideas:

• In one urban PDS, preservice teachers take a day-long tour of the community, hosted by high school students from the PDS.

• In another PDS, all preservice teachers begin their teacher preparation by doing a semester of teaching or tutoring in a non-school setting in the community—such as in a Saturday academy run by the NAACP or in classes for English-language acquisition at a community center.

• In one setting, arguing that teacher educators couldn't teach what they didn't know, the teacher education department of the PDS held a faculty meeting in the offices of its community partner, in a part of the city that many of the faculty did not regularly go to. The visit included a neighborhood tour that changed the perceptions of many of the white, mostly suburban faculty and led to numerous connections between those faculty and community members.

• In another PDS, school and university faculty met with the school's parent coordinator to brainstorm a list of what preservice teachers could do to expand their knowledge and contact with parents. That list, which included having interns meet with parents, assist in parent centers, conduct home visits, tour the community, engage in a family–community oral history project, conduct a community-service learning outreach project, and develop lists of community members as resources in their classrooms, has become part of the planning and discussion process of the PDS heading toward implementation.

Think creatively about the ways your partnership can do a better job of grounding your preservice teachers in the communities of their students. What ideas do you have?

4.11 Experienced Teacher Development in PDSs

PDSs provide a culture of support for many avenues of teacher growth and professional development, in addition to the learning that comes about through new roles. Use the following list to consider the kinds of development that is (or could be) going on in your PDS.

• Look at changes in your school culture for experienced educators, such as teacher study groups, curriculum writing groups, teacher research projects, peer observation, case conferences, program evaluation and documentation, trying out new practices (with collegial support), teacher resource centers, and participation in outside events and organizations (adapted from Lieberman & Miller, 1992). Look especially for factors that contribute to teacher development: colleagueship, space and time for teacher inquiry, focus on learning content in context, and opportunities for leadership and for networking activity that go beyond the bounds of the school.

• Look at changes in professional roles as teachers take more responsibility for their own professional development, through involvement in book clubs, presentations and attendance at regional and national conferences, visits to other schools, or provision of workshops to student teachers or other teachers.

• Look at changes as teachers take on deeper roles in supporting student learning, becoming curriculum developers and curriculum interpreters. Tailoring instruction to meet the needs of students, factoring in curriculum ideas brought by interns, and looking critically together at curricular innovation can be transformative professional development experiences.

As you use these ideas to consider teacher development in your PDS, do not forget about the development of university-based educators that can be triggered by the following:

• Roles as coteachers in classrooms with PreK–12 students
• Members and facilitators of inquiry teams
• Translators of theory into practice
• Researchers in context
• Leadership roles in the PDS

4.12 New Teachers' Benefits in a PDS

Take a look at the orientation and support you provide for new teachers in your school and compare that to what is needed for incoming interns. The grid on page 156 is a start of some of the knowledge and skills new teachers or new interns need to be effective in your school. Finish the left-hand column with specific items that apply in your setting. If you have a significant number of new faculty at the university, add another column on the grid for them. Use the grid to get started, looking for potential alignments that will save time and energy and produce benefits for each group.

Knowledge or Skills Needed for Those Teaching in Your School	How It Is Currently Done for New Teachers	How It Is Currently Done for Interns	Ideas for Potential Alignment
Physical orientation to the school			
Instruction on copy machines, etc.			
Interaction with nurse, special education, technology, and other offices or departments			
Classroom management			
School and district instructional approaches			
Observation and feedback procedures by mentors/supervisors			
School discipline code/policies			
Effective engagement with parents			
Others			

4.13 University Faculty Development

Are university faculty in your partnership being pushed outside of their ordinary practice and comfort zone? If so, how are they being supported, encouraged, and rewarded by the PDS and their university? (And if not, why aren't they being pushed?) Since the discomforts of change in their teaching practice can lead faculty members to withdraw—either disengage or even resist involvement in the PDS—what can your PDS do to encourage them? Here are a few ideas to consider:

- Make the changes (and challenges) in university teaching discussable in faculty and departmental meetings
- Organize faculty inquiry groups into the challenges of teaching either in the PDS or to groups that include PDS interns
- Arrange for peer observations and discussions
- Collect data on the impacts of having interns in classes on other teacher education students

4.14 Boundary-Spanner Challenges and Growth

Those individuals whose work crosses over and connects the different partnering organizations can face special stresses. They can become marginalized within their own organization if they are seen as going too far in their involvement in the PDS. PreK–12 teachers who get very involved in working with preservice teachers or in teaching university courses may be looked at askance by their colleagues. So might university faculty who spend most of their time at the PDS—they may be left out of important decision making and other aspects of the culture of the university.

Specific Challenges Faced by:	Support Needed by This Individual or Role	Support Offered to This Individual or Role
[Name of individual, or role]		
[Name of individual, or role]		
[Name of individual, or role]		

What is happening in your PDS for your boundary crossers and what can you do to support them? Use the grid below to get started assessing what you are doing (and what you could be doing) to support these critical individuals.

4.15 *Taking Control of Your Professional Development*

There is a tremendous amount of professional development that takes place as a normal part of the operation of a PDS. In addition, most schools and school districts (and some universities) often have professional development activities such as inservice workshops or ongoing study groups. In some PDSs, these are aligned so that, for instance, teacher inquiry groups fostered by the PDS count as part of the teachers' evaluation cycle (instead of being observed by an administrator every year, experienced teachers conduct research and report on it every other year). Another alignment would be the way some districts draw on the PDS work at their inservice workshops. Instead of hiring an outsider to provide a one-shot workshop, some districts use the day to have teachers, interns, university faculty, and community partners report out on best practices or share results of action research.

These two examples start the tables below. Take this opportunity to see how aligned your school, district, or university's formal professional development agenda is with the informal ongoing PD that takes place in the PDS.

Use the two grids below as a starting point for checking this alignment.

PD Activities Embedded in the PDS	*Existing Connections to School, District, or University PD Structure*	*Potential Connections to District, School, or University PD Structure*
Teacher inquiry groups	Part of alternative year evaluation cycle	
Sharing best practices		
Producing teaching portfolios (by interns and experienced school and university teachers)		
Conducting and reporting action research findings		
Other		

Formal PD Activities Sponsored by School, District, or University	Existing Connection to PDS	Potential Connections to PDS
Staff inservice time	PDS reports of best practices or action research	
Staff evaluation	Use alternate cycles of to conduct inquiry groups	
Mentoring and peer coaching		
Orientation for new teachers		
Other		

4.16 Who Benefits From PDS Professional Development and Who Doesn't?

Make a list of the teachers in your PDS and next to each name indicate the degree to which that person is engaged in and benefiting from the PD activities of the PDS. If your PDS is like many others, there will be some who are heavily benefiting, some occasionally, and maybe even some that are not benefiting at all. Look at the list you have generated and then work with your steering committee to extend the benefits to all. As you do this, ask yourself why some are less engaged than others. (It also helps to ask the others who are not as engaged what keeps them out and what would help draw them in.) In mapping a strategy to spread the engagement and the benefits, ask yourself tough questions: Do you have an insider's group that others feel left out of? Are there people you have written off ("Oh, she'll never change")? Are your planned PD activities based on a thorough needs assessment of the entire faculty or based on the feelings of a few insiders?

4.17 Is Everyone Learning in the PDS?

Central to any PDS is the professional development of educators which, at least in theory, is for all educators—teachers as well as administrators and other education personnel, at the university as well as at the school. Yet often, professional development focuses on PreK–12 teachers, with less attention paid to the professional development of university faculty and even less to that of administrators at either institution or other partnering organizations. Does this imbalance exist in your partnership, suggesting the possibility that there may be differing perceptions of the need for and importance of continuing professional development for all participants in your PDS?

If this is the case, how do you address it? (See also *Including All PDS Partners in Professional Development* below and the preceding section on *Who Benefits From PDS Professional Development and Who Doesn't?*

4.18 *Including All PDS Partners in Professional Development*

This expands the notions from *Who Benefits From Professional Development and Who Doesn't?* to include all the adults who are part of your PDS partnership—teachers, administrators, and other staff at the school and university, community partners, union leaders, parents, and central office personnel. List the categories of potential beneficiaries of professional development, indicating who is benefiting, who could be, and what steps would need to be taken to maximize impacts. Explore the same questions about why some are less engaged and benefiting less than others from the PDS's professional development opportunities. Again, as you develop strategies to change this, ask the tough questions: is professional development for

Possible Professional Development Beneficiaries	Who Is Benefiting?	Who Could Be?	What Steps Need to Be Taken to Expand Impacts?
New teachers			
Experienced teachers			
Teacher education faculty			
Arts and science faculty			
Parents			
Community members			
Administrators			
Others			

all? (See *Is Everyone Learning in the PDS?* on p. 159.) Are some partners left out? Do some feel left out because their voices are not heard?

4.19 Restructuring and Reculturing

You may find the distinction Michael Fullan (2000) uses between these terms useful. In "Three Stories of Educational Reform," he notes that in high-performing schools, teachers and administrators form a professional learning community, focus on student work (through assessment), and change their instructional practices to get better results. "Restructuring" involves changes in structure and roles, along with related formal elements of the organization, such as setting up a school site council or mandating high test scores. This is relatively easy, can be mandated, and by itself does not necessarily have an impact on teaching and learning, although it may be helpful. "Reculturing," which Fullan defines as the process of developing professional learning communities, is, on the other hand, much harder. It includes increased attention to assessment and pedagogy and the development of norms that support improving teaching.

Take a look at the innovations that have come about as a result of your PDS. Which would you characterize as the restructuring that is necessary but not sufficient and which as the reculturing that brings the changes into the classroom?

4.20 Bumping Into the Regularities of Schooling

As you have moved forward on some of the new approaches to teaching, learning, and leadership, you probably have run into some forms of opposition. Whether it is self-imposed limits (as in, "That's a good idea, but we wouldn't be allowed to do it") or more overt forms of resistance, it can create some real tensions in your PDS. Take this opportunity to name the limits—publicly identifying the "regularities of schooling" that you are (or might be) bumping into.

Use the following grid to track the changes you are putting into place and the opposition any of the partnering organizations might provide. This list may end up being enormous—since there are probably dozens or even hundreds of things you are doing in your PDS that are different enough from existing practice to make some disturbances. Focus here on a few, but use the idea embedded in this exercise to periodically examine how your ideas are helping to change your partnering institutions.

PDS Approach to Teaching, Learning, or Leadership	Possible Obstacle in the Regularities of Current Practice	Strategies to Address the Problem
Year-long internships	Existing policies for student teaching	
University faculty spend much of their time in schools	Other requirements of their job descriptions, promotion and tenure policies	
Use of portfolio assessment of interns or of PreK–12 students	Existing evaluation procedures for each group	
Interns who are coteaching and then taking over classes	Union contract or other work rules	
Other		
Other		

4.21 Second "Marriages"—Learning From Partnering Mistakes

If yours is a partnership that has ended in a break-up, what have you learned from the experience? Some partners walk away from the entire concept with bitterness and distaste, never to partner again. Others try again. Many of those that do find that, by analyzing the breakdown, they can be much clearer and more focused in what they look for in a second partner and how they set things up from the beginning. They report (Teitel, 1998c) that they enter the new relationship able to clearly articulate what they hope to get from and hope to offer to the partnership. They are clearer about their expectations and less willing to settle for something less than they want.

If your PDS is not working as well as you would hope, what are you learning about partnership formation and expectations that will help you next time?

4.22 How Inevitable Is the Plateau Effect?

If you are experiencing a plateau effect, how inevitable is it? In some quiet way, is it possible that enough institutional needs have been met that you and your partner are satisfied enough not to push on to the harder challenges you might have laid out at the outset?

Use this opportunity to dig into the core motivations of each partner. Are the primary goals for the university to get better student teaching placements and offer higher-quality field experiences for preservice teachers? Are the primary goals for the school and district to improve the quality of their student teacher pool and provide professional development opportunities for their experienced educators? If so, is your PDS becoming institutionalized as a cluster site for student teachers, with strong involvement and interaction of classroom teachers with preservice teachers and college faculty? Although this is an improvement over traditional student teaching, is that as good as it gets? What about student learning gains or equity issues?

When do you periodically reexamine your goals and discuss with your partners where you are going and whether you have become stuck along the way? Does your PDS have processes that allow for, and even require, honest reflection and dialogue? Make a list of the opportunities you have to have these discussions, when you ask people to step back from the day-to-day concerns of the partnership, sometimes with outside facilitating or sometimes through the use of a network or of critical friends.

CHAPTER RESOURCES

This section includes a brief annotated bibliography of text and Web resources. The full citations for the text references are in the back of the book.

There are many additional sources that describe various aspects of the PDS learning community; they are the most common kinds of journal articles about PDSs. For an overall grounding and multiple examples of what PDSs are doing for students and for preservice and experienced educators, see my own literature review (Teitel, 1998b).

For a broad overview concerning student learning, see Kimball et al. (1995) and supplement with more recent articles on reading improvement (Frey, 2002), impacts of counseling (Silva & Gimbert, 2001), character education (Esters & Douet, 2001), and so forth.

To get the same broad grounding on preservice teacher experiences in the PDS, see Zeichner and Miller (1997) and supplement with Grisham, Berg, and Jacobs (2002) on impacts on new teacher beliefs, Rock and Levin (2002) on impacts of action research as a part of new teacher preparation, or Voltz (2001) on preparing new teachers to work with special education students.

To follow-up on experienced educators, see Darling-Hammond, Cobb, and Bullmaster (1995), or Teitel (1996c) for a broad base and supplement with Molseed (2000) on the by-products of teacher growth in a PDS or Silva and Dana (2001) on supervision as professional development.

For synergistic connections among the different members of the learning community, see Thompson, Bakken, and Clark (2001) or Middleton (2000).

Several case studies of PDSs, with considerable detail on the learning community aspects of each, are available in Levine and Trachtman's *Making Professional Development Schools Work*—see King (1997), Lancy (1997), and Snyder with Goldman (1997).

For more on the notions of restructuring and reculturing, and what those inside and outside of schools can do, see Fullan (2000) or www.pdkintl.org/kappan/kful0004.htm.

For updates on text and Web sources related to this Standard, see http://pds.edreform.net/home/ and click on Learning Community.

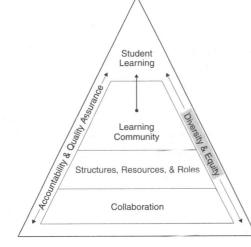

5

Diversity and Equity

Preparing a Diverse Group of Educators to Teach All Students

Picture the following scenes from PDSs around the country addressing diversity and equity:

- Where the approach to student learning seems (to use a sports metaphor) like a "full-court press"—where each student is listed in the principal's notebook along with his or her test data and where each has an individualized learning plan that draws on all the resources of the PDS—teachers, aides, parents, interns, college faculty, and other students (peers)

- Where, through diligent recruiting, use of stipends, tuition remission, and focusing their teacher education program in urban schools with large populations of color, the cohort of students enrolling in the (predominantly white) university to become interns in the PDS is increasingly diverse—more than half students of color last year, with more and more applicants of color each year

- Where teachers and administrators from school and university, along with parents on the school improvement team, pore over student test data, looking carefully at the reading acquisition of African American and Latino children, studying different approaches being tried in the PDS, and assessing the outcomes

- Where prospective teachers intern in an afterschool or Saturday school program of a community-based organization before ever setting foot in the school-based partnership that is part of the PDS

- Where multiple initiatives for the recruitment of teachers of color are in place, ranging from future educator clubs, to charter high schools for the preparation of teachers, to mentoring of undergraduate preservice teachers of color—providing a depth and range of experience that is transforming the university

- Where peer groups of students of color meet with interns to study together, discuss school problems, and develop more school-success-oriented rituals and behaviors

- Where faculty from school and university are in study groups that look at the achievement gap and try different approaches to curriculum and instruction in their classes and discuss results

Each of these scenarios represents examples of partnerships moving toward increased diversity and equity. Yet in a way, each of these is also about student learning and the preparation of a diverse workforce which has the vision, skills, and courage to make schools work well for all students. In this sense, the Standard for diversity and equity is closely intermeshed with all aspects of the PDS that focus on student learning. Despite what should be a tight link to the overall purposes of the PDS, of the five PDS Standards, Diversity and Equity is probably the least understood and most unevenly implemented. The language of the PDS Standards reads:

> PDS partners and [teacher] candidates develop and demonstrate knowledge, skills, and dispositions resulting in learning for all PreK–12 students. PDS partners ensure that the policies and practices of the PDS partner institutions result in equitable learning outcomes for all PDS participants. PDS partners include diverse participants and diverse learning communities for PDS work. (NCATE, 2001b, p. 16)

The subheadings (elements) of the Standards call for ensuring equitable opportunities to learn, evaluating policies and practices to ensure equitable learning outcomes, and recruiting and supporting diverse learners.

OVERVIEW AND HISTORY

The Holmes Group, whose reports (especially *Tomorrow's Schools*, 1990) provide powerful intellectual impetus for PDSs, makes very clear the commitment of the PDS as an institution to remedy societal inequities as they get played out in education. Nonetheless, there are often differing views among PDS participants of what equity means. I have worked with or documented PDSs where, put simply, there has been no real diversity or equity agenda. On the other hand, I have seen PDSs that have systematically reduced the achievement gap among students by careful, focused, coordinated, and collaborative action. My reviews of the literature in 1996 and 1998, as well as those of Ismat Abdal-Haqq (1998) and Linda Valli and her colleagues (1997), found little evidence of progress toward those equity goals or even of a great deal of understanding and process (that might lead to progress eventually). Abdal-Haqq and Valli and her colleagues, along with Peter Murrell's *Like Stone Soup* (1998), have provided thoughtful and influential critiques of the PDS movement. Their works raise concerns that need to be considered here. Some key elements of their critiques are next, followed by some suggestions for how PDSs can and should respond.

Valli and her colleagues (1997) distinguish between equality (where everyone is treated the same) and equity, which brings in "notions of fairness and justice, even if that requires an unequal distribution of goods and services" (p. 254). They go on to make a useful differentiation among three forms of equity:

- *Access:* Providing appropriate routes, including adaptations or accommodations so that everyone can take advantage of the educational opportunities that are offered
- *Participation:* Ensuring that the structures and processes of schools—curriculum, instruction, assessment, tracking, or grouping arrangements—do not privilege one group over another
- *Outcomes:* Reducing or eliminating the gaps in intergroup achievement, attitudes, graduation and college-going rates, and employment (pp. 254-255)

Valli and her colleagues also address the degree of change on the agenda of the PDS, using Cuban's (1988) first- and second-order changes (discussed in Chapter 4) as a guideline. They draw heavily on the language of the Holmes report *Tomorrow's Schools* (1990) to outline the intention of PDSs in reference to equity and then use their review of the literature to identify the many ways in which the intentions have not yet been met.

Abdal-Haqq (1998) defines equity in ways that distinguish it from a term it has sometimes been combined and confused with—parity. Parity addresses the issues of equal voice and status between the school and university partners. Abdul-Haqq notes the high level of attention that has been given to establishing parity and changing the historically "colonizing" relationship between schools and universities, but adds that less energy and focus have been spent on equity issues such as increasing diversity in the teaching force or preparing teachers to work in more culturally responsive ways with students. The notion of diversity can itself get watered down by looking at all forms of diversity, such as when you hear someone saying, "we have a diverse pool of interns because some are young and some are old, and they come from all parts of the state," even though they are all white, middle-class women.

If Abdal-Haqq and Valli and her colleagues challenge those in the PDS community to be true to the roots and stated mission of the PDS, Peter Murrell (1998, 2001) takes the critique further and suggests that PDSs might be part of the problem if they are not part of the solution. His critical look at PDSs suggests that the problem goes beyond the lack of pursuit of equity concerns, to the ways in which the PDS model cuts out other partners. He suggests a number of factors that make it problematic for PDSs to address diversity and equity issues, including the following:

- As a structural design, PDSs are inherently neutral both culturally and politically in urban communities where, Murrell argues, the status quo must be questioned and challenged vigorously.
- The bilateral nature of PDSs (schools and universities) makes it harder for parents and community stakeholders to have meaningful roles in schools and teacher preparation.
- Preestablished roles outlined in PDS agreements will not allow enough fluidity to really bring in all voices and improve schools and teacher preparation.
- The focus of PDSs on teacher professional development takes place at the expense of the development of parents, schools, neighborhoods, and children.

In response, others (including myself) counter with examples of the many PDSs that have in fact been successfully addressing the diversity and equity agenda, and argue further there is nothing inherent or structural in a PDS that makes it "part of the problem." (See Teitel in Foreword to Murrell, 1998.) At the same time, there is no question that the critiques of Murrell, Valli and colleagues, and Abdal-Haqq have brought important attention to issues of diversity and equity in PDSs. They have shaped my thinking and suggested ways that I believe PDSs can and must respond to meet the broader goals of providing high-quality learning for all students. Specific ideas follow, mapped onto the PDS Standards Student Learning Pyramid that is the organizing theme of this book. The Diversity and Equity Standard is displayed on the Pyramid as angling up the side. The issues related to it cut through every aspect of the partnership and, as shown below, provide opportunities to connect at each level with the important suggestions of Murrell, Valli and colleagues, and Abdal-Haqq.

• At the Collaboration level, an initial question focuses on who are involved as a partner and who is not. Is the partnership solely a dyadic relationship (between school and university) or are others—parents, community agencies, unions, and so on—at the table and involved (see Murrell, 1998, 2001)? What is the racial, ethnic, and cultural diversity of the participating institutions, and what is their commitment to using the partnership to promote equity and social justice?

• The intersection with the Structures, Resources, and Roles Standard focuses attention on the extent to which the PDS's organizational structures create parity and reciprocity among the partners (so that if there are diverse partners there is equality and voice from all) *and* address issues of equity, including prioritizing the use of resources to address issues of equity. It addresses the different roles taken by participants and how diverse and equitable those roles are as well as how diverse the pools of interns, mentors, and faculty are (see Abdal-Haqq, 1998).

• In the Learning Community Standard, key issues to examine include the philosophy undergirding the partnership and how it shapes curriculum, instruction, and assessment as well as the development of community among the teachers, interns, and students. How do issues of diversity and equity drive the content and process of the curriculum and instruction for PreK–12 students, interns, faculty, and administrators at all participating institutions? How are equitable opportunities to learn for all ensured (see "equity of participation" in Valli et al., 1997)?

- At the apex of the Pyramid, impacts on students become paramount. The intersection of diversity and equity with the Assessment Standard (angling up the other side) suggests the critical focus on reduction of the achievement gap and evaluation of policies and practices to support equity (see "equity of outcomes" in Valli et al., 1997).

The process of mapping the critiques of PDSs concerning diversity and equity onto the PDS Student Learning Pyramid underscores my conviction in the importance of making sure PDSs are responsive to these sets of issues. The current high level of focus on the achievement gap in many sectors of the educational community and society can provide important support for ensuring that PDSs move toward this direction. The work of K–16 networks and the Education Trust help bring about an important confluence of interest and concern about achievement gap issues. PDSs can serve as an excellent mechanism for trying to bring about the second-order changes necessary to make a difference on tough issues such as the achievement gap, since when properly configured and focused, they can influence teacher preparation, as well as schools and communities.

START-UP TASKS AND CHALLENGES

Six overarching questions guide my thinking about start-up issues and the Equity and Diversity Standard.

- Who is at the table (and who is not)? At the most basic collaboration level, who are your partners? If faced with choices, does your university opt for a mostly white, suburban school or an urban or rural school that is more racially and economically diverse? If your school has choices for partners, do you choose a teacher preparation program that is racially diverse and has a commitment to diversity and equity? How does each partner think about those choices? Also, who is not a part of the partnership that could and should be? See, on p. 39 in Chapter 2, *Finding a Partner: Sources*, *Evaluating a Potential Partner* and *Scanning the Environment for Potential Partners: Who Is Missing?* on p. 50.

> One of the perennial questions that shows up among university teacher educators who are forming PDS partnerships concerns the quality of the school with whom they might partner. Teacher educators seeking the best placements for their students may sometimes express a preference for a suburban school over an

urban or rural one, arguing that more suburban teachers are better exemplars of practice and that the schools have a greater capacity to be good partners and to provide good experiences for the preservice teachers. Others advocate for placement in an urban or rural school, arguing that being part of a PDS indicates an important turnaround for the school and provides rich opportunities for preservice teachers to work with diverse populations and participate in a school being transformed. I have seen these arguments paralyze university faculties, preventing them from moving ahead on developing a partnership. Resolution of the differences can be quite complex and requires examination of the core values of the teacher education program, as well as opportunities to engage with possible partners, examine stereotypes, and form relationships.

• Are issues of diversity and equity clearly understood and on the agenda, and is there the will to keep them there? How much is explicitly discussed at the beginning about what either of the terms means and what implications there are for the partnerships and the individual partner institutions? See *What's Your Partnership's Understanding of Diversity and Equity?* on p. 183.

Although some of the PDSs I document or participate in as a consultant have little idea or clarity about equity and diversity, there are some that are quite sophisticated. One college that I have done some documentation with over the past 10 years has really transformed itself and its partnerships in relation to these efforts. Formerly having a mostly white, middle-class student body and faculty, with most teacher education placements in the suburbs, the college looks very different now. With a significant number of administrators and faculty members of color on board, there has been a constant process of "interrogating the curriculum" and reviewing all aspects of structure and placement. The college has developed strong partnerships with urban schools where faculty from school and college are deeply involved with issues of student learning and reduction of the achievement gap.

• Having clear answers to the questions about partners and commitment is necessary but not sufficient for change. Your partnership also needs a clear set of strategies to address issues of equity and diversity. What you choose will be based on your local circumstances, the core values of your partnership, and your beliefs about what the underlying causes and solutions are for a host of diversity- and equity-related issues. For instance if you choose to focus on increasing the racial diversity of the teaching force, you may choose to put more energy into recruitment. That might take the form of setting up long-range "pipeline programs" as some PDSs have done, developing future teacher clubs in schools with high populations of students of color. Or it might lead to mid-career programs where your PDS draws prospective teachers from an older pool—from the military, for example. Or you might notice that your PDS doesn't have as much trouble recruiting preservice and experienced teachers of color as it does retaining them, so you might focus on providing mentoring and other support. You might do them all and then some, but the point here is you need strategies to plan and implement. Similarly, if you are focusing on the achievement gap, you might think that the major point of intervention is with teachers on developing relationships with students (Ferguson, 2001) or the importance of cultural connections (Gay, 2002), peer group support (Tresiman, 1992), or other issues such as parent engagement, school organization (tracking), culturally relevant teaching or curriculum, and so forth. To plan your strategies, see *Developing Strategies to Address Diversity and Equity* on p. 184.

• Are there data sources that will help assess the effectiveness of any strategies? Any strategies that are new will need to be assessed for tune-ups and overall effectiveness. For many PDSs this has required a closer look at data, often requiring disaggregated data by racial group to get a fine analysis of impacts. See *Assessing Impacts of Equity and Diversity Strategies and Policies* on p. 186.

• Changing policies or approaches to recruitment, curriculum, instruction, or assessment can be touchy issues at all the partnering institutions. Is there a sufficiently trusting relationship between the partners to work on tough issues within and across the organizational boundaries? See *How Deep Is Your Trust?* on p. 188.

A dean in a long-standing (five-year) partnership told me that he was upset about how kids of color were being treated in his college's partner PDSs, but simply felt "We cannot go there. We think our thoughts, but if we ever brought them up, it would be all over."

• Are there resources (or a strategy to get them) to support the work outlined in the strategies above? In some cases, policies and practices can be changed without any influx of resources, but more often than not, any of the strategies called for in this section will require, at the minimum, some support and professional development for the adults involved. Others, such as tuition remission or stipends to attract prospective teachers of color, will have longer-term and possibly larger needs of resources. See *Resource Suggestions for Getting Started on a Diversity and Equity Agenda* on p. 186.

ISSUES AND CHALLENGES IN SUSTAINABILITY

As your partnership moves into the sustainability phase, the same six issues apply, but you can look at each at a more complex or deeper level.

• As the partnership deepens, look again for who should be at the table. Most PDSs are dyadic relationships between schools and teacher education programs. How can you expand the clinical triad pool, as Murrell suggests, to include parents, community-based educators, and arts and science faculty? Further, look at roles and power dynamics within partnerships. Who speaks and who remains silent? Who has power, and whose knowledge counts? See *Expanding the Circle of Practice* on p. 188.

The guidelines for the federal Teacher Quality Enhancement grants (Title II) required that partnerships seeking funding be expanded from teacher educators and school personnel to include arts and sciences faculty at the universities. One of the state consortia that applied for and received a grant decided to go further and designed a process to include parents and community members in the planning and implementation of the grant. Using a logo that shows all four constituent groups (teacher educators, families and community members, arts and science faculty, and school personnel) as equal partners, the partnership has struggled to make that a reality. It has been a slow and uneven process of engagement and connection with some important gains made, and much still to be done.

• Is there the will to keep on pushing issues of diversity and equity, even as the partnership is developing greater clarity about what the implications of that are? Are participants willing to look closely at the their own practices, as well as those of their partners? See *Addressing Deep-Seated Change on Diversity and Equity* on p. 189.

A PDS in one of the networks that I am in shared this story. The university liaison talked about how there was a growing concern among his faculty colleagues about the tracking at the high school with which they had been partnered for five years. For two years, the issue was back-burnered, with college faculty afraid to rock the boat by bringing it up. When the liaison finally broached it with his counterpart, it turned out faculty from the school had concerns about the college's totally white faculty and how the high costs of the college meant that the graduates of their own high school and other poor and working-class students in the area could not attend. When the partners began to talk to each other about this deeper level of mutual concerns about equity and diversity, they began to develop some joint strategies about how to move forward.

• Are the strategies for addressing diversity and equity issues comprehensive, sustained, and central to the PDS and its partners? See *Sustaining and Integrating Diversity and Equity Strategies* on p. 189.

I made a site visit to a PDS that had a strongly integrated approach to issues of equity and diversity that was central to the core mission of the university and the schools. It included working with teachers at all partner institutions on "culturally responsive teaching," mentoring preservice teachers of color, and recruiting future teachers of color through future educator clubs. A separate office was set up to coordinate these and other related activities and, due to sustained high-level support and a strong commitment by partnership members, has managed to keep a strong focus on the diversity and equity agenda without becoming marginalized.

• Are documentation approaches in place to learn from the strategies that are implemented? How are the documentation efforts tied to decision making about structures, roles, and resources and how are the inquiry and assessment processes themselves maintained and supported? When done well, inquiry about equity can help provide accountability to various publics, which enhances sustainability. See *Connecting Equity, Inquiry, Accountability, and Sustainability* on p. 190.

• How have the conversations on the tough issues worked out? Is there sufficient safety and reciprocity? Are the hard discussions left up to

committed individuals to bring up or are there structures in place to talk
about equity and diversity? What does your ability (or inability) to have
these conversations say about the underpinnings of collaboration (trust),
roles, and structures in your partnership? What topics seem sealed off or
too touchy to discuss? See *Honest Talk About the Undiscussable Issues in
PDSs* on p. 105 above the undiscussable issues in PDS in Chapter 3.

> Three years into a very successful partnership between a
> nationally known university and an urban high school, one of
> the veteran teachers, herself strongly committed to the part-
> nership and to equity issues in her school, put it quite simply:
> "If the university math and science faculty come into our
> classrooms or to this school to tell us how to fix the achieve-
> ment gap in math and sciences, it will provoke anger and
> resentment by teachers. With all due respect, what do they
> know about the kids we have in this school? How else can we
> move on this?" Rather than torpedoing the possibility of
> discussion of the achievement gap issues, the statement was
> a realistic appraisal that helped redirect the strategies for
> bringing those content area "experts" into the discussion of a
> problem central to the school.

• Are resources adequate? Are they external and "soft" or do they
represent commitment within the partnership? Is there a plan that reallo-
cates internal resources, that draws on external grants, and that connects
to existing decision-making structures for implementation and sustainability? See *Strategies for Supporting and Sustaining Equity and Diversity
Work* on p. 191.

Focus on Student Learning

Ken Sirotnik (1988, p. 181) has a simple but powerful definition of
equity: "Imply[ing] a commitment to excellent education for all students
regardless of race, ethnicity, gender, family income, religion, eye color,
or any other extraneous variable." In this sense, any efforts done under
the Diversity and Equity Standard automatically connect with student
learning.

An example that illustrates the connection between equity and
student learning, even as it shows how professional development schools
can be effective mechanisms for addressing equity issues, comes from
Boston. The Boston Public Schools, which has pledged to reduce the
achievement gap among its students, funded professional development

school partnerships with three universities with a clear focus on developing and implementing strategies for improving the achievement of African American and Latino students. Below, I include an excerpt from the assessment plan for that PDS initiative since it shows how the different partners that comprise a PDS can be brought to bear on a challenging problem; it also shows how solutions to that problem can ripple through the PDS in ways that extend the impacts (to other preservice teachers, for instance, not only those involved in the Boston PDSs). The language is somewhat formal, and the excerpt comes from the beginning of the assessment plan, which defines what being a Boston Public Schools PDS means.

> Being a professional development school partnership within Boston permeates every facet of the school and the higher education partner, fundamentally transforming the teaching and learning that goes on in both institutions and leading to a sense of caring and responsibility for the achievement of all students. Being a PDS in Boston means that the school, the university, and community partners are institutionalizing procedures and practices that let them, in a focused and sustained manner, think about, and work on improving (and documenting the improvement of) teaching and learning in K-12 settings, with a particular focus on using research and expert knowledge to help African American, Latino, and other students achieve at high levels. In PDSs, we expect to see focused and coordinated changes in curriculum, instruction, assessments, and the organizational structures that support them at the school and university. We expect these changes to begin to affect the achievement of BPS students on summative and formative measures. We expect interns who learn to teach in these PDSs to be better prepared to work effectively with African American, Latino, and other students, and to be more likely to continue to teach in Boston. Finally, we expect university partners to be deeply engaged in this work and to use their involvement to improve their own teacher education programs.

This language sets a high bar for what a PDS's focus on equity and diversity should look like, even as it illustrates the powerful connections that can and should be made among equity, diversity, and student learning.

ASSESSMENT

Form 5.1   Quick-Check Self-Assessment Framework

For each statement below, assess the response that best describes your partnership, using a scale ranging from Strongly Disagree (SD), to Disagree (D), to Agree (A) to Strongly Agree (SA). Use NA for items that are not applicable in your context. Use the space below each item to list a few indicators that give evidence to support your assessment and to explain any questions you felt were not applicable.

1. There is a clear understanding   SD   D   A   SA   NA
   of what diversity and equity
   means in the PDS.
   Indicators:

2. The PDS has in place a set of   SD   D   A   SA   NA
   strategies to address issues
   of diversity and equity.
   Indicators:

3. The PDS includes a diverse set   SD   D   A   SA   NA
   of partnering organizations,
   including those representing
   parents and community
   stakeholders.
   Indicators:

4. The voices and perspectives of   SD   D   A   SA   NA
   all PDS partners are heard and
   respected within the partnership.
   Indicators:

5. The diversity of the preservice   SD   D   A   SA   NA
   teachers and faculty at school
   and university match that of the
   students and community.

   Indicators:

6. There is a strong commitment to   SD   D   A   SA   NA
   issues of diversity and equity, and
   the collective will to follow through,
   even if changes are difficult.
   Indicators:

7. Trust exists between and among   *SD   D   A   SA   NA*
   the partners that enables them to
   talk honestly with each other, even
   about deep-seated issues.
   Indicators:

8. A good documentation plan is in   *SD   D   A   SA   NA*
   place to assess the impacts of
   diversity and equity strategies.
   Indicators:

9. There is a coherent plan for addressing   *SD   D   A   SA   NA*
   diversity and equity that is at
   the core of the partnering
   organizations, not marginalized.
   Indicators:

10. Adequate resources are committed to   *SD   D   A   SA   NA*
    address diversity and equity
    approaches.
    Indicators:

DIVERSITY AND EQUITY ASSESSMENT TEMPLATE

The following template closely adheres to the discussion of how the Diversity and Equity Standard cuts through all the other Standards, advanced in the introduction to this chapter, showing how the critiques of PDSs can and should be incorporated. It is presented here in bare-bones form, since it repeats some of what was in the text, and it is followed by a detailed example fleshed out for UTTC.

Diversity and equity issues should cut through every aspect of the partnership:

• At the Collaboration level, documentors should focus on who are involved as partners and who are not. Is the partnership solely a dyadic relationship (between school and university), or are others—parents, community agencies, unions, and so on—at the table and involved? What is the racial, ethnic, and cultural diversity of the participating institutions, and what is their commitment to using the partnership to promote equity and social justice?

• At the Structures, Roles, and Resources level, documentors need to address how the organizational structures put into place create (or do not create) parity and reciprocity among the partners. Documentation should note the different roles taken by participants and how diverse and equitable those roles are (such as how diverse the pools of interns, mentors, and faculty are) as well as how resources are used and issues of equity prioritized.

• In the Learning Community, key issues to examine include the philosophy undergirding the partnership and how it shapes curriculum, instruction, and assessment, and the development of community among the teachers, interns, and students. How do issues of diversity and equity drive the content and process of the curriculum and instruction for PreK–12 students, interns, faculty, and administrators at all participating institutions? How are equitable opportunities to learn for all ensured?

• At the apex of the Pyramid, impacts on students become paramount. The intersection of Diversity and Equity with the Assessment Standard (angling up the other side) suggests the critical focus of documentation here is reduction of the achievement gap and evaluation of policies and practices to support equity.

DOCUMENTATION EXAMPLE

Like the UTTC excerpt in Chapter 4, the following segment from the assessment framework for the Urban Teacher Training Collaborative is a detailed elaboration of the Diversity and Equity Assessment Template, based on suggestions and applications from the UTTC Assessment Group. Only some portions of the documentation called for in it currently exist; the rest is to be developed. It is included here as illustrative, not as a complete or finished example of an assessment.

Diversity and equity issues cut through every aspect of the UTTC. Suggestions for documentation are in italics. Starting at the bottom right of the Pyramid, and working up:

- At the **Collaboration** level, look at the background and commitments of each partner to issues of diversity and equity.

  - *Insert here background demographics of partner institution students, faculty, staff, and administrators (include five-year trends). Also insert any policy statements or other pieces of relevant histories of any of the partners in relation to diversity and equity.*

- How did diversity and equity factors influence the decision to form a partnership? How did each partner see the partnership as contributing to its own diversity and equity agenda?

  – *Insert here documentation about the decision to partner. For example, Tufts made the decision to partner with the Fenway and Boston Arts Academy and Mission Hill to move to a greater racial, ethnic, and cultural diversity, as opposed to continuing or deepening partnerships with suburban schools. Include the rationale for this, and also document number of teacher ed placements in suburban vs. urban schools over the last five years and other relevant information.*

- Which issues around diversity and equity were explicitly on the PDS agenda when the partnership was formed? What joint understandings or agreements existed about the direction the partnership would be taking? Were there explicit discussions of this at the beginning?

  – *Insert documentation of any agreements for directions of the partnership made at the outset, in relationship to diversity and equity.*

- At the **Structures, Resources, and Roles** level, there are many connections as roles have shifted to focus on equity and incorporate a more diverse intern group.

- A big connection, that itself has had many additional ripples of effect, is the enrollment of significantly more interns of color in the partnership, attracted in part by the placements in urban diverse settings.

  – *Document the numbers and demographics of the Tufts intern pool and teacher education candidates for the last five years.*

  – *Document (from student interview comments and other sources) that many of the interns were attracted by placements in those particular, diverse, settings.*

- Impacts on roles: Some important issues of equity in roles have emerged as interns of color have taken on real responsibilities, enabling students and others to see people of color in authority positions.

  – *Document with reflections by interns, students, and other PDS participants.*

- Impacts on roles: These new roles of interns (and interns of color) have had impacts on Fenway and Boston Arts Academy and Mission Hill faculty teams, as experienced teachers, accustomed to working in certain ways, have needed to adapt to new sources of input.

  – *Document with intern and faculty reflection, notes from teacher team meetings, and observations of coordinator.*

- Impacts on roles: The practical experiences and perspectives of the interns in their classes at Tufts challenged the authority of the faculty and shifted some of the power dynamics in the relationship.

- *Document with intern exit surveys and course evaluations, and reflections by faculty.*

- Roles: Impact on hiring of faculty of color at Fenway and Boston Arts Academy and Mission Hill schools.

  - *Document numbers up, graduates hired; include five-year trend.*

- Roles: The discussion of equity and diversity increases the attention given to the (mostly white) faculty at Tufts.

  - *Document with the faculty roster, five-year hiring trends, and notes from discussion of increasing the diversity of Tufts faculty.*

- Structures: The increased focus on diversity draws attention to the mostly white steering committee.

  - *Document with membership list, document efforts to rectify expansion of committee to include faculty and administrators of color.*

- Structures: Impact on schoolwide meetings of having ten additional adults in these small schools—the interns form a significant percentage of addition people who are "transient."

  - *Document the pattern of faculty meetings that include interns in most, but not all, faculty retreats and meetings.*

- Resources: Money allocated for recruitment of diverse pool of interns, scholarships (especially for interns of color).

  - *Document monetary allocations and five-year trends.*

- At the **Learning Community** level, again there were many impacts, starting with the presence of a talented group of interns of color and rippling out in several directions. This group had impacts on the following:

  - The white interns at Fenway and Boston Arts Academy: the impacts of being a part of the cohort, and having close learning relationships with interns of color. The interns of color comprised a majority within the cohort and, themselves strong leaders, helped those white interns with little exposure to people of color learn how to "be with" children (students) of color.

    - *Document with reflection papers, exit interviews, course evaluations.*

  - The other (mostly white) preservice teachers at Tufts: through interaction with interns of color in seminars, through on-site courses and attending events like the play, and through deeper discussions in classes about race, gender, and class.

    - *Document with reflection papers, exit interviews, course evaluations.*

  - The (mostly white) Tufts faculty: who engaged in deeper discussions of race, class and gender in their own courses, in part driven by the interns.

> – *Document with teaching notes, reflection papers, exit interviews.*

- The Fenway and Boston Arts Academy and Mission Hill students (mostly students of color): impacts by role modeling, informal college counseling, choice of readings, special events the interns organized.

  > – *Document with roster of special activities done by interns (especially those of color); document interest and applications to historically black colleges and universities, also student interviews, reflection papers after events.*

- For the interns themselves, key learnings included:

  - For some of the interns of color, insights into the challenges of developing rapport with students, and being a teacher who is an authority figure with high expectations of them.

    > – *Document with intern reflections, notes from seminar discussion on "difference between being a school teacher and being a cool teacher."*

  - How to interact with student support teams, participate in parent conferences, work effectively with special needs students and the teachers and support systems available to help them.

    > – *Document with rosters, schedules and rotations, as well as intern reflections, exit interviews, course evaluations.*

  - Being a generalist as well as a content specialist by doing some teaching and learning in areas outside the intern's disciplinary strengths.

    > – *Document through intern reflections, exit interviews, course evaluations, especially looking at how this helped interns understand student learning, by working in areas of their own weaknesses*

At the intersection with **Assessment: Accountability and Quality Assurance,** there are a number of things to follow.

For the interns as well as the faculty and administrators from all partnering institutions, there have been important learnings about the following:

- Using a variety of student assessment approaches to understand the learning needs of diverse learners.

  > – *Document with descriptions of portfolios, exhibitions, and other forms of assessment used, and their impact on diverse learners, through reflections and interviews of students, interns, faculty and administrators, exit interviews, etc.*

- Achievement gap issues, how they affect diverse learners, and strategies to close the gap, through discussion groups and the systematic review of disaggregated achievement data by teams, houses, and other groups in the school.

> – *Document with agendas and minutes of the groups focusing on this, reports, summaries of student data, reflections, and exit interviews.*
>
> • How issues of diversity and equity drive the content and process of the curriculum and instruction for PreK-12 students, interns, faculty and administrators at all participating institutions.
>
> – *Document with agenda and minutes of forums in which these curriculum and instruction discussions take place, including agendas and minutes, course syllabi and teaching notes, reflections, and exit interviews.*

Toolkit

5.1 What's Your Partnership's Understanding of Diversity and Equity?

It is hard to talk about diversity and equity without having some consensus on what is meant by these terms. Start by asking your colleagues and partners what definitions they are using. You might draw on the work by Valli and her colleagues (1997) as a jumping-off point for getting an agreed-upon definition of equity. The grids below will get you started, but there could be many more variations (focus on curriculum, etc.).

Equity as . . .	What does this mean in your PDS?	How can you get a more widespread understanding of this?	What is your PDS doing to address this form of equity?
Access			
Participation			
Outcomes			
Other			

Diversity in . . .	What does this mean in your PDS?	How can you get a more widespread understanding of this?	What is your PDS doing to address this form of equity?
Racial			
Social class			
Disability			
Gender			
Other			

5.2 Developing Strategies to Address Diversity and Equity

What drives your partnership's development of strategies around equity? Having a clear consensus about a definition is an important starting point, but where do you go from there? If, for instance, your focus is on equity outcomes, and thus on the achievement gap, you will still have to choose among a number of competing (and sometimes complementary) analyses. Do you focus your efforts on students—setting up peer support networks to develop study skills and provide challenging work (Tresiman, 1992)—or examine the curriculum for cultural relevance or the skills of the teachers to ensure cultural relevant teaching (Gay, 2002)? Do you work with teachers to help them develop stronger relationships with students, as Ron Ferguson (2001) does in the Minority Student Achievement Network? Do you focus on quality teaching and high standards, like Kati Haycock of the Ed Trust (Haycock, 2001)? Do you look at organizational structures, such as tracking, or how involved parents are in the school? I could go on, but the point is about the importance of you and your partners drawing on your values and beliefs, internal data, and external literature, and developing your own hypotheses and strategies about what will make a difference in your community.

Take the time to discuss this fully. Many PDSs share articles, offer study groups, and sponsor think tanks and preliminary pilot research before embarking on any strategies. Developing a community advisory board and drawing on a range of perspectives, including those of the students, are key planning strategies. Use a grid like the one below to get some of the options organized.

Hypothesis	Foundation for Hypothesis	Implied Strategy to Address	Resources Needed to Get Started	Data Needed to Assess Success (by what date?)
Kids need peer groups	Treisman			
Kids need curriculum that addresses their culture	Gay			
Parents need to be actively involved	Internal hunch (data from successful school in area)			
Teachers need to learn culturally relevant teaching approaches	Gay			
Kids need basic skills	Internal hunch			
Teachers need to build stronger relationships with kids	Ferguson			
Kids need high standards and challenging curriculum	Haycock			
Other				

The focus here has been on reducing the achievement gap, but your partnership could (and should) do a similar chart for recruiting and retaining a diverse workforce and for other issues of equity and diversity.

5.3 Assessing Impacts of Equity and Diversity Strategies and Policies

What tracking systems do you have in place for assessing your diversity and equity efforts?

List each specific strategy your PDS is working on and how you are assessing it. For some more ideas on efficient strategies for data collection, see *Gathering Data Efficiently and Effectively* on p. 221 in Chapter 6.

Equity and Diversity Initiatives	Documentation Currently in Place	Suggestions for What We Might Do
For students		
For preservice teachers		
For experienced educators and other adults		

5.4 Resource Suggestions for Getting Started on a Diversity and Equity Agenda

As you seek resources to develop and implement a diversity and equity agenda, draw on the previous toolkit suggestions to have a clear view of what you are proposing to do, what the theory in action behind it is, and how you will assess its progress. Expand the "Resources needed to get started" column from *Developing Strategies to Address Diversity and Equity* on p. 184 by thinking of the resources you need not just as monetary, but in terms of people, passion, purpose, and power. If your partnership is a broad one, with community and other noneducator partners, and you have also sought allies in a variety of places, you will be well positioned to seek the additional resources needed. For each strategy you are considering, use the grid below to help you get started, plotting the resources you need (going down) with the potential sources of the resource (going across). I have started filling this one out for recruiting and retaining prospective teachers of color into the PDS.

Resources Needed	School	School District	Teacher Education Program	University	Community Partner(s)	Outside Funders
Money for stipends				X		X
Provide mentors of color	X	X	X		X	
Recruitment outreach		X		X		X
Set up future teacher club						
Review of teacher education curriculum	X		X		X	
Develop culturally respectful teaching course	X		X	X	X	
Other aspects of strategy						

The X's I have placed are just for illustrative purposes. Use this as a process for diversifying your base of support by drawing collaboratively on your partners, looking for opportunities elsewhere in your partnership organizations (for instance, your university partner may have money for stipends or recruitment travel to increase enrollment of students of color) as well as for external funds and support.

5.5 How Deep Is Your Trust?

Poking at the sometimes controversial and challenging issues of diversity and equity requires a high level of trust in a partnership. How deep does the trust run in yours? To assess this, sort through the list of tough topics that have been successfully dealt with at the partnership level, but also look at the ones that one partner or another has backed away from or that you know are being avoided. The following grid may help you get started. Use it with your steering committee as a way to open discussion about trust.

Name A Tough Topic. . .	. . .That You Discussed and Resolved	. . .That You Backed Away From or Avoided	So What? What Did You Learn From Each?

5.6 Expanding the Circle of Practice

Peter Murrell (2001) suggests that "community teachers" cannot be prepared in the traditional triad of clinical practice—of preservice teacher, cooperating teacher, and teacher educator. Rather, he argues that this circle of practice, whose aim is the development of the student teacher, must be enlarged to include parents, community-based educators, and arts and sciences faculty. The aim of the larger circle is much broader, including inquiry about the efficacy of instruction of students and the development of practice for student teachers, cooperating teachers, and other participants.

Has your PDS altered the basic clinical triad relationship? If so, in what ways? Some PDSs have successfully engaged arts and sciences faculty, but have not included parents and community members in any meaningful way. Have you? What would it mean to really engage parents and community members?

5.7 Addressing Deep-Seated Change on Diversity and Equity

How deeply do your diversity and equity initiatives go? Ismat Abdal-Haqq (1998) suggests that, in many PDSs, it is not deep enough to make meaningful change. After noting that some PDSs offer coursework on multicultural education and placements in diverse schools as ways of preparing "culturally responsive" teachers, she notes,

> What is not equally evident is whether the content and focus of this coursework or field placement are designed to challenge underlying assumptions that govern how schools are structured, who controls them, their purpose, how they relate to students and families, and how they support societal inequities. (pp. 67-68)

If this quote raises a responsive chord in you, consider using it as a discussion starter in your next steering committee meeting, or use it to open a forum on the progress of the PDS that includes parents and community members.

5.8 Sustaining and Integrating Diversity and Equity Strategies

How are you coordinating your diversity and equity efforts? To what extent are they seamlessly integrated into all aspects of what your PDS does and to what extent are they separate, both from each other and from the mainstream of the PDS? How are you organizing to support them?

As you think about coordinating these activities, you may want to think through the advantages and disadvantages of each approach and figure out one that works best for you. I have started that comparison below and invite you to finish it and apply it in your context.

Here are some advantages of a separate office coordinating diversity and equity issues:

- Committed focus of individuals for whom it is a primary part of their job description
- Coherence among activities (e.g., recruitment of prospective teachers of color can be tied to mentoring and to development of culturally responsive teaching courses for faculty and school and university)
- Administrative gains of having an office that can apply for and handle grants, publicity, and so on

Some disadvantages of a separate office include:

- Potential marginalization from the mainstream of the PDS, unless highly visible, could be an out-of-sight, out-of-mind phenomenon
- Sense on the part of PDS participants that someone else is addressing diversity and equity issues
- If issues are not deeply supported by people in high places, possible loss of power or access due to separate status

5.9 Connecting Equity, Inquiry, Accountability, and Sustainability

The eight partnerships in the Bay Area School Reform Collaborative (including five universities, two school districts, and 18 schools) have focused on equity for the past five years. After developing some common definitions of equity, each partner in the network developed its own accountability plan that focused on student learning, adult learning, and institutional learning. They connect the four "Y's," as they call them, of equity, inquiry, accountability, and sustainability, noting that their inquiry into equity helps hold themselves accountable to their various stakeholders, thus increasing their sustainability (Hammond, Whitenack, & Whittaker, 2002).

The connections they make among the four Y's provide sparks for a few questions you may want to consider in your PDS:

1. Are you using inquiry to document your equity?

2. In what ways do you hold yourselves accountable for equity?

3. Who else holds you accountable for your partnership's progress on equity?

4. If you were documenting progress on equity would it enhance your ability to show your ability to be accountable for your own progress to outsiders?

5. If you were able to show gains on equity, would that enhance your sustainability?

5.10 Strategies for Supporting and Sustaining Equity and Diversity Work

As you settle in for the long-range support of diversity and equity work, what are some sources of continuing and renewing resources for the work? A few suggestions follow; use them as a springboard for your own development of ideas for supporting and sustaining this work.

• Ensure that school improvement plans for the PDS schools and long-range plans in the universities are clearly aligned with these activities.

• Look together for supplemental monies to support these activities and the professional development and infrastructure development needed. This may include tapping existing monies that are already involved in the PDS (such as Title II), as well as seeking additional funds together. Having clear, focused, assessable plans backed by research and supported by a diverse set of partners, including parents and community members, should enhance the chances of successful outside funding.

• Set up an advisory committee of persons knowledgeable about developing cultures of achievement for African American, Latino, and other students and about developing and institutionalizing PDSs and other partnerships with schools, universities, families, and communities.

• Schedule public forums to report PDS experiences in addressing equity and diversity concerns to broader audiences.

• Develop research strands in the participating (and other) universities relating to this work to engage faculty and doctoral students in this.

• Develop "critical friends" visiting teams and other audiences for reports and other documentation of student progress, school improvement, PDS development, and the impact of teacher education curriculum changes on interns' ability to teach African American and Latino students more effectively.

• Connect to policy issues at the universities, including recruitment and retention of potential teachers of color.

What ideas does a review of this list trigger in your collaborative?

CHAPTER RESOURCES

This section includes a brief annotated bibliography of text and Web resources. The full citations for the text references are in the back of the book.

To obtain elaborations of the critiques of PDSs that were mentioned in the text, follow up with Murrell (1998, 2001), Valli and colleagues (1997), and Abdal-Haqq (1998, 1999).

For a good overall summary of different theories explaining the achievement gap, see "The Canary in the Mine: The Achievement Gap Between Black and White Students" (Singham, 1998).

For different detailed approaches to addressing equity issues, see Gay (2002) on developing, designing, and demonstrating culturally relevant teaching or Tresiman (1992) on the use of peer groups to enhance study skills and achievement for students of color.

For a variety of interesting equity approaches being used in the San Francisco Bay area, see Hammond, Whitenack, and Whittier (2002); see also resources on the Bay Area School Reform Collaborative Web site, www.basrc.org/resources/index.html.

If you are interested in work on relationship building between teachers and students, see Ferguson's (2001) strategies being used in the Minority Student Achievement Network; also see his research on the role teacher expectations play in the achievement gap (Ferguson, 1998).

For suggestions (and other Web links) on developing and using a variety of data, including student performance, perception, demographics, and school processes, to drive decision making around equity, visit http://eric-web.tc.columbia.edu/digests/dig177.html for *Data-Driven Equity in Urban Schools*, an ERIC digest of the Clearinghouse for Urban Education.

For a primer on approaches to reducing the achievement gap, check out another publication of the ERIC Clearinghouse for Urban Education, at http://eric-web.tc.columbia.edu/digests/dig169.html, "Closing The Achievement Gap: Principles for Improving the Educational Success of All Students" (2001).

The Clearinghouse for Urban Education also maintains a portal expressly for achievement gap links, http://eric-web.tc.columbia.edu/pathways/achieve_gap/index.html, and it is good source for recent reports on how achievement is affected by teaching quality, school organization, policies, curriculum reform, and so forth.

Another Web site to watch for achievement gap focus, one that carefully marshals data on the impacts of teachers, standards, and so on, is that of the Education Trust at www.edtrust.org.

One of the specific ongoing projects of interest may be "Dispelling the Myth," which draws on examples of high-poverty and high-minority schools achieving at high levels. See www.edtrust.org/main/main/DTM. asp.

For updates on text and Web sources related to this Standard, see http://pds.edreform.net/home/ and click on Diversity and Equity.

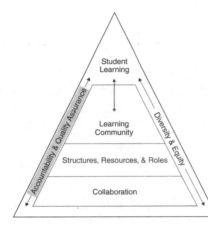

6

Accountability and Quality Assurance

Assessing the Partnership and Its Outcomes

Assessment takes on many meanings in professional development schools, ranging from the relatively informal action research that might be conducted by interns to large-scale summative and formative evaluations designed to meet the needs of the internal and external stakeholders of the PDS. Assessment is closely interwoven with the notions of accountability and quality assurance in ways that will be outlined in this chapter.

The PDS Standard for Accountability and Quality Assurance reads:

> PDS partners are accountable to themselves and to the public for upholding professional standards for teaching and learning. They define clear criteria at the institutional and individual levels for participation. PDS partners collaboratively develop assessments, collect information, and use results to systematically examine their

195

practices and establish outcome goals for all PreK–12 students, candidates, faculty, and other professionals. The PDS partnership demonstrates impact at the local, state, and national level on policies and practices affecting its work. (NCATE, 2001b, p. 13)

There are three major roots for the ideas explored in this chapter:

- Accountability and quality assurance
- Summative assessment of the professional development school as an innovation
- Inquiry into what works and what doesn't in PDSs, with an eye to formative improvement

The first is the deepest and oldest of the roots, harking back to the early days of schooling. I remember learning that periodically the local school boards would come en masse, or send some of its members, to check up on the quality of the schooling. They would, as I recall, descend on the one-room schoolhouse and ask the students to stand and deliver—declaim in Latin, or do some computations. The modern day equivalent of this would be high-stakes standardized testing. I have collapsed a considerable amount of history and many strongly held and disputed views into these short sentences—the full story falls out of the scope of this book, but the notion of accountability and quality assurance is key. How it is being defined, and by whom, is an important part of the debate.

One of the roots of PDSs is the professionalization of teaching. One of the hallmarks for being a professional is the setting of standards for what it means to join (to become an architect, a lawyer, a doctor). If PDSs become the entry point into teaching, teaching as a profession has taken a major step toward setting the standards for entrance. The Standard calls for developing "professional accountability" and ensuring "public accountability"—in other words replacing (or at least augmenting) the outsiders-checking-up-on-the-schools process with one that shows the profession can take care of its own standards (and can work with outside stakeholders so they are assured of quality). Key elements to that strategy are the development, collection, and sharing of assessment data on outcomes the public cares about.

Linda Darling-Hammond addresses this when she notes that PDSs

offer the possibility for socializing new teachers to a different set of expectations about practice within and outside the boundaries of their classrooms. . . . If PDSs become the doorways that all new teachers pass through as they launch their careers, they can transform the culture of teaching and the expectations for collaboration along with the nature of teaching and learning in individual classrooms. (1994, pp. 8-9)

These issues of professionalization apply to induction of new teachers as well as experienced teacher development as Darling-Hammond (1992) defines what professional accountability for teachers might look like, anchoring her discussion in a review of the advantages and limits of other forms of accountability—legal, political, bureaucratic, and market driven. She identifies professional development schools as the places best suited to provide accountability for professional teachers, "by ensuring that they have the tools to apply theory in practice and by socializing them to professional norms and ethics" (p. 91).

The second strand that drives assessment looks at the PDS as an innovation—as an approach to improving schools and teacher education and development. It asks, in a summative way, what the impacts of PDSs are—on PreK–12 students and on the preparation and professional development of educators. Implicit (and sometimes explicit) in the question is a comparison: Are PDS partnerships better at what they do than traditional schools and university programs are separately? This question is of interest and concern to those inside and outside the PDS.

The final strand is formative assessment—how do you do what you are doing in the PDS and do it better? This looks at impacts (like the second strand), but also at processes. What, for instance, are you doing in the PDS that supports the kinds of reading skills and levels you hope to get from students? The primary audiences for this kind of question are the insiders. Key connections need to be made between processes and products, so assessment can work in a formative way.

All three of these strands must be kept in mind when thinking about any kind of assessment in PDSs. Knowing the various audiences and what they care about is essential. It shapes the choice of data to be collected and analyzed, as well as the formats in which the data are shared. Engaging with those stakeholders—inside and outside the PDS—at all points in the process is a critical part of thinking holistically about assessment, accountability, and quality assurance.

OVERVIEW AND HISTORY

The history of the assessment of PDS impacts has been a spotty one, with only a handful of well-done studies. There were a number of reasons that this was difficult during PDSs' first decade. Below is a list I developed when I did assessment workshops in the mid-1990s, followed by some of the reasons I am hopeful that many of these obstacles are disappearing.

Producing careful documentation and assessment of the impacts of professional development school partnerships was challenging in the mid-1990s for several reasons:

- There was no clear, agreed-upon definition of what it meant to be a professional development school.

- PDSs were moving targets, changing and evolving so fast that no evaluation could capture what they were doing.

- It was premature to measure PDS partnerships, which are long-term systemic changes, until the changes were in place and had had an adequate chance to make a difference.

- PDS relationships were fragile and might easily be damaged by a premature evaluation or one that was not sensitive to the need to nurture the relationship.

- It was difficult to establish comparison or control groups in PDS evaluations since those who participate are usually self-selected.

- There were different perceptions of what outcomes matter in teaching and teacher education and student learning, as well as how to measure these outcomes, especially among the different stakeholders involved in the educational process.

- Some outcomes were particularly difficult to measure—for instance, getting consensus on how to measure good teaching as an outcome for preservice teachers; or guaging increased student learning without relying solely on standardized test scores.

- Participants in PDSs were often too busy making the partnership happen to document their work.

Several years later, I am more optimistic that many of these challenges have been addressed. Three important sets of developments in the past several years contribute to my sense of hope (Teitel, in press):

- Clearer connections are being made between PDS processes and outcomes.

- The development and release in 2001 of Standards for Professional Development Schools by the National Council for Accreditation of Teacher Education show a maturation of the PDS partnership movement. The Standards represent a critical convergence of what it means to be a PDS, with profound implications for documenting and assessing PDS-type partnerships.

- The climate of increased accountability has led to an abundance of student test data and some emerging assessments of teacher quality.

Better Process and Product Links

In the early to mid-1990s, much of what was listed as research on professional development schools was really about process—stories of the development of PDSs. Few outcome data were available. The few studies with some sort of outcome data frequently presented findings without context—"black-box" studies—providing no underlying definition of what might have been going on in a PDS partnership to lead to those outcomes (Teitel, 1998b).

In the past few years, more studies have been making important links between process and product—looking at partnership formation as one link in a chain that, for instance, leads to improved student learning because the partnership is changing the experience that students are having. Some have found a "conceptual framework" or "logic model" developed with members of the Massachusetts PDS steering committee helpful in designing and implementing impact research studies. The broad strokes of that framework are included in Table 6.1; for more detail and examples of how it has been used, see Teitel (2001a) or Teitel with Abdal-Haqq (2000).

The chief value of the model is that it steers researchers away from black-box studies and provides a framework to help organize and conceptually link the various kinds of process and product data that exist in partnerships. In a research environment where establishing causality through randomly assigned treatment and control schools is virtually impossible, it provides opportunities for researchers and their audiences to make plausible links that suggest, for instance, that preservice teachers who have spent substantial portions of their internships working on collaborative teams with special education teachers will prove to be stronger collaborators and more skilled in working with a range of students than their peers who have not.

Table 6.1 Conceptual Framework

Organizational Desired Outcomes Innovation: Partnership Development	Adaptations in Roles, Structure, Culture	Best Practice in Teaching, Learning and Leadership	Improved Learning for
School PDS	Changes in governance, decision making, leadership	Classroom approaches: teaching for understanding and constructivism	All students
⟨⟩	Use of time, roles, and rewards	Different expectations for teacher professional development	Experienced teachers and other education personnel
Teacher education program ⟨⟩	Views of collaborative relationships, field work, expectations	Different approaches to preservice teaching	Preservice teachers and other education personnel
Communities, districts, unions, parents, arts and science faculty			

SOURCE: Adapted from Teitel (2001a).

Similarly, the model offered in this book, the PDS Standards Student Learning Pyramid, provides process and product connections, allowing logical links to be made.

PDS Standards

In the mid-1990s, merely agreeing on what was and was not a PDS was a major challenge to serious research on impacts. In her review of the literature for the *Handbook of Research on Teacher Education*, Cassandra Book (1996) identifies this problem:

> The operationalization of what is meant by a professional development school continues to plague researchers' ability to clearly explain what impact the activities of a PDS are having on teaching, learning, school organization, and teacher education. As researchers and teacher educators, we are often at a loss to define when a school is actually a professional development school. (p. 204)

The Professional Development School Standards Project of the National Council for the Accreditation of Teacher Education has taken a major step to change that. The existence of the Standards settles the question of what it is that a PDS should be and do. Even though the Standards are not yet officially part of the NCATE Accreditation process, their impact has already been felt. Many PDS partnerships (including those not involved in the field test of the Standards) have used them to self-assess, to examine issues of sustainability, and to focus research (see, for instance, Rosselli, Brindley, & Daniel, 1999). Some states, such as New Jersey, have incorporated the Standards into the language of their grant proposal requirements. Others, such as Maryland, have adapted the Standards and woven them into state policy as part of the redesign of teacher education.

As the Standards gain wider acceptance, their impact on research will continue to grow. They reduce the dilution of the effects of PDSs that comes about when impact studies are done on schools that are paper PDSs, where the name is changed but little or no PDS-like innovations are in place. Taken one step further, the Standards may also have another profound effect on assessing PDSs. The wider adoption and use of the Standards, over time, will permit comparisons of impacts of PDSs that meet the Standards with those school or college settings that do not (or those that are in earlier stages of meeting the Standards). Just as there are now research findings that compare National Board Certified Teachers in terms of their impact on student learning (Bonds, 2000), it is easy to imagine the day comparable studies available on PDS impacts make use of the Standards. Since current reviews of the literature on the impacts of PDSs are limited by the lack of knowledge of whether the partnership in a particular research report is truly a PDS, this will be an important long-term benefit of the Standards.

The Climate of Increased Accountability

The strong debate in the larger educational community about outcomes and accountability can help the development of good assessment and accountability measures in PDSs, although it also has the risk of hindering it. The opportunity to draw on the wealth of student and teacher test data now available (requiring little or no effort to develop instrumentation or collect and aggregate the data) adds important options for researchers. The risk is that poorly constructed tests or narrow-dimensioned examinations become stand-ins for student learning, for teacher quality, or for both.

The availability and increasing sophistication of the test data will grow. As the Standards suggest, the PDS should play important roles in developing and augmenting those test data with other forms of assessment. With care to maintain a focus on a range of outcome measures, and to look critically at the underlying tests and what they measure, this accountability climate has great potential to enhance impact research for PDSs. More districts and states will develop sophisticated assessments of teacher quality by looking, for instance, at the notion of value added by teachers. Sanders (1997) provides some compelling examples of this, documenting the positive (and negative) impacts teachers have. At this point, most of the findings from these studies are reported in black-box style. We know that teachers in the top value-added quintile boost student achievement on test scores tremendously over those in the bottom quintile, but we do not really know why. The logical next step in this is to look at how the approaches and the preparation of top quintile teachers differ from those in the lowest segment, something Sanders reports he is undertaking. Since one of the central questions in PDS impact research is whether preservice teachers prepared in a PDS are better than those in traditional programs, the value-added data systems may provide some additional resources to find out.

Assessment Matters

Although many of those involved in PDSs feel strongly that their partnerships are improving the learning of prospective and experienced teachers at the K–12 level, teacher educators, and K–12 students, they need to have credible evidence to document those impacts and assure their various publics. As the movement grows and receives increasing national recognition as a key to the future of teacher preparation and school improvement, and as the costs of PDSs become better understood, more stakeholders become involved and the need for documentation of impacts becomes more urgent. Those inside PDSs also need data on the impacts of this educational reform in order to understand better what they do, to fine-tune it, and to justify sustaining their own high levels of personal effort. Finally, and to me most important of all, PDSs need good information about their processes and the impacts they are having on students to stay focused on the equity and student learning focus that gives them reasons to exist.

START-UP TASKS AND CHALLENGES

When I am asked to conduct a workshop or speak about assessment in PDSs, I usually find I am addressing one of three broad areas of consideration in starting up PDS assessment.

- The first is motivational, shaped by the often unspoken question of the audience of "Why bother?" The argument runs like this—"We are too busy making the PDS work to research it. Aren't there others who can do this?"
- The second challenge that shapes the discussion is procedural—addressing who is involved and who should be involved in the assessment. I often frame this by asking, "Who cares about your assessment? And who should care?"
- The final area is technical. Questions include the how-to aspects of conducting and sharing research, as well as the underlying question "How can we do this, given the resource constraints and other demands on our time?"

Think about these three types of questions as they apply to your PDS—your sense of where your PDS is in relation to these three questions becomes a good springboard for addressing your PDS's start-up assessment tasks and challenges.

Suggestions for Designing PDS Research

In the opening part of this chapter I suggested a number of reasons to take the trouble to develop and implement a thoughtful assessment for a

PDS. I have argued that assessment matters, that a focus on outcomes for students is important, and that looking at process and product together is critical. What follows are some specific suggestions on connecting these ideas in your PDS.

- *Focus on outcomes that matter.* In keeping with the framing purposes from the beginning of this chapter, what questions need to be asked to address any accountability and quality assurance concerns? What summative questions do you need to have answered to let external stakeholders know that the PDS is having positive impacts? And what do you need to focus on to allow you to fine-tune the way your PDS works? For example, brainstorm summative questions on the research team, but also with the various stakeholders. For each area of summative interest (impact on preservice teachers, on PreK–12 students, etc.) develop a list of outcome attributes, the presence (or absence) of which would help determine success of the PDS. As part of the brainstorming process, think expansively about this list and then narrow it down to focus it on the core outcomes your program seeks. Get buy-in from stakeholders that these are what matter. See *Sample Outcomes for Preservice Educator Preparation* on p. 217 and *Team Planning Sheet* on p. 217.

- *Use a conceptual framework to guide the work.* Your backward mapping approach to each major area of desired impact of the partnerships could be the four-column model shown in Table 6.1 (see Teitel, 2001a, for a fuller explanation), the PDS Standards Student Learning Pyramid of this book, or something else that makes connections among the partnership formation, the processes, and the outcomes of PDSs. Try not to look at any of the outcomes in isolation from the changes that might be leading to it. So, for instance, if the data show growth and professional development of experienced faculty, map backward to look at what activities, approaches, attitudes, and structures contributed to those gains. Or, if you are looking at developing positive attitudes of teacher education candidates toward urban schools, look for what experiences would lead preservice teachers to develop these attitudes and document the connection.

Once at an assessment workshop I was leading, a university faculty member told me a great story illustrating connections in her PDS experiences. She was working on a particular approach to reading and writing with six of the experienced elementary teachers in the PDS. As part of the inservice course, the teachers were implementing a form of the readers and writers workshop approach in their classes. They noticed how much their students seemed to like the approach and appeared to be learning. When the schoolwide reading test scores came back, the principal was very excited when scores for the students of all six of the teachers rose dramatically and showed significantly higher gains than the reading scores of the students of any of the other teachers in the school. Needless to say, I urged her to pull the data together and think about which audiences, beyond her, her students, and the principal, should learn about it.

• *Engage stakeholders early and often in the documentation process to build ownership of the efforts and to ensure collection of data that are seen as credible at the local and state levels.* There is no sense designing and implementing an assessment only to find that the audience that matters (internal or external stakeholders) did not buy-in to the assessment design. Early and frequent engagement in assessment also develops interest and connection, and sometimes commitment, to the underlying efforts. See *Who Cares?* on p. 218 and *What Do Stakeholders Care About?* on p. 219.

• *Include a range of qualitative and quantitative measures to document the impacts.* Think about the information you want to collect, selecting from a broad array of data sources and always keeping in mind what will be seen as credible by various stakeholders inside and outside the PDS. Think imaginatively about archival data, and try to turn information you are collecting anyway and things you are doing anyway into data for your impact study. For example, if teacher education candidates present portfolios as part of your program, use them to help document some of the attitudes and perhaps some of the professional relationships or reflective practices exhibited by the teacher education students. If you need to collect some data on a specific question, think about how to incorporate it into something educationally useful (or at least interesting). For example, if you want to get teacher education student attitudes on a variety of topics, consider having them write educational platforms articulating their views. If this is done early in the year, and then again near program completion, it not only provides good comparative data over time, it can also promote reflection that helps students develop and prepare for job interviews. See *Gathering Data Efficiently and Effectively* on p. 221.

• *Plan and provide adequate resources to design, collect, analyze, and share findings.* Be sure, in all your planning, to identify who will do the collecting, sorting, and analyzing. There is no point in designing an assessment you do not have the capacity to implement. Even if you make the best possible use of the ideas in the tips for *Gathering Data Efficiently and Effectively*, it takes effort and time (or money to buy time) to conduct this work. Some strategies include putting in place support for the basic collections of data and then being creative about using personal interest, mini-grants, graduate classes, and other ways to get focused pieces of assessment work done within your partnership. See *Suggestions for Supporting Assessment* on p. 222.

• *When it comes to your PDS's assessment design, think big, long-term, and conceptually, but act in the short term in focused, manageable ways.* If you use this book as a way to frame your assessment design, you will have an excellent big-picture, long-term assessment strategy in place. But it may seem overwhelming, and indeed it would be, if you pictured doing all of it each year. Keep in mind that in any given year, you will probably only be doing some pieces of the assessment, not the whole thing, and your challenge is to focus on the pieces that make the most sense for you at any given time. See *Thinking Big, Acting Focused* on p. 225.

• *Present research findings in a variety of engaging ways to different audiences.* Think of "presentation" as the continual and iterative engagement of a variety of stakeholders with the findings, not a one-shot formal presentation or written product. Think about this as ongoing connections, making sure to reach the people who care (or should care) about what you found. If you have already made sure to get consensus that the outcomes mattered and that the information you collected is seen as credible to each, the key work becomes sharing, engaging, and analyzing. Think about the best way to reach each stakeholder group. When and where? See *Sharing Findings With Stakeholders* on p. 226. Also tie whatever research is being done to decision making. See *Connecting Research, Assessment, and Decision Making* on p. 226.

ISSUES AND CHALLENGES IN SUSTAINABILITY

Assessment, accountability, and sustainability are closely linked. Some of the things you might hope your accountability and assessment processes will do in sustaining your PDSs include the following:

• Providing for ongoing inquiry in and on the PDS to ensure that institutionalization does not lead just to new structures and policies that appear innovative but do not improve the learning of students and adults
• Checking back to make sure the PDS is meeting the original or evolving mission and goals for the partnership

- Helping to ensure public accountability (often this is linked to locating and sustaining stable funding and support from outside funders and from decision makers at the district and university levels)
- Developing a culture of inquiry and data use, so research findings are routinely used to shape policy and decision making

Within that broad framework here are two challenges you may face concerning data collection, followed by several suggestions to enhance the collection, analysis, and use of data in your partnership.

- *No baseline of data collection from the beginning.* It is not uncommon that, during the start-up phase, there was not the motivation or sufficient capacity to begin collecting data and thinking about how they will be organized and used. If you are at the point of thinking about sustaining your PDS but have no data, you are not alone, but you will have some catch-up work to do.

> A few years ago, I was asked near the end of the first year of a three-year funded PDS initiative to help design an assessment tool. It was a multisite PDS partnership based around a school district that was funding stipends for interns. Since the partnerships had been started without a great deal of clarity about or process on goals, we had to back up. The assessment planning group functioned for several months as a retroactive design team—by specifying what the goals of the PDS were and getting buy-in from all stakeholders, the assessment group spelled out and developed consensus on what the goals of the partnership were; only then could they go forward and document what was happening in any kind of meaningful way.

- *Too much data.* Your PDS may have the opposite problem—plenty of data collected during the start-up years. The first challenge is to make sure the information gathered is being used. Questionnaires collected but unanalyzed can create ill will on the part of those who took the time to fill them out. Having the capacity to use longitudinal data is wonderful, but make sure you have a handle on what you have coming in and what you can use.

> In another consulting situation, I faced quite the opposite problem. In operation for almost a decade, the partnership (a multisite one centered around a university in a rural area)

had years of data collected—survey forms, interview notes, questionnaires, and accumulations of test scores. The challenge was to focus—to build on what was there, while acknowledging that some of what had been collected would never be used. At the same time, the assessment group needed to look at what the partnership's current research needs were and to figure out how to balance depth and breadth, as well as current interests versus longitudinal data.

Other suggestions for the sustainability phase include the following:

• *Widen the audience to connect more to stakeholders.* Unless your assessment process was launched with an unusual amount of buy-in and connection with stakeholders, use the opportunity to share what you have and revisit and rebuild connections. See *Who Cares?* on p. 218.

• *Strengthen the conceptual links.* If your assessments so far can best be characterized as black-box studies, use the chance to revise them to include clearer process and product connections using a conceptual framework. See *Integrating Multiple Studies Conceptually* on p. 227.

• *Use the assessment processes for decision making.* If assessment is divorced from decision making at your PDS (as it is in many places), bring them together. One way to start is to look at the connections made on the PDS Standards Student Learning Pyramid—at the intersections on the graphics between the Assessment Standard and each of the other four. See elaboration of this in the assessment section of this chapter. See *Connecting Research, Assessment, and Decision Making* on p. 226.

• *Take stock of your partnership.* One way to move toward using data for decision making is to analyze what you have. Use the framework of the PDS Standards to assess where your partnership is on the Standards. You could do all five Standards, or even just look at one of them this year— collecting evidence, for instance, on where the partnership is on the Diversity and Equity Standard. The *Handbook for the Assessment of Professional Development Schools* (NCATE, 2001a) has a very specific process to guide you through collecting evidence, forming conclusions, and making statements of standing as part of the self-study process. It also has some suggestions on how to use the findings to promote PDS development and accountability. See *Using Evidence to Form Conclusions in the Self-Study Process* on p. 228.

- *Tune your assessment to meet the partnership's evolving needs and leverage points for change.* Think strategically about the kinds of changes that are going on (or should be) in your PDS or in your partnering institutions. For example, if there is a strong interest in reducing the achievement gap in your school, you might use the process–product ideas embedded in this book and target your data collection to look at programs and initiatives that might increase the learning of low-performing students, assess their impacts, disaggregate data to focus on the specific questions your partnership has, and so forth. See *Doing Research That Matters: Key Leverage Points for Change* on p. 228.

- *Look for unanticipated consequences.* In PDSs, as in the rest of life, there are often side effects—some good, some bad—of decisions, policies, and initiatives. For example, many PDSs have shifted to yearlong internships. This has many positive impacts but also can have a negative impact on a key equity issue, since some students have enough trouble supporting themselves through shorter student teaching and can certainly not afford a year without pay. Some of the PDSs have tried to address this by offering stipends, but my point here is about the importance, as you move into the sustainability phase, of systematically using research to identify and address consequences. See *Checking for Unanticipated Consequences* on p. 229.

Focus on Student Learning

At a recent PDS summer retreat of a statewide PDS initiative, I saw dozens of ways in which inquiry and assessment were being used to connect to student learning. In one of the partnerships, not only were the interns required to conduct an action research inquiry project on some aspect of student learning, but the school-based faculty members were also encouraged to do the same by their district office. The range of studies was impressive—inquiry into the learning challenges of low-performing fifth-grade readers, or evaluations of strategic interventions, such as the use of graphic organizers for third graders, the use of literature maps for African American male students who struggle with text comprehension, and the use of paired reading for children for whom phonics instruction has not been successful. Even more impressive was the use these studies were being put to. In many of the PDSs, the final product was not simply a report to the course instructor, but a presentation to the school improvement team. And in some cases, preservice teachers, experienced classroom teachers, and university faculty were doing the research collaboratively. Not only were the inquiry projects modeling the way good teaching connects to student learning, but, taken together, they were serving as an important research and development engine for the PDS.

ASSESSMENT

Form 6.1   Quick-Check Self-Assessment Framework

The following self-assessment checklist may be used by PDS partnerships in assessing the implementation of their impact research; it may also be a useful lens with which to view plans for designing and implementing PDS impact research (adapted from Teitel with Abdal-Haqq, 2000).

For each of the steps outlined below, assess how well your impact research addresses the question, using a scale of 1 to 5, with 1 as poor, 5 as excellent, and NA for items that are not applicable in your context. Use the "Planned" category if this aspect is already planned. List a few indicators that give evidence to support your assessment. If you indicated that an item was being planned, give some indication of what the planning stage is.

1. The impact research questions are clear and focused.
   1   2   3   4   5   NA   PLANNED
   (Poor)   (Excellent)

2. There is a widespread sense of the importance of the research question(s) by PDS stakeholders.
   1   2   3   4   5   NA   PLANNED
   (Poor)   (Excellent)

3. The design and implementation of the documentation effort involve all partners from school and college in ways that reflect collaboration and parity.
   1   2   3   4   5   NA   PLANNED
   (Poor)   (Excellent)

4. There is a broad range of data sources being utilized to provide multiple measures.
   1   2   3   4   5   NA   PLANNED
   (Poor)   (Excellent)

5. The data sources being used are seen as credible by all stakeholders.

   1 2 3 4 5 NA   PLANNED
(Poor)   (Excellent)

6. The documentation plans specify who will do the data collection analysis and presentation, and those individuals have the needed skills and the time or other compensation to properly do the work.

   1 2 3 4 5 NA   PLANNED
(Poor)   (Excellent)

7. The findings are grounded in some sort of conceptual map or framework, and are not just outcomes or processes in isolation from each other.

   1 2 3 4 5 NA   PLANNED
(Poor)   (Excellent)

8. The presentation stage (whether it has happened yet or not) includes a continual and iterative engagement of stakeholders with the findings.

   1 2 3 4 5 NA   PLANNED
(Poor)   (Excellent)

9. There is a clear plan for multiyear, ongoing documentation.

   1 2 3 4 5 NA   PLANNED
(Poor)   (Excellent)

10. There are clearly delineated resources to provide time or other compensation to those engaged in the documentation.

   1 2 3 4 5 NA   PLANNED
(Poor)   (Excellent)

11. The assessment process provides assessment on the internal processes of the PDS.

   1 2 3 4 5 NA   PLANNED
(Poor)   (Excellent)

12. Assessment data are used for decision making.

   1 2 3 4 5 NA   PLANNED
(Poor)   (Excellent)

ACCOUNTABILITY AND QUALITY ASSURANCE TEMPLATE

Documentation of this Standard focuses on how the partnership uses inquiry and assessment processes at all stages and levels. Like the Diversity and Equity Standard, it starts at the bottom of the pyramid and cuts through and intersects with all the others. As in Chapter 5's treatment of the Diversity and Equity Standard, this template is "bare bones," since it is followed immediately by a detailed example, drawn from the continuing example we are using of the Urban Teacher Training Collaborative. Read this section for the broad ideas and then go on to the UTTC example for details and specific suggestions about data sources.

• At the Collaboration level, documentation needs to ensure accountability to the partnership's various stakeholders, including the accreditation of the participating institutions.

• At the Structures, Roles, and Resources level, the partnership can use assessment to reflect on and improve its own processes. This includes assessing whether new roles are clear and people in them are supported and rewarded and whether partnership structures and the effective use of resources move the partnership toward its goals.

• At the Learning Community level, documentation should assess the learning of all participants in ways that are useful for internal and external stakeholders. This means blending the use of external accountability measures with other forms of authentic assessment, using inquiry and action research as teaching and learning tools for students and adults, and connecting to professional accountability systems for adult learning.

• Documentors should be addressing the Diversity and Equity Standard by looking at data on any achievement gaps, participation rates, and other data.

DOCUMENTATION EXAMPLE

What follows is the final example from the Urban Teacher Training Collaborative assessment framework. (See Chapter 2 for introduction and background.) Developed in collaboration with the UTTC Assessment Group, the excerpt highlights areas of inquiry that have been suggested as possibilities to follow in that partnership; again, it is included here for illustrative purposes only.

Documentation of this Standard focuses on how the partnership uses inquiry and assessment processes at all stages and levels. Suggestions for documentation are in italics. Starting at the bottom left of the pyramid, and working up:

At the **Collaboration** level,

A critical task is ensuring accountability to the partnership's various external stakeholders—those not personally or organizationally involved in the partnership, but with an interest in successful outcomes for some part of the population affected. This includes:

- The superintendent and central office, Boston Public Schools—*Document with the BPS PDS Annual Reports, and their accounting of impacts on PreK-12 students.*
- Tufts University—*Document with memos and correspondence about the decision to place interns in Fenway and Boston Arts Academy and Mission Hill schools, the decision to keep them there, what kinds of resources have been required, and what kinds of impact the intern model is having on Tufts preservice educators.*
- The parents and local boards of the schools—*Document with internal memos, minutes of meetings and discussions, connecting to the accountability for the successes of students.*
- The state department of education—*Document with teacher test pass rates, other observation reports and requirements needed to get and maintain program approval from the state for the Tufts teacher education program.*
- Ensuring for the internal stakeholders of the partnership (those active in it) that the collaboration is meeting their needs and that the benefits of being involved exceed the costs—*Document with minutes, agenda items, data that are gathered on successful outcomes for various participants, and of the costs, or downsides, to engagement in the partnership.*
- Assessing partnership formation and collaboration, for the internal stakeholders, to fine-tune the collaborative

process, and to learn from the collaboration among Tufts and Fenway, and BAA, and learn about how to best expand to include Mission Hill and art schools, as well as Malden and any other potential partners. *Document with "tent meeting" notes, and other data that are used for assessing existing collaboration, and proposed expansions of UTTC.*

At the **Structures, Resources, and Roles** level, assessment includes what those in the partnership need to reflect on and improve their own processes, as well as what information their organizations need to support the partnership work, and, if necessary, to adapt to changes that the partnership is bringing about. This includes:

• Assessing whether new roles are clear and people in them are supported and rewarded. This includes the collection of data that lead to changes in role descriptions that come about as a result of the partnership (e.g., adapting different roles for university supervisors in observing and giving feedback to preservice teachers in the partnership, adaptations in roles for mentor or cooperating teachers, etc.). Part of this assessment is understanding the evolution of roles over time, how they are fluid at first, then clarified and institutionalized, and how they remain sufficiently flexible to adapt to the uniqueness of each school setting (so, for example, the site coordinator role will not look exactly the same at all sites).

  – *Document with data collection on needs for role changes, minutes or agenda items that show the discussion of such changes, as well as the revised job descriptions or other records of the changes.*

• Examining whether partnership structures effectively move the partnership toward its goals. This includes both the organizational structures and policies of the partnership, and those of the participating institutions. Changes in the former may bump into and require changes in the latter. For example, the scheduled courses that preservice teachers take during their internship are established at the university and are aligned to state standards and requirements by decisions of the teacher education faculty. If once the partnership is in place it turns out that the interns are too overloaded with courses, and changes are needed, what data are collected and analyzed (and by whom) to make those policy changes? This form of assessment and the process for using it for decision making becomes particularly important as UTTC seeks to include other organizations and other units within the existing partners' own organizations (for example, expanding to include other schools like Malden, or other teacher education programs within Tufts).

> – *Document with types of informal and formal data collected to reflect on how well policies and practices are working and how they are aligned with the state standards for teacher education; also minutes and agenda items of meetings where policies and practices are reviewed, and changed as needed. These data might come from faculty, administrators, interns, or graduates (reflecting back on the course sequence and what might have improved it).*

- Ascertaining if the resources of the partnership as a whole, as well as those of the individual partner institutions, are utilized most effectively to help the partnership achieve its goals. This includes time as well as money, and data on effective use of resources are closely tied to outcomes, as well as analysis of roles and structures detailed above.

> – *Document with analyses that connect resource uses with outcomes and processes; also minutes and agenda items of meetings where resource uses are reviewed, and changed as needed.*

- At the **Learning Community** level, assessing the learning of all participants in ways that are useful for internal and external stakeholders. This means blending the use of external accountability measures with other forms of authentic assessment; using inquiry and action research as teaching and learning tools for students and adults, and connecting to professional accountability systems for adult learning. Specifically:
- Using a variety of assessment techniques including, but not limited to, high-stakes testing to address student learning and achievement gap issues.

> – *Document with examples of the range of assessment used, including portfolios, and exhibitions, the perceived validity of those approaches to various internal and external stakeholders, as well as the connection of the use of the range of assessment devices to student learning.*

- Assessing the impact of involvement in the partnership on preservice educators, and ultimately on the impacts they have on student learning after they graduate.

  - *Document with scores or pass rates of graduates on various teacher or other professional educator tests, as well as follow-up outcomes that assess their impact on students, like test scores and other achievement gains for students the interns go on to teach, and placement and hiring rates in specified target communities (like urban schools). Connect with BPS PDS documentation, as well as MetLife follow-up study grant.*

- Tracking professional development and continued learning on the part of the adults in the partnership—parents, community members, novice and experienced educators on the faculty and staff of the partnering institutions.

  - *Document with number of articles presented and conferences attended by faculty and administrators, reflections of adults on their own learning in the partnership, and for teachers, the connection those learnings make to their classrooms.*

- Tracking the development and sustenance of the *community* part of learning community—looking at the collaborative culture that has developed and helps support all the other changes.

  - *Document with school culture and climate surveys and reflections of participants over time.*

- At the **Diversity and Equity** level, assessment addresses all the connections with other topics on the pyramid highlighted above—gathering data to track the diversity of the partners and their commitment to equity; looking at structures, and roles, and resources to see how the partnership is moving to better address these issues; looking, at the learning community level, at improvements in curriculum, instruction, and at data on the reduction of the achievement gap. [These are not repeated here—see Chapter 5.]

Toolkit

6.1 Sample Outcomes for Preservice Educator Preparation

A key element in assessing how successful your PDS is in achieving its goals is to have a clear articulation of what those goals are. If you and your partners talk about "doing a better job at preparing teachers" or "improving student learning" how do you measure either of those important ideas? A few years ago, when I was helping a PDS consortium design a multiyear, multisite impact research study, we spent quite a bit of time gaining consensus on what it meant to "better prepare new teachers." We identified four major categories that we cared about: teaching skill and repertoire (including content knowledge), attitudes and beliefs about students, professional relationships, and resiliency and personal professional development. We fleshed these out and provided bullets and definitions under them (see Teitel with Abdal-Haqq, 2000, pp. 30-31). Committing to paper what we cared about as outcomes was important for several reasons:

- It enabled us to get buy-in from key stakeholders on the goals before we collected the data and did the hard work of analyzing it.

- It gave us a framework for looking for the kinds of data we needed to ascertain whether, in fact, teachers were being better prepared in our partner schools. This allowed us to draw on a variety of sources, including those that were available anyway (see *Gathering Data Efficiently and Effectively* on p. 221).

- It enabled us to coordinate the collection and analysis of data among the several partnerships participating in the study. See *Integrating Multiple Studies Conceptually* on p. 227.

Identify one or a few key goals for your PDS, and develop a list of outcomes that would tell you and your stakeholders whether you have attained your goal.

6.2 Team Planning Sheet

What follows is a planning framework for team discussion I use in assessment workshops for partnership in the early stages of focusing their assessment interests. Use the guide below to start the discussion at your site that can lead to a timetable and work plan for impact documentation.

1. What question(s) about impacts need to be asked? Use some sort of conceptual framework (the four-column model, the Standards Pyramid, or something else of your choice) to locate the impact you are seeking to document. If it is a column 4 impact (say on experienced educators), look across the other columns to see what other relevant changes also need to be documented. If using the Standards Pyramid, look down to see what other Standards also need to be documented.

2. What sources of information can help answer the question(s)? Use a grid of potential data sources to ensure a broad range of measurements.
   a. What information do you already have on this?
      How are you sorting through and analyzing what you already have, to help answer the question?
      Who is, or will be, doing the work, and do they have the needed skills, time, compensation to do it?
   b. What information do you want to collect specifically to answer the question?
      How are you going, or will you go, about doing it?
      Who is, or will be, doing the work, and do they have the needed skills, time, compensation to do it?
   c. When you have collected it, how are you sorting or will you sort through and analyze it?
      Who will do it?

3. Who are the people who care (or should care) about what you are documenting?
   a. Is the information you are planning to collect credible to each?
   b. What is the best way to reach each?
      When and where?
      Who will do it?

What additional knowledge, skills, staff, or other resources do you need to make this documentation effort a success?

6.3 Who Cares?

Who cares (and who should care) about the work you are doing in your PDS? Take the time to make a list of those in each category. Think big. If you find it helpful, you can use the four main purposes of PDSs as triggers (as shown), or you can view it more holistically.

Aspect, Program, or Goal of Your PDS	Who Cares?	Who Should Care	Ideas About Getting Those Who Should Care to Know and Care About Your PDS
Improved student learning			
Better preparation of prospective educators			
Inquiry and assessment on best practices			
Improved professional development			
Other			

6.4 *What Do Stakeholders Care About?*

Build on the *Who Cares?* list and think about the different audiences, what outcomes they might care about for your partnership, and what measurements they might find compelling. Here is the start of a chart that lists the audience (stakeholders) with a place for possible outcome measures. If this is helpful, you might want to have your colleagues make some notes and bring them to a steering committee or an assessment design meeting.

	Qualitative	Quantitative
Internal stakeholders		
• Teachers and administrators in participating institutions		
External stakeholders		
• Parents		
• Community members		
• Other (uninvolved) faculty in school or university		
• University administrators		
• School department administrators		
• Grant funders		
•		
•		
•		
•		
•		
•		

6.5 Gathering Data Efficiently and Effectively

When you are planning a comprehensive assessment, I find it helpful to think of four categories of data needed for this assessment.

Category 1 includes the existing mandated assessments and reports—data that are already being collected and will need to continue to be, due to external requirements. Examples would be your local standardized test data, state educator certification exams, department of education program approval reports, other school or district required reports, and so on.

Category 2 represents the assessments and data sources that are not mandated by others, but are regularly done by the partnership or the individual partners. This includes portfolio presentations, exhibitions, project assessments, junior review, and graduation committee as well as exit interviews with interns, reflective exercises that are collected, and so on.

Category 3 is comprised of archival data—information that is collected and stored for purposes other than assessment, but that can be useful in an assessment. This includes demographic information on students, interns, faculty, and administrators (and changes over time) as well as assignment rosters, schedules (that show number of electives taught by interns, for instance), syllabi, minutes of meetings, job descriptions, and the like.

Category 4 represents the data sources that are collected and compiled just for the assessment. This includes surveys, questionnaires, and interviews done specifically to find answers to questions that cannot be addressed in the first three categories.

The goal is to keep category 4 as small as possible. Strategies for doing this include first trying to frame questions to draw on the existing data in categories 1–3 and, when that does not work, weaving the questions needed into some existing function or purpose. For example, if one of the important impacts of having a number of young interns at the school has been the connections they have made with high school students, then figure out how to capture student reactions to this. If the contact is in the form of afterschool activities such as plays and cultural events, for data collection purposes it would be useful to have some student perspectives on these activities and what they meant to them, their connection to schools and to the interns, and the impacts on their engagement and aspirations. One solution is to conduct a survey (category 4—just for the assessment purposes) asking students to reflect back over the year, on their extracurricular experiences with the interns, and respond to some questions. Another way to approach it is to figure out how to weave the reflections into the afterschool experiences themselves, asking students, as a matter of course, to do some written reflections on their involvement in the play as it comes to an end and then using those for a debriefing discussion among the students. This now shifts it to a category 2 and it becomes a "two-fer"—something that is educationally useful but also contributes to the assessment.

A variation on this strategy is to align category 2 data with the questions that need to be answered for the assessment. So if exit interviews for the interns are being conducted anyway, or follow-up is being done on graduates, ensuring the questions are targeted and aligned with the overall assessment framework makes a great deal of sense.

One way you can address the overall task of thinking about all the data streams is to put them on a grid, like the one on page 223. This is not complete or comprehensive, but it is illustrative of an approach your PDS could use to develop a big overall list of data sources that would be helpful for any assessment efforts.

6.6 Suggestions for Supporting Assessment

Unless your PDS were to have an unusual influx of resources (time or money), it would be impossible for you to follow up on all the areas of the assessment outlined in this book at any one time. Rather, it is useful to think about how assessment might evolve over the next several years and how it could be done in a way that complements the evolution and growth of your partnership.

If you have very few resources available for assessment, think about supporting data collection and analysis on at least a maintenance basis. This would probably require the dedicated time of one or more archivists—individuals who need to have time built into their jobs, or additional compensation for the work, to keep track of and organize the data. Thinking creatively now about where data are stored can save a great deal of trouble later. The assessment framework (Pyramid) itself might serve as an organizing instrument for archiving the data about your partnership, possibly using a Web site or some other forms of electronic storage to simplify retrieval for analysis.

With data organized and available for analysis, your partnership might then commit to one or two research efforts a year and provide incentives for individuals or groups interested in supplementing this with other research you need. You might set aside a small pool of money to offer mini-grants in the several hundred to several thousand dollar range

Target Population	Category 1 *Mandated*	Category 2 *Regularly Done*	Category 3 *Archival*	Category 4 *Developed for the Assessment*
Students	Stanford 9 Formative and summative district assessments Grades	Portfolios Junior reviews Graduation panels Exhibitions Internship portfolios	Demographics College applications and acceptances Courses enrolled in	Student reflections on intern impacts on academics, personal connections, role modeling, and so forth.
Interns	State teacher tests State standards for program approval District-required reports	Supervisor evaluations Mentor evaluations Portfolios Video papers	Demographics Hiring rates of grads Follow-up impacts on Follow-up impacts on student learning	Intern reflections on the impacts of their experiences.
Experienced educators	State recertification (schools) Promotion and tenure (university)	Supervisor evaluations Annual faculty reviews Course evaluations	Demographics Rehire/renewed contracts Rosters/schedules Syllabi Job descriptions	Teacher exit interviews, reflecting on their own learning, new practices, the impacts of yearlong interns have on university faculty, etc.

to provide support—stipends or release time—to PDS participants and other potential researchers interested in doing this work. Take advantage of teachers who wish to do teacher inquiry or action research as part of their professional development cycle, or interns looking for topics for research papers, or doctoral students looking for dissertations. If you keep a clearinghouse for research being conducted on or in the PDS, and make sure it ties to the stated needs of the PDS (and the school improvement plan), you will make the greatest use of the resources you have available.

Source or Type of Data	Resources (Persons, Time, Money) Needed to Maintain Archives	Resources (Persons, Time, Money) Needed to Conduct, Analyze, and Present Findings	Ideas of How to Get Additional Resources to Do This Well
Demographics of students, interns, faculty in partnering organizations			
Meeting minutes			
State teacher licensure test scores			
Intern reflections			
Student test score data			
Other			

6.7 Thinking Big, Acting Focused

Throughout the book, I have suggested you think broadly and conceptually about where you are going with your PDS and how your assessment connects to that. The key to doing that, and remaining sane, is to focus on specific areas of interest within the larger framework. The choice about which specific areas to drill down on might be driven by issues of immediate interest to the steering committee—to solve a problem of practice or to learn about the impacts of a new approach. It might be in response to the request of a funder or external stakeholder, or to provide data organized in a way that will help your PDS get additional funds. The focus areas might also capitalize on the personal interest of one or more individuals within or affiliated with the partnership—teachers, university faculty, or graduate students who seek to do some research, write a paper for a course, or do a dissertation. The framework provides a context and some conceptual glue for smaller studies within it.

List some areas to drill down on within your PDS, what the impetus for each is, and how you think you might find the resources to focus on it.

Topic to Focus on	Impetus—Why Now? Why Is This Important?	Resources That Can Be Brought to Bear on This

6.8 Sharing Findings With Stakeholders

Preparing a report, writing a paper, or giving a talk about your findings at a regional or national conference can be energizing, helpful to others, and possibly even useful to yourself for purposes of promotion and tenure. However, if your PDS stakeholders don't read the report or go to the conference, the work may have no real effects on your PDS community. What are you doing to make sure that those who care about this work (and those who should care) engage with it in a variety of interactive ways? Think about what venues will truly reach people and what formats work best, and develop strategies to get on the agendas of various groups, get into the newspaper, and, in general, do whatever it takes.

Findings or Other Data About Your PDS	Stakeholders Who Care (Or Should Care) About This Topic	Best Venues and Forums to Reach These Stakeholders	Action Strategies to Implement Interactive Presentations

6.9 Connecting Research, Assessment, and Decision Making

How many times have you filled out a time-consuming survey or worked on a taskforce that produced a report and then heard nothing more about it? Perhaps the survey never got analyzed and the report went to sit on a shelf somewhere. The biggest boost and support your PDS can give to research and assessment within it is to use your findings to shape discussions and guide decision making inside and outside of the PDS. Chances are that your PDS is at a point where there are decisions to be made—expansion or reallocation of resources, or decisions about which programs to keep and which to fine-tune or drop. Chances are that you have external issues of accountability and quality assurance that the skillful and complete collection of data could help address.

Make a list of all the research projects that have been conducted in your PDS (or in the partnering institutions) in the past two years. Then take a look at how each was used for internal decision making or for summative or formative evaluation purposes for an internal or external audience. If you find that research and inquiry are being underused in your partnership, consider the options. Some PDSs, for instance, set it up ahead of time so that all the action research projects conducted by the interns are on topics that the PDS steering committee or school improvement council has deemed important. When those results are completed, they are automatically shared with those governing bodies. Others use mini-grants on targeted issues to encourage research by experienced teachers and administrators at school and university. Some PDSs have found that the data they collect through these avenues get used in their school district reports, in requests for grant funding, and in the decisions they make about the PDS.

Discuss this at your steering committee—asking how you are doing at focusing, aligning, and using inquiry in your PDS—and if your partnership is not where you want it to be, develop some strategies to change it.

6.10 Integrating Multiple Studies Conceptually

Since some of your best resources for inexpensive research will be internal, you want to think about how to inspire, support, and coordinate the work. Perhaps the preservice teachers in your PDS need to conduct an action research inquiry, or your district encourages experienced teachers to engage in teacher action research as a part of the evaluation cycle, or you have doctoral students who are looking for dissertation topics. As part of thinking big and acting focused, think through how you can integrate multiple small studies. The conceptual framework discussed earlier in this chapter or the pyramid that is used throughout the book can be helpful here. Since a key aspect of these frameworks is the connectedness of process and product, you can use them to help organize and conceptualize a broad range of impact documentation studies.

For example, consider the case of the Urban Teacher Training Collaborative, segments of whose assessment framework have been interspersed in this book. The presence of a critical mass of interns of color has had a significant impact on the collaborative and could trigger any number of fascinating studies. As noted in the Diversity and Equity excerpt, the presence of a critical mass of interns of color has had implications for all five Standards areas—and powerful and varied ripple effects on the learning of students, interns, and the adults associated with UTTC. Studies of those impacts, as well as what processes led to successful recruitment and retention of the students, could be powerfully linked by the conceptual framework of the PDS Standards Student Learning Pyramid.

In discussion with your partnership steering committee or assessment group, identify several broad issues that are important to your PDS and then work with the four-column model or the Pyramid to see what smaller studies might be spun from it and conceptually linked.

6.11 Using Evidence to Form Conclusions in the Self-Study Process

Would it be helpful to your PDS to assess its progress on one or more of the dimensions of being a PDS articulated by the Standards? Each Standard includes a set of development guidelines, allowing an assessment of whether your partnership is "Beginning," "Developing," "At Standard," or "Leading." A number of reasons your partnership might wish to conduct such a self-assessment are outlined in Chapter 7. If you decide to do this, the *Handbook for the Assessment of Professional Development Schools* (NCATE, 2001a) has some specific suggestions for how to take evidence from your PDS to form conclusions about your standing as a PDS.

What do you see as the advantages and disadvantages of doing this?

6.12 Doing Research That Matters: Key Leverage Points for Change

How can assessment help move your partnership in the direction you and your colleagues and partners wish it to go? Think strategically about the challenges facing your PDS and what it will take to bring about the kinds of change you think your PDS and your partnering institutions need. This is another approach to thinking about assessment and inquiry—let your strategic change agenda drive it.

Take some time to outline what you see as the toughest and most important changes on the agenda of your PDS (or its partnering institutions). Then, thinking creatively about how information can be used to drive change, align your research with the change agenda.

6.13 Checking for Unanticipated Consequences

You may want to periodically screen for the unintended consequences (positive and negative) of the work you and your colleagues are doing in the PDS. Use the grid below to get you started. The example of year-long internships (from the text) is used to illustrate.

PDS Action or Activity	Positive Consequences	Negative Consequences	Strategies to Mitigate Negative Consequences
Requirement of yearlong internships	Deeper connection of interns to the full life-cycle of the school	Makes it harder for less affluent students to give up income for so long	Stipends and other tuition waivers may be offered to offset the opportunity costs
Other			
Other			
Other			

CHAPTER RESOURCES

This section includes a brief annotated bibliography of text and Web resources.

For background reading on planning, conceptualizing, and reviewing PDS research you may want to read Dick Clark's (1995) "Evaluating

Partner Schools" or Ken Sirotnik's (1988) "The Meaning and Conduct of Inquiry in School-University Partnerships," or Ismat Abdal-Haqq's (1998) *Professional Development Schools: Weighing the Evidence.*

For an elaboration of the conceptual framework referred to in this chapter as well as an extended case example, see Teitel (2001a). For a variety of assessment strategies and sample instruments from PDSs around the country, see *Assessing the Impacts of Professional Development Schools* (Teitel with Abdal-Haqq, 2000).

For a summary of what impacts of PDSs have been reported in the literature for students and preservice and experienced educators, see Teitel's (2001b), *What Evidence Exists for the Effectiveness of Professional Development Schools?*

If you are interested in research data on teacher retention in PDSs, see Charlene Fleener's (1999) award-winning dissertation on *Teacher Attrition: Do PDS Programs Make a Difference?*

One of the most compelling studies of large-scale PDS impacts on preservice teachers and on children is W. R. Houston and colleagues' (1999) "Effects of Collaboration on Urban Teacher Education Programs and Professional Development Schools." This is a chapter in the Association for Teacher Education's Yearbook, which focused on research on PDSs (Byrd & McIntyre, 1999).

If you are interested in comparative studies to determine the level of teaching quality of teachers prepared in a PDS versus those who were not, see Neubert and Binko (1998). It is a small-scale study, but the authors use rubrics and a trained observer blind to the purposes of the experiment to document impacts.

For a nice compendium of Web sites focusing on student learning, and how to best assess it, see the "Web wonders" put out by Educational Leadership, at www.ascd.org/readingroom/edlead/0002/webwonders. html.

For an online course in conducting the cycle of inquiry, see www.basrc.org/resources/onlineCOI.htm.

For a good discussion (and some links to Web-based resources) of the different kinds of data that you may want to collect and analyze, see http://eric-web.tc.columbia.edu/digests/dig177.html.

For updates on text and Web sources related to this Standard, see http://pds.edreform.net/home/ and click on Accountability and Quality Assurance.

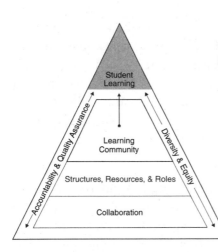

7

Next Steps for Strengthening Your Professional Development School

This chapter suggests some ways to use the materials in this book, as well as other resources for integration, planning, and follow-up.

USE QUICK-CHECKS TO KNOW WHERE YOU ARE AND WHERE YOU WANT TO GO)!

- The Quick-Checks help establish common language and vocabulary and focus on the essential components of PDSs.

- They can be used in a light pass for the PDS steering committee or comparable group at a meeting or retreat. You could pick one Standard and have people fill out their perceptions of where the partnership is, right there, and then discuss it.

- A more elaborate option is to plan ahead and have a range of participants respond to one of the Quick-Check sections, collate the responses, and then bring them to a meeting to discuss.

- You could also have students in a research class conduct a survey with the questions, noting the categories of respondents (i.e., tabulating the comparative response of school-based versus university-based faculty or of students versus parents versus teachers), and prepare a report to be shared with the PDS.

USE CASE STUDIES TO FOSTER COMMUNICATION

This can be done at the local level or with a network. A central theme in this book is that for PDSs to be effective in the simultaneous renewal of schools and universities, partners have to be able to talk honestly with one another about the tough issues that will come up along the way. One way to foster that honest dialogue is through the use of short trigger cases—portraying difficult issues between or among partners in a PDS setting. The cases I recommend (a couple are in Appendix B) are about a page in length and set the stage for dialogue about the key issues, followed by a role-play and a debriefing. They can be used in several ways (adapted from Teitel, 1996a):

- The cases can be used as a communications sensitivity-training workshop for one side of a collaboration. This might be appropriate for a school or university in an early stage of getting involved in a PDS. For instance, a university department of education about to embark on establishing PDS sites might use the case and discussions it triggers to anticipate questions and problems, air them, and lead to clearer communication with the school from the beginning. This is a valuable activity since the worlds of schools and universities are so different that some university faculty members do not know how to talk to or about schoolteachers without being (unconsciously) offensive.

- Teams from a school and its partnering university can use the cases to open up a difficult discussion. Working with one's counterpart can be a particularly fruitful way to use the case to immediately open communication. It is helpful to have a neutral facilitator, especially in the beginning. Ideally a case used for this format is close, but not identical, to real issues that have emerged in your PDS. This provides an opportunity for your colleagues and partners to look together at a situation that is like yours, laying the basis for carry-over without dealing with the tensions of directly dealing with real conflict.

- At a conference or retreat setting, PDS participants from several different PDSs can choose one of the trigger cases and share strategies across PDSs for how to best address the case's underlying challenges.

CONDUCT AN INFORMAL SELF-ASSESSMENT

You can use this book with a PDS steering committee to conduct several levels of self-assessment.

- Use the Quick-Check questions to identify an area on which the committee wishes to work and follow it up in steering committee meetings for a set time.

- Use the start-up or sustainability challenges to take a more detailed look at one or more aspects of your PDS.

- Do some action planning, asking participants to take turns picking out a toolkit sample to read before each meeting and discuss briefly.

- Plan and conduct an overall assessment or a smaller action research project using the assessment framework of the book.

CONDUCT A FORMAL
SELF-STUDY USING THE PDS STANDARDS

The book is highly compatible with the PDS Standards and you may wish to consider doing a self-study. Use the *Handbook for the Assessment of Professional Development Schools* (NCATE, 2001a). This outlines a format, a procedure, and suggestions for collecting evidence and ways of drawing conclusions about your partnership's standing on each of the Standards. Doing this formally is a large undertaking, with many benefits. Some of the benefits, adapted here from those noted in the *Handbook* (p. 3), include the following:

- Supporting and modeling the development of one of the key characteristics that successful PDS partnerships share: the ability to use inquiry to assess and drive PDS practice.

- Deepening connections among institutional and individual partners. When done as suggested in this *Handbook,* the self-study reinforces and models another key characteristic of successful PDSs, that the responsibility for conducting PDS work is shared by an extended learning community, including families, districts, and arts and sciences faculty, as well as school and professional education faculty.

- Strengthening collaborations by drawing on a wide range of stakeholders. It raises stakeholder leadership awareness and buy-in and helps everyone see how the PDS efforts fit in with, and support, other institutional priorities.

• Demonstrating to inside and outside stakeholders how well the PDS is meeting internal and external standards, in part by collecting and examining a variety of accountability data.

• Keeping the partnership focused on what matters in professional development schools—the improvement of learning for PreK–12 students. Because the *Handbook* is closely linked to the Standards, which keep children at the center of PDS work, partnerships conducting a self-study will find themselves continually coming back to this important focus.

FOLLOW UP YOUR SELF-STUDY WITH A THOUGHTFUL ACTION PLAN

Whether you conduct a full formal self-study or some other less formal inquiry, your partnership will reap even more benefits from carefully planned follow-up activities. Producing a document that assesses where a partnership is in its development as a PDS helps a partnership grow if the document is used well. The *Handbook* lists a number of benefits of follow-up plans after a self-study. I include them here because even if you do not do as complete a process as a PDS Standards self-study, but do one of the less formal suggestions above, you may find some of these ideas helpful:

• Bring the self-study document back to an all-PDS annual retreat and use it to inform next steps of the overall partnership or the work of its subcommittees.

• Use the lessons of the self-study to guide the hiring and use of consultants or other efforts to improve the partnership in ways that are suggested by the recommendations of the study.

• Share the self-study within a PDS network or with a set of critical friends or cooperating PDSs in ways that help the partnership move forward with its objectives.

• Use the self-study as a basis for arranging a formal visit from a team of PDS educators experienced in working with the Standards. This external validation and feedback to the partnership can make important contributions to its continuing development and other follow-up efforts. It may be possible to arrange visits through the National Council for the

Accreditation of Teacher Education or other collaborating state agencies or PDS networks. (NCATE, 2001a, pp. 3-4)

If you find the developmental guidelines of the Standards helpful you might want to think about how any follow-up action plan should help move your partnership to the next stage on the developmental guidelines. Regardless of how formally you do this, consider combining your action plan with a specified review cycle, so the issues raised, especially the follow-up on the recommendations made in the self-study, are returned to by your partnership in a set period of time. It may help to have whatever review cycles you set up tied to the larger organizational structures in your district, university, and community. For example, you might tie it into your school's annual report to the school board or the deans' council.

WORK WITH THE IDEAS OF
THIS BOOK AS PART OF A NETWORK

Many of the suggestions above that involve some level of self-reflection and study, and the use of critical friends, can be best facilitated in a network setting. Some networks do that now. In addition to sharing best practices, the members of the Bay Area School Reform Collaborative hold one another accountable for progress on the equity agenda that each partnership has developed. The Benedum Collaborative in West Virginia uses regular retreats to document and refocus its PDSs on its set of core beliefs. The St. Louis PDS Consortium uses the national PDS Standards as a framework for the annual report each constituent partnership completes. The reports require PDSs to conduct thoughtful reflective inquiry into their own practice, focusing on how they met their own stated goals and the Standards. In Maryland, where there is a statewide commitment to Maryland's own version of the PDS Standards, teams of PDS educators from around the state have conducted four-day site visits to look at the fit between the visited PDS site and the draft Maryland standards.

If you are currently in a network or a multisite PDS partnership, you may want to consider adding the reflection, documenting, and action planning to your network or multisite partnership agenda. If not, you may want to join one. It is one of the most powerful ways for PDSs to help one another stay focused on equity and student learning.

CONCLUSION

Professional development schools matter, and the efforts that you and your colleagues are making can have powerful impacts. You have in your grasp the possibilities of shaping the most important thing in this country—the education of its children and youth. I hope this book has provided some small assistance in helping you start, sustain, and assess your professional development school. Most important, I hope it has helped you think about and connect with the greatest potential for professional development schools—the education of all our nation's students and the preparation of teachers who have the vision, courage, and skill to address the equity challenges embedded in this task. Please keep your eyes on that prize—and hold on. It is the most important thing you can do.

Appendix A

Applying the Framework to Multiple School Partnerships

Since an increasing number of PDS partnerships involve more than a single school, it makes sense to explore how the suggestions outlined in this book can be modified to apply to multiple school PDS (MSPDS) partnerships. Applying the Standards to an MSPDS only makes sense if certain characteristics are valued within the multisite partnership and there is a common vision for the partnership. Specifically, applying this framework assumes that all the members value having shared goals, policies, and expectations for outcomes; that they choose to function as a learning community; that there is collaboration among the members; that they have common mechanisms for accountability and quality assurance; and that they are committed to diversity and equity. It assumes that the multisite PDS partnership creates structures and roles to support itself as a partnership with many members, that it uses resources to sustain itself, and that sites in a multiple school PDS partnership are engaged in common work.

With some important modifications, the assessment process described in this book will work for multiple school PDS partnerships that either have the above characteristics or aspire to develop them. A key step is to clarify the history and the nature of the MSPDS partnership: how it got started, the nature of the joint work and activities, and the glue that keeps it together. Guiding questions include the following:

Note. This section is an adaptation of a similar section at the end of the *Handbook for the Assessment of Professional Development Schools* (NCATE, 2001a, pp. 42-45).

- How does the MSPDS function as a learning community across the partnership?

- How do the multiple school, university, and other partners collaborate within the partnership?

- Does the MSPDS have a common approach to accountability and quality assurance?

- Has the partnership constructed roles and structures to support work among its members?

- How does the MSPDS partnership use its resources to support its goals?

- What is the shared work of the MSPDS partnership?

- In what ways is the partnership committed to equity and diversity?

Other adaptations include the following:

- Understanding the nature of the PDS work to be considered. Shared PDS work may be more general than that of the individual PDSs (e.g., focused on the general notion of the functions of a PDS—supporting the preparation of candidates, preparing mentor teachers at all schools, supporting PreK–12 student learning) or it may be more specific (e.g., closing the achievement gap among PreK–12 students in the various school partners). The PDS work shared among partners is joint initiatives that exist across the PDS partnerships.

- Looking at various sources of evidence for the collaborative and the partnership operating as a whole. These sources might include, for example, minutes of the MSPDS group meetings, interviews and observations about contributions from leadership in the school and university, changes in roles and structures to support the partnership's initiatives, details about how committee assignments are made, types of professional development opportunities offered to PDS members, and attendance at these sessions by PDS participants. The various reflective and assessment activities in the book would be explored by looking at

MSPDS partnership activities and events

Input from a range of PDS participants about the nature and joint work of the MSPDS partnership

Examination of contracts, agreements, and resource commitments that undergird the MSPDS partnership

Looking at the degree to which the partnership revolves around one partner (the university, if there is one university with a number of schools) and how much each of the schools connects with one another

Investigation through interviews, observations and document analysis, and decision-making processes of the MSPDS partnership

Examination of how the Standards are applied across the MSPDS partnership

Questions that are particularly pertinent to MSPDS partnerships include the following:

- How does the partnership function as a learning community? Are all partners being supported as learners? Do all partners share a common vision of teaching and learning? Do the results of inquiry-based learning get shared and used across the partnership schools? Does the learning community extend beyond the individual schools in the partnership?

- As a multiple school PDS partnership, what are the assurances of accountability and quality? Are all PDSs contributing to and operating consistently with the criteria established for being part of the partnership? How is the broad partnership supporting capacity building for "younger" PDS partners?

- What are the examples of partners engaging in joint work across the broad partnership? Are the roles, resources, and structures at the broad partnership level supportive of collaboration and parity? How does the partnership recognize in an official manner the contributions of all PDSs?

- Are all publics being served equally and equitably? Is there an effort to seek diverse participants when developing new PDSs?

- Does the MSPDS partnership governance structure support PDS work being shared across PDSs? How do new roles get created? How are they supported? Where is the funding coming from for the partnership operation? Who schedules meetings and are they at a time that ensures opportunities to participate by all PDS partners?

Appendix B

Using Cases to
Facilitate Discussion
of PDS Partnership Issues

Because some of the most important issues and conflicts that arise in PDS partnerships seem difficult or impossible to discuss, I have found the use of short cases to be helpful triggers for discussion. These are referred to in the book under the "Honest Talk" toolkit entry. I include two samples here, along with the guidelines I use in a workshop. Other short cases are available in "Getting Down to Cases: Tackling the 'Undiscussable' Issues of Professional Development School Partnerships" (Teitel, 1996a); in addition, you can write your own.

I usually offer participants in a workshop setting a choice of four or five cases, so they can pick something that they care about. Once people have read the cases, each case serves as a trigger for a role play of a dialogue on a difficult issue that has built into it the requirement for honest communication; each will also serve as the framework for analyzing the underlying dynamics of parity, power, and voice. After break-out groups role-play and discuss cases, the entire group usually reconvenes to discuss the communication issues that arose in the case discussion groups and to identify key strategies for promoting honest communication in PDS partnerships.

The first case I include here addresses a concern I brought up at the end of the Learning Community chapter—about the notion of a plateau that limits how far PDSs go. The second is a more basic case about communication and expectations. The two cases are followed by a set of questions I usually use for discussion.

Getting Beyond the Plateau:
Reconnecting With PDS Visions and Goals

John and Mary sat in the teachers' room at the Johnston School drinking coffee and reflecting on the progress of their PDS initiative. "In just three years we've involved almost half the teachers here," said John. "We've got teachers as mentors and coaches, as collaborative inquirers, with everybody doing a lot of learning and growing themselves."

"I'm even starting to see some changes at the college," said Mary. "More of my colleagues are willing to place student teachers here, or in one of our other PDSs. Even the ones who were reluctant in the beginning are starting to come around; they see it is a better placement for student teachers. I've even gotten a couple of arts and science faculty involved, and that's tough."

"Yeah," said John, "but do you remember that conference we went to a year and half ago on the whole professional development school model? They had that guy talking about the four goals of PDS and how lots of partnerships mostly do two of them—the preservice teacher part and professional development for experienced teachers. The other two—improved learning for kids and inquiry—he said lots of places don't really do much of that—and he's right. Look at us. And he talked about how the partnership should really improve the school and transform the teacher education experience, so new teachers come out really prepared to teach in real schools, with real kids."

"I remember that, too," responded Mary. "You're right. In a way what we have is a better model for student teaching, with some professional development thrown in for the veteran teachers. We're not really making any major changes at either of our institutions, but everybody's happy with what we have done. And we are all so busy—going further would be tough. I remember at that conference, on the way home you and I plotted out how we could make this thing more than good, clustered student teaching. We were going to involve parents and community organizations. We were going to do a study of tracking in the school and how it adversely affects kids of color. We were going to form study groups. Do you remember?"

"Yeah . . . " said John, quietly. "If only I could find my notes from then . . . Well, I gotta go to my class."

As they went their separate ways each wondered about the conversation.

John realized how touchy Mary was whenever he or any of the teachers at Johnston made any comments about how the teacher ed courses at the college needed to be more practical, more reality based. The college always seemed to resist really getting input into teaching or redesigning any of the college courses, even though John and several other teachers had volunteered to help. He wondered if he should bring it up again at the steering committee meeting next week.

Mary wondered about the attitudes of the mostly white teaching staff toward students of color. The heavy tracking in the school, and the poor achievement of many of the African American students seemed like undiscussable topics—she remembers the first time she brought it up as a concern at a PDS steering committee meeting—all the teachers looking down, obviously uncomfortable with the subjects. She wondered if she dared bring it up again, and if so, how?

"They Still Don't Get It"—Issues in Communication and Supervision

"They still don't get it." Pam Berliner was angry after a second upset cooperating teacher had buttonholed her in the hallway. It was already the second year of the PDS partnership and Pam, the teacher coordinator at the school site, was frustrated because the college supervisors still had not adequately communicated their expectations of the cooperating teachers and of the student teachers. The cooperating teachers were upset when the student teacher evaluators came in and didn't seem to have any understanding of the PDS concept or of what roles the cooperating teachers should play in evaluation. "Oh well," Pam sighed, "looks like another call to the college liaison."

As she braced herself for what might be a difficult telephone call, Pam reviewed the litany of teacher complaints: Despite several meetings about communication and expectations, the supervisors still were breezing in, observing, meeting with the student teachers, and waltzing out without explaining what they were doing, let alone giving serious value to the comments and input of the teachers. "Several of our teachers," mused Pam as she punched in Sharon Hinds's number, "are trying out some new models of coteaching with their interns but the supervisors don't seem ready to adapt to that."

When the phone rang in the college field placement liaison's office, Sharon Hinds was reflecting on an upsetting conversation she had heard at lunch. The three supervisors who worked in the college's three PDS sites were grousing about how this new PDS model wasn't really changing anything:

"All this talk about working collegially to help student teachers— in a lot of cases it's just talk," said one. "There are some exceptions, but most of these teachers are too busy to really mentor a student teacher."

"Yeah," another supervisor agreed. "They mostly want another set of hands in the classroom. And I can't blame them—the class sizes are getting ridiculous. Some of them use the student teacher to split the class. That may help them with their class size problems, but it means they can't do much observing or coaching of the student teacher."

"Their primary focus is on their students," added the third. "That's perfectly reasonable, just like our primary focus is on the student teachers."

When Pam identified herself on the telephone, Sharon snapped out of her reverie, wondering how much of this she should or could share with Pam.

Case Discussion Questions

About the Case

1. What is this case about?

2. What is the key information you have about the case?

3. What don't you know that you think is important?

4. What is (are) the key communication problem(s)?

Recommendations for Action

1. What advice would you give the protagonists about talking to each other?

2. What should they say to their colleagues at their own institutions?

3. How can they support each other in making change in their respective institutions?

Role Play

Planning

Decide on next steps for any of the protagonists—when and where they will talk and to whom. Divide into subgroups to prepare the roles of each of the protagonists you plan to include in a role play.

Role Play

Role-play the next conversation the two of them might have.

Follow-Up Reflective Questions

1. For those involved in a PDS, how "close to home" are the issues expressed in this case?

2. What are some other "sticky" issues that are hard to talk about in your partnership?

3. What are follow-up strategies you would like to initiate in your own PDS on these or other difficult communication issues?

4. What would help you promote "honest talk" about the issues that are difficult to discuss in your partnership?

References

Note that portions of this book are drawn, with permission, from the following.

Teitel, L. (1996c). *The transformation of school leadership in professional development schools* [Monograph]. New York: National Center for Restructuring Education, Schools, and Teaching.

Teitel, L. (1997b). The organization and governance of professional development schools. In M. Levine & R. Trachtman (Eds.), *Making professional development schools work: Politics, practices and policy* (pp. 115-133). New York: Teachers College Press.

Teitel, L. (1998a). *Governance: Developing professional development school governance structures.* Washington, DC: American Association of Colleges for Teacher Education.

Teitel, L. (1998b). Professional development schools: A literature review. In M. Levine (Ed.), *Designing standards that work for professional development schools* (pp. 33-80). Washington, DC: National Council for Accreditation of Teacher Education.

Teitel, L., with Abdal-Haqq, I. (2000). *Assessing the impacts of professional development schools.* Washington, DC: American Association of Colleges for Teacher Education.

* * *

Abdal-Haqq, I. (1998). *Professional development schools: Weighing the evidence.* Thousand Oaks, CA: Corwin.

Abdal-Haqq, I. (1999). Unraveling the professional development school equity agenda. *Peabody Journal of Education, 74*(2), 145-160.

Bonds, L. (2000). *Accomplished teacher validation study.* Greensboro: University of North Carolina Press.

Book, C. (1996). Professional development schools. In J. Sikula, T. J. Buttery, & E. Guyton (Eds.), *Handbook of research on teacher education* (2nd ed.). New York: Macmillan.

Byrd, D., & McIntyre, J. (Eds.) (1999). Research on professional development schools. In *Teacher education yearbook VII.* Association of Teacher Educators. Thousand Oaks, CA: Corwin.

Cameron, K. (1984). Organizational adaptation and higher education. *Journal of Higher Education, 55*(2), 122-144.

Case, C. W., Norlander, K. A., & Reagan, T. (1993). Cultural transformation in an urban professional development center: Policy implications for school-university collaboration. *Educational Policy, 7*, 40-60.

Clark, R. (1988). School-university relationships: An interpretative review. In K. A. Sirotnik & J. I. Goodlad (Eds.), *School-university partnerships in action* (pp. 32-65). New York: Teachers College Press.

Clark, R. (1995). Evaluating partner schools. In R. Osguthorpe, C. R Harris, M. Harris, & S. Black (Eds.), *Partner schools: Centers for educational renewal.* San Francisco: Jossey-Bass.

Clark, R. (1997). *Professional development schools: Policy and finance.* Washington, DC: American Association of Colleges for Teacher Education.

Clark, R. (1999). School-university partnerships and professional development schools. *Peabody Journal of Education, 74*(3-4), 164-177.

Clark, R., & Pilecki, M. (1997). Professional development schools: Their costs and financing. In M. Levine & R. Trachtman (Eds.), *Building professional development schools: Politics, practice and policy.* New York: Teachers College Press.

Collay, M. (1995). Creating common ground: The facilitator's role in initiating school-university partnerships. In H. G. Petrie (Ed.), *Professionalization, partnership, and power: Building professional development schools* (pp. 145-158). Albany: State University of New York Press.

Collinson, V. (1994). *Changing context for teachers roles: Teachers as learners and leaders in universities.* Paper presented at the annual conference of the Association for Supervision and Curriculum Development, Chicago. (ERIC Document Reproduction Service No. ED347 091)

Cuban, L. (1988). A fundamental puzzle of school reform. *Phi Delta Kappan, 70*, 341-344.

Darling-Hammond, L. (1992). Accountability for professional practice. In M. Levine (Ed.), *Professional practice schools: Linking teacher education and school reform.* New York: Teachers College Press.

Darling-Hammond, L. (1994). *Professional development schools: Schools for developing a profession.* New York: Teachers College Press.

Darling-Hammond, L., Cobb, V., & Bullmaster, J. (1995). Rethinking teacher leadership through professional development schools. *Elementary School Journal, 96*, 87-106.

Dempsey, V. (1997). The nature of professionalism in the context of school reform. In N. Hoffman, M. Reed, & G. Rosenbluth (eds.), *Lessons from restructuring experiences: Stories of change in professional development schools* (pp. 9-31). Albany: SUNY Press.

Dixon, P., & Ishler, R. (1992a). Acceptable approaches to alternative certification. *Teacher Education and Practice, 8*, 29-35.

Dixon, P., & Ishler, R. (1992b). Professional development schools: Stages in collaboration. *Journal of Teacher Education, 43*, 28-34.

Eckel, P., Green, M., & Hill, B. (2001). *Riding the waves of change: Insights from transforming institutions.* Washington DC: American Council on Education.

Ellsworth, J., & Albers, C. M. (1995). Tradition and authority in teacher education reform. In H. G. Petrie (Ed.), *Professionalization, partnership, and power: Building professional development schools* (pp. 159-176). Albany: State University of New York Press.

Esters, I. G., & Douet, K. P. (2001). Influencing student achievement through counseling: The story of a commonsense professional development school. *NASSP Bulletin, 85*(624), 38-45.

Ferguson, R. (1998). Teachers' perceptions and expectations and the Black-White test score gap. In C. Jencks & M. Phillips (Eds.), *The Black-White test score gap* (pp. 273-317). Washington DC: Brookings Institution.

Ferguson, R. (1999). Conclusion: Social science research, urban problems, and community development alliances. In R. F. Ferguson & W. T. Dickens (Eds.), *Urban problems and community development.* New York: Brookings Institution.

Ferguson, R. (2001). *A project framework for developing routines in teacher-student relationships that foster high achievement.* Cambridge, MA: Wiener Center for Social Policy, Harvard University.

Fleener, C. (1999, February). *Teacher attrition: Do PDS programs make a difference?* Distinguished Dissertation in Education Award Winner, Association of Teacher Educators Annual Conference, Chicago.

Frazier, C. M. (1994). Two education reform trains: Standards/assessment and simultaneous renewal. *Record in Educational Leadership, 14*(2), 15-17.

Frey, N. (2002). Literacy achievement in an urban middle-level professional development school: A learning community at work. *Reading Improvement, 39*, 3-13.

Fullan, M. (2000). Three stories of school reform. *Phi Delta Kappan, 81*(8), 581-584.

Gay, G. (2002). Preparing for culturally responsive teaching. *Journal of Teacher Education, 53*(2), 106-116.

Gold, G., & Charner, I. (1986). *Higher education partnerships: Practices, policies, and problems.* Washington DC: National Institute for Work and Learning.

Goodlad, J. (1988). School-university partnerships for educational renewal: Rationale and concepts. In K. Sirotnik & J. Goodlad (Eds.), *School-university partnerships in action: Concepts, cases and concerns* (pp. 3-31). New York: Teachers College Press.

Grisham, D. L., Berg, M., & Jacobs, V. (2002). Can a professional development school have a lasting impact on teacher beliefs and practices? *Teacher Education Quarterly, 29*(3), 7-24.

Hammond, Z., Whitenack, D., & Whittaker, A. (2002, April 1). *What can be learned about equity through inquiry? Cases of school-university partnership.* Paper presented at the annual meeting of the American Educational Research Association, New Orleans, LA.

Harris, C., & Harris, M. (1995). Launching and sustaining a partner school. In R. Osguthorpe, C. R. Harris, M. Harris, & S. Black (Eds.), *Partner schools: Centers for educational renewal.* San Francisco: Jossey-Bass.

Haycock, K. (2001, March). Closing the achievement gap. *Educational Leadership, 58*(6), 6-11.

Hess, F. M. (1999). *Spinning wheels: The politics of urban school reform.* Washington, DC: Brookings Institution.

Holmes Group. (1986). *Tomorrow's teachers: A report of the Holmes Group.* East Lansing, MI: Author.

Holmes Group. (1990). Statement of principles. *Tomorrow's schools: Principles for the design of professional development schools.* East Lansing, MI: Author.

Holmes Group. (1995). *Tomorrow's schools of education.* East Lansing, MI: Author.

Hord, S., Rutherford, W. L., Huling-Austin, L., & Hall, G. E. (1987). *Taking charge of change*. Alexandria, VA: Association for Supervision and Curriculum Development.

Horsley, D. L., & Loucks-Horsley, S. (1998). CBAM brings order to the tornado of change. *Journal of Staff Development, 19*(4), 17-20.

Houston, W. R., Hollis, L. Y., Clay, D., Ligons, C., & Roff, L. (1999). Effects of collaboration on urban teacher education programs and professional development schools. In D. Byrd & J. McIntyre (Eds.), *Research on professional development schools*. Teacher Education Yearbook VII, Association of Teacher Educators. Thousand Oaks, CA: Corwin.

Hovda, R. (1999). Working on a public school calendar: Reflections on the changing role of a university faculty member in a professional development school. *Peabody Journal of Education, 74*(3,4), 85-94.

Kimball, W. (1999). Changing roles of teacher education students. *Peabody Journal of Education, 74*(3,4), 95-108.

Kimball, W., Swap, S., LaRosa, P., & Howick, T. (1995). Improving student learning. In R. Osguthorpe, C. R. Harris, M. Harris, & S. Black (Eds.), *Partner schools: Centers for educational renewal*. San Francisco: Jossey-Bass.

King, J. (1997). The Thomas Paine Professional Development School. In M. Levine & R. Trachtman (Eds.), *Making professional development schools work: Politics, practices, and policy* (pp. 194-214). New York: Teachers College Press.

Klaumeier, R. L. (1990). Four decades of calls for reform of teacher education: The 1950s through the 1980s. *Teacher Education Quarterly, 17*(4), 23-64.

Kyle, D., Moore, G., & Sanders, J. (1999). The role of the mentor teacher: Insights, challenges, and implications. *Peabody Journal of Education, 74*(3,4), 109-122.

Lancy, R. (1997). The Thomas Jefferson Professional Development School. In M. Levine & R. Trachtman (Eds.), *Making professional development schools work: Politics, practices and policy* (pp. 215-233). New York: Teachers College Press.

Levine, M. (Ed.). (1992). *Professional practice schools: Linking teacher education and school reform*. New York: Teachers College Press.

Levine, M. (Ed.). (1998). *Designing standards that work for professional development schools*. Washington, DC: National Council for Accreditation of Teacher Education.

Lieberman, A., & Miller, L. (1992). Teacher development in professional practice schools. In M. Levine (Ed.), *Professional practice schools: Linking teacher education and school reform*. New York: Teachers College Press.

Little, J. W., & McLaughlin, M. (Eds.). (1993). *Teachers' work: Individuals, colleagues and contexts*. New York: Teachers College Press.

Loving, C., Wiseman, D., Cooner, D., Sterbin A., & Seidel, S. (1997, March 26). *The evolution of a research design: Evaluating professional development schools in the NEA Teacher Education Initiative*. Paper presented at the annual meeting of the American Educational Research Association.

Maryland State Department of Education. (2001, Spring). *Professional development schools: An implementation manual*. Annapolis, MD: Author.

Middleton, V. (2000). A community of learners: Colorado State University Professional Development School Partnership. *Educational Leadership, 57*(8), 51-53.

Miller, L., & Silvernail, D. (1994). Wells Junior High School: Evolution of a professional development school. In L. Darling-Hammond (Ed.), *Professional development schools: Schools for developing a profession*. New York: Teachers College Press.

Mitchell, T. R., & Torres, L. A. (1998). Something, but not very much: School-university partnerships in historical perspective. In P. M. Timpane & L. S. White (Ed.), *Higher education and school reform* (pp. 15-39). San Francisco: Jossey-Bass.

Molseed, T. (2000). Redesigning pre-service teacher practices through staff development: Serendipitous growth for classroom teachers. *Education, 120*(3), 474-478.

Muchmore, J. A., & Knowles, G. J. (1993, April 12-16). *Initiating change through a professional development school: Three teachers' experiences*. Paper presented at the Annual Meeting of the American Educational Research Association, Atlanta, GA. (ERIC Document Reproduction Service No. ED 364500)

Murray, F. (1993). All or none: Criteria for professional development schools. *Educational Policy, 7*, 61-73.

Murrell, P. (1998). *Like stone soup: The role of the professional development school in the renewal of urban schools*. Washington, DC: American Association of Colleges for Teacher Education.

Murrell, P. (2001). *Community teacher*. New York: Teachers College Press.

National Center for Restructuring Education, Schools, and Teaching. (1993). NCREST Vision Statement. In *PDS Network News*. New York: Author.

National Council for Accreditation of Teacher Education. (2001a). *Handbook for the assessment of professional development schools*. Washington DC: Author.

National Council for Accreditation of Teacher Education. (2001b). *Standards for professional development schools*. Washington DC: Author.

Navarro, J. J. (1992). *Will teachers say what we want to hear? Dilemmas of teacher voice*. East Lansing, MI: National Center for Research on Teacher Learning.

Neubert, G., & Binko, J. (1998, February). Professional development schools: The proof is in performance. *Educational Leadership, 55(6)*, 44-46.

Neufeld, B. (1992). Professional practice schools in context: New mixtures of institutional authority. In M. Levine (Ed). *Professional practice schools: Linking teacher education and school reform*. New York: Teachers College Press.

Pugach, M. (1991). Changing the practice of teacher education: The role of the knowledge base. Washington, DC: AACTE. (ERIC Document Reproduction Service No. ED 339680)

Rock, T. C., & Levin, B. B. (2002). Collaborative action research projects: Enhancing preservice teacher development in professional development schools. *Teacher Education Quarterly, 29*, 7-21.

Rosselli, H., Brindley, R., & Daniel, P. (1999). *Beyond good intentions: Using standards to examine PDS sustainability through transitions*. Symposium #434A at the annual meeting of the American Association for Colleges of Teacher Education, February 1999.

Sanders, W. (1997). Teacher and classroom context effects on student achievement: Implications for teacher evaluation. *Journal of Personnel Evaluation in Education*. www.mdk12.org/practices/ensure/tva/contexteffects.html.

Saphier, J., & King, M. (1985). Good seeds grow in strong cultures. *Educational Leadership, 80*(1), 67-74.

Sarason, S. (1982). *The culture of the school and the problem of change.* Boston: Allyn & Bacon.

Schack, G. (1999). Multiple roles and relationships of professional development school liaisons: The struggle for collegiality within hierarchical settings. *Peabody Journal of Education, 74*(3, 4), 306-309.

Schaefer, R. J. (1967). *The school as a center of inquiry.* New York: Harper & Row.

Sewell, T. E., Shapiro, J. P., Ducett, J. P., & Sanford, J. S. (1995). Professional development schools in the inner city: Policy implications for school-university collaboration. In H. G. Petrie (Ed.), *Professionalization, partnership, and power: Building professional development schools* (pp. 179-198). Albany: State University of New York Press.

Shen, J. (1994). *A study in contrast: Visions of preservice education in context of a professional development school.* Paper presented at the annual meeting of the American Educational Research Association, New Orleans, LA. (ERIC Document Reproduction Service No. ED368677)

Silva, D. Y., & Dana, N. F. (2001). Collaborative supervision in the professional development school. *Journal of Curriculum and Supervision, 16*(4), 305-321.

Silva, D. Y., & Gimbert, B. G. (2001). *International Journal of Social Education, 16,* 18-33.

Singham, M. (1998, September). The canary in the mine: The achievement gap between black and white students. *Phi Delta Kappan, 80*(1), 8-15.

Sirotnik, K. A. (1988). The meaning and conduct of inquiry in school-university partnerships. In K. A. Sirotnik & J. I. Goodlad (Eds.), *School-university partnerships in action.* New York: Teachers College Press.

Smylie, M., & Denny, J. (1990). Teacher leadership: Tensions and ambiguities in organizational perspective. *Educational Administration Quarterly, 26*(3), 235-259.

Snyder, J. (1994). Perils and potentials: A tale of two professional development schools. In L. Darling-Hammond (Ed.), *Professional development schools: Schools for developing a profession* (pp. 98-125). New York: Teachers College Press.

Snyder, J. (1997). The Oak Street Professional Development School. In M. Levine & R. Trachtman (Eds.), *Making professional development schools work: Politics, practices and policy* (pp. 234-260). New York: Teachers College Press.

Snyder, J. (1998). Finance and policy structures. In M. Levine (Ed.), *Designing standards that work for professional development schools.* Washington, DC: National Council for Accreditation of Teacher Education.

Stallings, J. A. (1991). *Connecting preservice teacher education and inservice professional development: A professional development school.* Paper presented at the annual meeting of American Association of Colleges for Teacher Education, Chicago, IL. (ERIC Document Reproduction Service No. ED339682)

Stoddard, T. (1993). The professional development school: Building bridges between cultures. *Educational Policy, 7,* 5-23.

Stroble, B., & Luka, H. (1999). It's my life now: The impact of professional development school partnerships on university and school administrators. *Peabody Journal of Education, 74*(3-4), 123-135.

Sykes, G. (1997). Worthy of the name: Standards for the professional development school. In M. Levine & R. Trachtman (Eds.), *Building professional development schools: Politics, practice and policy*. New York: Teachers College Press.

Teitel, L. (1992). The impact of professional development school partnerships on the preparation of teachers. *Teaching Education, 4*(2), 77-85.

Teitel, L. (1996a). Getting down to cases: Tackling the "undiscussable" issues of professional development school partnerships. *Contemporary Education, 67*(4), 200-205.

Teitel, L. (1996b). *Professional development schools: A literature review.* Washington, DC: Professional Development School Standards Project, National Council for Accreditation of Teacher Education.

Teitel, L. (1996c). *The transformation of school leadership in professional development schools* [Monograph]. New York: National Center for Restructuring Education, Schools and Teaching.

Teitel, L. (1997a). Changing teacher education through professional development school partnerships: A five year follow-up study. *Teachers College Record, 99*(2), 311-334.

Teitel, L. (1997b). The organization and governance of professional development schools. In M. Levine & R. Trachtman (Eds.), *Making professional development schools work: Politics, Practices and Policy* (pp. 115-133). New York: Teachers College Press.

Teitel, L. (1998a). *Governance: Developing professional development school governance structures.* Washington, DC: American Association for Colleges of Teacher Education.

Teitel, L. (1998b). Professional development schools: A literature review. In M. Levine (Ed.), *Designing standards that work for professional development schools* (pp. 33-80). Washington, DC: National Council for Accreditation of Teacher Education.

Teitel, L. (1998c). Separations, divorces, and open marriages in professional development school partnerships. *Journal of Teacher Education, 49*(2), 85-96.

Teitel, L. (1999). Looking toward the future by understanding the past: The historical context of professional development schools. *Peabody Journal of Education, 74*(2), 6-20.

Teitel, L. (2001a). An assessment framework for professional development schools: Going beyond the leap of faith. *Journal of Teacher Education, 52,* 57-69.

Teitel, L. (2001b). *What evidence exists for the effectiveness of professional development schools?* Washington, DC: Professional Development School Standards Project, National Council for Accreditation of Teacher Education.

Teitel, L. (in press). Using research to connect school-university partnerships to student outcomes. In D. Wiseman & S. Knight (Eds.), *The impact of school-university collaboration on K-12 student outcome*. Washington: American Association of Colleges for Teacher Education.

Teitel, L., with Abdal-Haqq, I. (2000). *Assessing the impacts of professional development schools.* Washington, DC: American Association of Colleges for Teacher Education.

Teitel, L., Reed, C., & O'Connor, K. (1998). Institutionalizing professional development schools: Successes, challenges, and continuing tensions. In N. Lauter

(Ed.), *Professional development schools: Confronting realities* (pp. 1-63). New York: National Center for Restructuring Education, Schools, and Teaching.

Theobald, N. D. (1991). Staffing, financing, and governing professional development schools. *Educational Evaluation and Policy Analysis, 13*, 87-101.

Thompson, J., Bakken, L., & Clark, F. L. (2001.) *Teacher Educator, 37*, 49-57.

Torres, R. (1992). Evaluation of the professional development school effort. In C. Woloszyk & S. Davis (Eds.), *Professional development school handbook*. East Lansing: Michigan State University. (ERIC Document Reproduction Service No. ED 352319)

Tresiman, U. (1992). Studying students studying calculus: A look at the lives of minority mathematics students in college. *College Mathematics Journal, 23*(5), 362-372.

Tyack, D., & Cuban, L. (1995). *Tinkering toward Utopia: A century of public school reform*. Cambridge, MA: Harvard University Press.

Valli, L., Cooper, D., & Frankes, L. (1997). Professional development schools and equity: A critical analysis of rhetoric and research. In M. Apple (Ed.), *Review of research in education* (Vol. 22). Washington, DC: AERA.

Voltz, D. L. (2001). Preparing general education teachers for inclusive settings: The role of special education teachers in the professional development school context. *Learning Disability Quarterly, 24*(4), 288-296.

Walker, W. (1999). Collaboration: The faint of heart need not apply. *Peabody Journal of Education, 74*(3,4), 300-305.

Walters, S. (1998). Walking the fault line: Boundary spanning in professional development schools. *Teaching and Change, 6*, 90-106.

Williams, R. (1993). A professional development school initiative: Indiana State University story. *Contemporary Education, 64*(4), 210-214.

Wilson, P. (1993). Pushing the edge. In M. Milstein (Ed.), *Changing the way we prepare educational leaders: The Danforth experience*. Newbury Park: CA: Corwin.

Zeichner, K., & Miller, M. (1997). Learning to teach in professional development schools. In M. Levine & R. Trachtman (Eds.), *Building professional development schools: Politics, practice and policy*. New York: Teachers College Press.

Index

**CORWIN
PRESS**

The Corwin Press logo—a raven striding across an open book—represents the happy union of courage and learning. We are a professional-level publisher of books and journals for K-12 educators, and we are committed to creating and providing resources that embody these qualities. Corwin's motto is "Success for All Learners."